CRYPTOFINANCE

A New Currency for a New Economy

CRYPTOFINANCE

A New Currency for a New Economy

Editors

Stéphane Goutte
Université Paris-Saclay, CEMOTEV, France
Vietnam National University, Vietnam

Khaled Guesmi
Paris School of Business, France
Telfer School of Management, University of Ottawa, Canada

Samir Saadi
University of Ottawa, Canada
IPAG Business School, France

World Scientific

NEW JERSEY • LONDON • SINGAPORE • BEIJING • SHANGHAI • HONG KONG • TAIPEI • CHENNAI • TOKYO

Published by

World Scientific Publishing Co. Pte. Ltd.

5 Toh Tuck Link, Singapore 596224

USA office: 27 Warren Street, Suite 401-402, Hackensack, NJ 07601

UK office: 57 Shelton Street, Covent Garden, London WC2H 9HE

Library of Congress Control Number: 2021938611

British Library Cataloguing-in-Publication Data
A catalogue record for this book is available from the British Library.

CRYPTOFINANCE: A NEW CURRENCY FOR A NEW ECONOMY

ISBN 978-981-123-966-3 (hardcover)
ISBN 978-981-123-967-0 (ebook for institutions)
ISBN 978-981-123-968-7 (ebook for individuals)

For any available supplementary material, please visit
https://www.worldscientific.com/worldscibooks/10.1142/12353#t=suppl

Desk Editors: Balamurugan Rajendran/Sylvia Koh

Typeset by Stallion Press
Email: enquiries@stallionpress.com

https://doi.org/10.1142/9789811239670_fmatter

Preface

Since the creation of Bitcoin in 2009, hundreds of cryptocurrencies have emerged, thus becoming a common fixture of financial news bulletins. With a market capitalization of the five highest-valued cryptocurrencies exceeding $140 billion at the time of writing, these alternative currencies have caught the attention of both financial institutions and central banks with their innovative technological foundations and their potential to disrupt current financial institutional structures. This book provides a non-technical overview of the concept and current market structure of cryptocurrencies for researchers in economics, finance, mathematics, and computer science.

With the increased growth of Bitcoin, lawmakers and investors have been willing to define what Bitcoin is in an economic context. Is it a currency, an asset, or a commodity? How is it different from cryptographic money and other virtual currencies? Bitcoin is not considered to be a payment instrument within the meaning of the Monetary and Financial Code because it is issued without a deposit. In fact, digital storage of money in digital format allows the user community to exchange goods and services without using fiduciary currencies. In addition, unlike fiduciary brokers, Bitcoin does not provide the central bank trust, sellers or the purchaser may deny the use of money in their transactions, and virtual currency transactions are irreversible and do not identify Explicitly the payer or recipient, like money.

The digital platforms have been developed to allow people who have not participated in the Bitcoin creation process to provide from this virtual currency in exchange for fiduciary currencies such as dollars or euros. As a result, an exchange rate exists between the digital currency and the currency distributed by the central banks. Nevertheless, the latter do not have the power to define this exchange rate. It is regulated by market demand and supply, which leads to certain characteristics of the Bitcoin exchange rate.

Cryptocurrencies are witnessing a growing interest from investors and the media. They are increasingly perceived as a new class of assets through added benefits, such as hedging capabilities and diversification. However, this does not preclude the fact that cryptocurrencies can be risky assets. Within such a context, diverse studies were carried out at various risk levels.

Our book bridges this gap and tries to reconcile varying positions on risk across cryptocurrencies. Particularly, it provides a detailed overview of the main risks to be considered by crypto-traders, namely, technology, fraud, legal, market, liquidity, and COVID-19 pandemic risks.

This book shows that Bitcoin cannot be considered as a currency. The Bitcoin has excessive volatility that has no correlation with classical currencies and is not shocked by macroeconomic variables. Moreover, the author confirms that there is no chance for risk management with Bitcoins because of their non-compliance. However, central banks are concerned by this phenomenon: the European Central Bank (2012) confirms that virtual currencies depend on the confidence of investors and institutions. Compared to a gold standard, trust is not based on the intrinsic value of a currency, but rather on cryptography and technology. Indeed, Brière *et al.* (2015) show that Bitcoins appear to be a valued precious in diversification. They study the relationship between Bitcoin and other cryptocurrencies and find that during times when Bitcoin appreciates against USD, it also appreciates against other cryptocurrencies.

Kristoufek (2013) shows a very strong correlation between the Google Trends measure, the number of Wikipedia articles on Bitcoins, and the Bitcoin price. He shows that trade in Bitcoins is attracted by attention and uninformed and that it resembles speculation at the start of the Internet bubble 2000. With Bitcoin's volume of transactions mainly from misinformed speculators, the information efficiency of the Bitcoin price is interesting. This document contributes to this analysis.

References

Brière, M., K. Oosterlinck, and A. Szafarz. 2015. "Virtual currency, tangible return: Portfolio diversification with bitcoin." *Journal of Asset Management* 16(6): 365–373.

Kristoufek, L. 2013. "BitCoin meets Google Trends and Wikipedia: Quantifying the relationship between phenomena of the Internet era." *Scientific Reports* 3, Article number: 3415.

https://doi.org/10.1142/9789811239670_fmatter

About the Editors

Stéphane Goutte is a Full Professor at CEMOTEV, University Paris-Saclay, France. He has two Ph.D. degrees, one in Mathematics and one in Economics. He received his Habilitation for Supervising Scientific Research (HDR) in 2017 at University Paris Dauphine. He teaches mathematics and related topics in MSc and BSc. He is also a Senior Editor of *Finance Research Letters* (FRL); an Editor of *Energy Policy* (JEPO); an Associate Editor of *International Review of Financial Analysis* (IRFA) and *Research in International Business and Finance*; a Subject Editor of *Journal of International Financial Markets, Institutions and Money* (JIFMIM); and an Editorial member of European Management Review (EMR). His interests lie in the area of mathematical finance and econometrics applied in energy or commodities. He has published more than 50 research papers in international reviews. He has also been a Guest Editor of various special issues of international peer-reviewed journals and an Editor of many handbooks.

Stéphane Goutte is also the Editor-in-Chief of the *World Scientific Series in Energy and Environmental Finance* (WSSEEF). Stéphane Goutte is a visiting or adjunct professor of many international universities such as Université du Luxembourg, Luxembourg; Vietnam National University, Hanoi, Vietnam; Telfer University of Ottawa, Canada and University of Calgary, Canada.

Khaled Guesmi is Full Professor of Finance at Paris School of Business, Head, Department of Research, Economics, Energy and Policy, and Director, CRECC. He's also adjunct Professor at Telfer School of Management, University of Ottawa, Canada, and affiliate Professor at University of Luxembourg. He undertakes research and lectures on empirical finance, applied time-series econometrics, and commodity markets. Dr. Guesmi obtained his HDR in July 2015. He obtained his Ph.D. in Economics from the University of Paris Nanterre in 2011, and his MSc in Finance from Paris I University of Sorbonne in 2005. Previously, he served as Professor of Finance and Head of the Environment, Climate Change and Energy Transition Chair at IPAG Business School, and as associate research positions at "EconomiX" laboratory at the University of Paris Ouest La Défense and "ERF" (Economic Research Forum), Egypt. In 2003 Dr. Guesmi joined UNESCO as a Research Manager, and in 2008, he joined "Caisse de Dépôts et Consignations" as a Financial Analyst.

Dr. Guesmi is the co-author of the book *Cryptofinance and Mechanism of Exchange* (Springer), as well as the book *Risk Factors and Contagion in Commodity Markets and Stocks Markets* (Word Scientific). He has published articles in leading refereed journals, including the *Energy Journal*; *International Review of Financial Analysis*; *Journal of International Financial Markets*; *Institutions & Money*; *Annals of Operations Research*; *Energy Economics*; and *Energy Policy*. Furthermore, Dr. Guesmi currently serves as Associate Editor at *Finance Research Letters*, and as international advisory board member at *The International Spectator*. In addition, Dr. Khaled Guesmi is the founder of the *International Symposium on Energy and Finance Issues* and Project Manager of the European Commission's Horizon 2020 Program for Research and Innovation. This program has focused on new models of cooperation between EU and the south-eastern Mediterranean region, which are expected to promote a radical re-design of these countries' energy strategies, focusing on sustainability and efficiency policies.

Dr. Khaled Guesmi applies modern financial econometrics tools to examine a broad set of topics related to the commodity markets. His research interests include topics such as the financialization of commodities and contagion effect between stock markets and energy markets. Dr. Khaled Guesmi holds the 4th best world researcher in Energy Finance: Frontiers and Future Development in Beijing in 2018.

Samir Saadi is an Associate Professor and Ian Telfer Fellow in Behavioral Finance at the Telfer School of Management, University of Ottawa. He is also an Affiliate Research Fellow at IPAG Business School. Before his current appointment, he was a Visiting Scholar at leading research-intensive institutions such as the Stern School of Business of New York University and INSEAD (France). His research interests include behavioral finance and Fintech. He has held several external grants from the Social Sciences and Humanities Research Council of Canada (SSHRC) among others. Besides publishing 12 book chapters, Professor Saadi has published more than 50 articles in refereed journals such as *Contemporary Accounting Research, Financial Management, Journal of Corporate Finance, Journal of Banking and Finance, Journal of Financial Research, Journal of Business Ethics*, and *Journal of Business Finance and Accounting*. He is an Associate Editor of *Financial Research Letters* and *Journal of Risk and Financial Management*. He is the founder and lead organizer of the Telfer Annual Conference in Accounting and Finance. Professor Saadi has served as a consultant for more than a dozen organizations in the government and private sectors as well as for non-profit entities. He is involved in CFA training programs in Europe and North Africa. He has been interviewed numerous times in live radio programs and newspapers. He has also served as an expert witness before the Senate of Canada. Professor Saadi holds a Ph.D. in finance from the Smith School of Business at Queen's University.

https://doi.org/10.1142/9789811239670_fmatter

About the Contributors

Aida Allaya is an Assistant Professor of Management at the Carthage Business School of the University of Tunis Carthage (UTC). She holds a Ph.D. degree in management from Faculty of Economics and Management of Tunis. Before joining UTC, she held faculty positions at the higher business studies of Sousse. Her research interests include cross–cultural and international joint-venture performance. Dr. Allaya has taught a variety of courses such as principle of management, international management, and fundamentals of management.

Ibrahim Arpaci is an Associate Professor of Educational Technology at Tokat Gaziosmanpasa University. He holds a BSc in Computer Education and Instructional Technology (2005) from Anadolu University, an MSc in Information Systems (2009) and a Ph.D. in Information Systems (2013) both from Middle East Technical University. He was a visiting scholar at Ryerson University, Ted Rogers School of Information Technology Management, Toronto, ON, Canada (2012 2013). His academic work focuses on how computational technology interacts with psychological, educational, and cultural dynamics. His research interests are in Computational Intelligence, Instructional Systems Design and Technology, Cyberpsychology and Behavior, Culture, Learning, and Technology. His publications have appeared in leading academic journals including *British Journal of Educational Technology, Telematics & Informatics, Computers in Human Behavior, Medical Internet Research, Personality and Individual Differences, Internet Research, and Cyberpsychology, Behavior, and Social Networking*. He received the Best Paper Award in the European and

Mediterranean Conference on Information Systems (EMCIS, 2009). He received the Distinguished Researcher Award from London Journals Press (UK, 2019).

Sonia Arsi holds a Ph.D. (finance) from IHEC Carthage, Tunisia. She is currently an Assistant Professor of Finance at Carthage Business School, University of Tunis Carthage; she teaches topics of international finance, asset pricing, corporate finance, and treasury management. Her research interests include behavioral finance, derivatives, commodities, and international finance.

Khouloud Senda Bennani is an Assistant Professor of Management and Head of Lectures at the Carthage Business School of the University of Tunis Carthage (UTC). She holds a Ph.D. in management sciences from the Higher Institute of Management of Tunis (ISGT) and the National School of Public Administration of Montreal (ENAP). She is a member of the laboratory of Interdisciplinary Research on Changes in Economies and Enterprises (LARIME). She is also a reviewer for several international scientific meetings. Her areas of expertise and teaching focus on public management, strategy, entrepreneurship, and human resources management.

Usman W. Chohan is a Public Value Theorist and the Director for Economics and National Affairs at the Centre for Aerospace and Security Studies (CASS). He writes extensively for the public interest on issues pertaining to cryptocurrency regulation.

Devinder Gandhi is the founding Director of the Executive MBA program at the Telfer School of Management. Given his expertise in corporate and international finance, he has taught and led several advanced workshops internationally and in Canada. Gandhi, formally an associate editor of the *Journal of Banking and Finance*, has published in numerous leading North American journals and is a recipient of best paper awards and honoraria at national and international conferences.

Yosra Ghabri earned a Ph.D. in Finance from IHEC Carthage, Tunisia, in 2017. She is currently an Assistant Professor of Finance at Carthage Business School, University of Tunis Carthage. Her teaching interests include Portfolio Management, Corporate Finance, Financial Markets, and Financial Management. Her research areas are Corporate Governance, Market Microstructure, Portfolio Management, and Energy Economics.

Rafla Hchaichi is an Assistant Professor of Economics at the Carthage Business School of the University of Tunis Carthage (UTC) and a Research Fellow of ESCTRA lab IHEC Carthage, Tunisia. She holds a Ph.D. in Economics from the Faculty of Economics and Management of Tunis El Manar. Her research includes topics such as cryptocurrency, energy, environment, climate change, and commodity market.

Shaista Jaffer is a student of a Master's in Finance at the Telfer School of Management. Her work focuses specifically on the economic implications of externalities in finance, particularly on that of cryptocurrencies. She also owns and manages her own successful small family business, using her background in mathematics and economics to engineer strategic interactions between the establishment and her clients. Shaista hopes to continuously grow her business and contribute her knowledge and expertise to empirical academic research.

Soumaya Ben Khelifa is Assistant Professor of Finance at Carthage Business School, University of Tunis Carthage. She earned a Ph.D. in Finance from IHEC Carthage, Tunisia, in April 2016. Her areas of research are Asset Pricing, Hedge Funds, International Finance, Market Finance, Financial Inclusion, and Energy Market.

Chen Liu is Associate Professor of Finance and Associate Director of the MBA Program at Trinity Western University. Dr. Liu's recent research focuses on corporate finance, valuation, and blockchain. She has published in *Small Business Economics*, *Financial Management* and numerous books and journal articles on FinTech and blockchain. Dr. Liu is a consultant and a frequent speaker at events and conferences on the topics of blockchain and finance. Dr. Liu also serves on the editorial board of the *Journal of the British Blockchain Association*. Dr. Liu received a Ph.D. in finance from Queen's University.

Janelle Mann is an Associate Professor at the University of Manitoba and holds a Ph.D. from Smith School of Business at Queen's University. Her research passion includes commodities, arbitrage, and financial instruments (including cryptocurrencies), but she enjoys any research that involves a time series. Dr. Mann's research has been published in quality journals such as *Energy Economics, the Canadian Journal of Economics*, and Empirical Economics and her research has been presented at dozens of conferences. In 2019, Dr. Mann was nominated for the CWEC Young Researcher Award.

Hela Mzoughi is currently a Ph.D. and Assistant Professor at Carthage Business School, University of Tunis Carthage. She earned her Ph.D. in Management from Higher Management Science of Sousse in January 2016 and she has specialized in Quantitative methods. Her Master's Research degree is in Actuarial Sciences and Finance from High Commercial Studies Institute of Sousse. Her research interests include quantitative finance, portfolio management, and actuarial science.

Octavian Nica holds a B.A. in Economics from the University of Manchester and a Master's Degree in Economics and Finance from the Barcelona Graduate School of Economics. Alongside his studies, he gained research experience in both academic and policy contexts, having worked as a Research Assistant for the University of Manchester and Romania's Ministry of Public Finance. He is currently working as an Economic Consultant, being based in Bucharest.

Karolina Piotrowska holds a B.A. in Economics from the University of Manchester and an M.Phil. in Finance from the University of Cambridge. At university, she was Vice President of the Student Society Blockchainers, Student Venture Capital Associate at Campus Capital, the first on-campus venture capital fund in Europe, and worked as the investment research analyst for Inflection Point Capital Management, part of the global asset manager La Française Group. She is currently Associate Partner Manager at Amazon UK HQ in London.

Sihem Ben Saad is an Assistant Professor of Marketing at the Carthage Business School of the University of Tunis Carthage (UTC). She holds a Ph.D. degree in Marketing from the Institute of Higher Business Studies of Carthage. Her research interests include digital marketing and child behavior. Dr. Ben Saad has presented papers at several national and international conferences such as the French Association of Marketing and the Tunisian Association of Marketing.

Klaus Reiner Schenk-Hoppé is Professor of Financial Economics at the School of Social Sciences, University of Manchester, and Adjunct Professor at the Department of Finance, Norwegian School of Economics. He holds a Ph.D. in Mathematics. His current research interests include financial markets and trading, evolutionary finance, computational economics and finance, dynamic economic theory, and random dynamical systems theory.

Sahar Shabani is a Ph.D. student at the Telfer School of Management in Finance specialization. Her current research is focused on corporate finance. Since her background is in Industrial engineering from which she learned many statistical and optimization methods, her goal is to combine her interdisciplinary major with Finance. Sahar is dedicated to her research, and her expertise from working for Kerman Motor Company in Iran will contribute to her theoretical and experimental framework used in her future research.

Fayda Taârit has a Ph.D. in Economic from the University of Tunis El Manar. She is a Professor of Economics at the Carthage Business School of the University of Tunis Carthage (UTC). Her research interests include banking productivity, information technology, monetary policy, and financial fragility.

Siavash Taheri is an IIROC registered investment specialist and holds a Master of Arts degree in Economics from the University of Manitoba. His main research area is labor productivity. He enjoys exploring new research methods and approaches including mechanism design and game theory. Siavash is looking to further his career in the financial industry as a fund manager. He intends to continue his research to support the use of cryptocurrencies as an alternative investment in modern portfolio management theory.

Austin McWhirter is an Economist at the Bank of Canada. He holds a Master of Arts degree in Economics from the University of British Columbia. His research interests are in applied macroeconomics and monetary policy, with a special interest in the relationship between business cycles and inequality. While attending UBC, Austin was the recipient of a Canada Graduate Scholarship (CGS-M).

Ralf Wandmacher is Professor of Finance and Entrepreneurship at accadis University of Applied Sciences in Bad Homburg, Germany. The focus of his research is blockchain finance — cryptocurrencies, digital asset management, security token, and tokenization.

Prof. Ralf Wandmacher is a researcher in the field of token models and tokenization. He has founded German Crypto Tech GmbH and FairTable GbR and is a board member at Bo1 AG and Coinmat AG. Furthermore, he is a senior advisor at Roots Advisory, Frankfurt, and an advisor at Boerse Stuttgart Digital Ventures and Phlow Ltd.

Prof. Ralf Wandmacher has more than 20 years of experience in derivatives trading, structuring, and sales at Goldman Sachs and Deutsche Bank in Europe. In his last position in banking, he was a Managing Director with teams in London and Frankfurt working on the European structured products market.

Prof. Ralf Wandmacher earned a Ph.D. in Finance, with a thesis about implied volatility theories, from the University of Cape Town in 1999. In addition, he holds the title of a Diplom-Kaufmann in Business Administration from the University of Göttingen with a thesis about neural networks.

https://doi.org/10.1142/9789811239670_fmatter

Contents

https://doi.org/10.1142/9789811239670_0001

Chapter 1

Cryptocurrencies: Concept and Current Market Structure

Octavian Nica[*,‡], **Karolina Piotrowska**[*,§], **and Klaus Reiner Schenk-Hoppé**[*,†,¶]

[*] *Economics, School of Social Sciences, University of Manchester, UK*
[†] *Department of Finance, NHH — Norwegian School of Economics, Bergen, Norway*
[‡] *octavian.nica.96@gmail.com*
[§] *kk.piotrowska@cjbs.net*
[¶] *klaus.schenk-hoppe@manchester.ac.uk*

Abstract

Since the creation of Bitcoin in 2009, hundreds of cryptocurrencies have emerged, thus becoming a common fixture of financial news bulletins. With a market capitalization of the five highest-valued cryptocurrencies exceeding $140 billion at the time of writing, these alternative currencies have caught the attention of both financial institutions and central banks with their innovative technological foundations and their potential to disrupt current financial institutional structures. We provide a non-technical overview of the concept and current market structure of cryptocurrencies for researchers in economics, finance, mathematics and computer science.

Keywords: introduction to cryptocurrencies, blockchain, mining, governance

1. A Brief History of Cryptocurrencies

Cryptocurrencies are generally characterized in the academic literature as a subtype of alternative currencies (Hileman, 2014; Nian and Kuo Chuen, 2015; Wood and Buchanan, 2015). Alternative currencies — "*any medium of exchange other than legal tender*" (Hileman, 2014, p. 7) — are not a new concept, as they have recurrently been present over the last few centuries, sometimes bearing a significant role in the economy (Hileman, 2014). What differentiates cryptocurrencies from any other alternative currency (or digital currency, for that matter) is that they are a medium of exchange that, in its purest form, does not require any central authority that accomplishes transactions or manages the currency supply. This level of decentralization is made possible through the use of cryptography. Cryptography can be used for two general purposes. The first one is to conceal (or partially conceal) the identity of participants in the market. The second use of cryptography is to require participants to solve a cryptographic puzzle. By solving the puzzle, users collectively validate the transactions that occur on the market, thus making safe transactions in the currency without the need of oversight from a trusted third party agent, and also receive units of currency as a reward, thus establishing a rule for the creation of currency (Nian and Chuen, 2015). Since 2009, the number of cryptocurrencies has surged, and many of them have moved away from this pure model.

1.1 *The Precursors of Bitcoin*

The idea of a cryptocurrency first appeared in Chaum (1982), who was motivated in his endeavor by the fact that electronic payment systems could impact personal privacy (Chaum, 1982). His solution to these issues was a "blind signatures cryptosystem," a system where cryptographic functions are used to conceal the identity of the payers and payees, while offering them the possibility to verify if the transaction has been completed. In a subsequent paper, Chaum introduced the concepts of "electronic wallets," and "public and private signatures" (Chaum, 1983), which are two ideas that are fundamental to cryptocurrencies in use today. Thus, Chaum created the first digital currency that made use of cryptography, called eCash, in 1990. Unlike most cryptocurrencies today, eCash was a centralized currency and it used cryptography to conceal the identity of users (Nian and Chuen, 2015).

In the 1990s and early 2000s, cryptocurrencies continued to be of academic interest. Szabo (1998, 2002) published extensively on the concept of money and devised a concept of cryptocurrency in Szabo (2008) just before the appearance of Bitcoin. In 1991, Haber and Stornetta (1991) introduced the idea of a blockchain that uses timestamping to authenticate authorship of intellectual property. Dwork (2006) and Back (2002) created a cryptographic proof-of-work algorithm called Hashcash which, even though not initially conceived for cryptocurrencies, later became the cryptographic puzzle used in many currencies, including Bitcoin, to allow networks of users to verify transactions in a decentralized manner.

In parallel, the technology behind Internet payments improved with the emergence of a series of digital currencies based on gold. These currencies were essentially asset-backed payment systems (Nian and Chuen, 2015). Of these gold standard digital currencies, the most popular was e-gold which, before its closure in 2008, was processing more than $2 billion per year. E-gold's popularity decreased as the currencies faced attacks from hackers and cases of Internet fraud, and it was shut down as it did not comply with the legal requirements imposed by US authorities.

1.2 *The Emergence of Bitcoin*

Bitcoin appeared in 2008, when an anonymous group, working under the pseudonym of Satoshi Nakamoto, published a whitepaper detailing the design of the currency (Nakamoto, 2008). Bitcoin is the first fully decentralized currency, and it can be operated by anyone who downloads its open-source software. This means that the currency is essentially a peer-to-peer network where all the users are connected with each other and can make transactions without the need for any third party, such as a bank. Bitcoin uses public-key cryptography in order to make transactions computationally impractical to reverse, thus, in theory, protecting users from fraud and preventing double spending. The supply of currency is determined by a predefined algorithm and new currency is released through a process of "mining," which means that certain users are rewarded with new currency units for performing computationally intensive tasks that are necessary for the Bitcoin system to function. Mining rewards stop after a ceiling of 21 million bitcoins is reached. From this point forward, Nakamoto (2008) argues that transaction fees can become a sufficient incentive for miners to keep performing their work.

After publishing the 2008 paper, Nakamoto (2009) popularized the new currency on online forums and mined the genesis block of Bitcoin in the same year, but Bitcoin remained a fringe phenomenon until about 2011. At that time, the currency suddenly gained traction, helped in part by the decision of Mt. Gox, a Japanese-based exchange for fantasy games cards, to allow trading in Bitcoins (Yermack, 2015). The sudden growth of cryptocurrencies from 2011 onwards can also be explained by the fact that Bitcoin was the first online currency to publish its entire source code online and– allow for it to be used and modified freely.[1] This has fostered the creation of alternative currencies based on its code. Some of these new currencies exist totally separated from the Bitcoin environment, having their own genesis block, while others are simply branches of the blockchain of Bitcoin. By the end of 2011, Tarasiewicz and Newman (2015, p. 202) reported that there were already 10 alternative cryptocurrencies in use, while at the end of 2013 the number of alternative currencies reached 215.

There are different reasons that explain the sudden rise in interests for cryptocurrencies. Hileman (2014, p. 164) presents a list of these reasons, mentioning, among others, the following: inefficiencies in the current financial system (long waiting times for transactions, high transaction fees), disbelief in the current political system (especially in the relations between the government and large financial institutions), technological innovations (cryptographic advances, increase in computational power) and speculation.

Among these diverse driving forces, the one that received the most attention in academic publications and in the media is the political foundation of the cryptocurrency movement. From its inception, the cryptocurrency community was associated with libertarianism (Huckle and White, 2016; Ametrano, 2016). A survey conducted in 2014 on the Bitcoin community shows that almost 60% of the respondents self-identify as libertarians, whereas 27% of them define themselves as anarchists (Lustig and Nardi, 2015, p. 9). Gavin Wood, one of the founders of Ethereum, another popular cryptocurrency initiative, is critical of the role of both the government and banks, arguing, in a paper, for the *"decentralisation of authority"* (Wood and Buchanan, 2015, p. 387) in the financial system.

[1]The Bitcoin source code is currently available from its Github repository at https://github.com/bitcoin/bitcoin.

Nakamoto himself shares the same view with the libertarian community when it comes to economic matters:

> *The root problem with conventional currency is all the trust that's required to make it work. The central bank must be trusted not to debase the currency, but the history of fiat currencies is full of breaches of that trust. Banks must be trusted to hold our money and transfer it electronically, but they lend it out in waves of credit bubbles with barely a fraction in reserve.* (Nakamoto, 2009)

The political foundations of Bitcoin are reflected in the way its currency supply is managed. The fact that the creation of new currency works according to an unalterable algorithm, which is only an intermediary phase until the 21 million bitcoins limit is reached, can be partially explained through the anti-central banks rhetoric that criticizes the system of centralized fiat currencies that has been in place since the complete abolishment of the gold standard in 1971 (Golumbia, 2016).

The increased popularity of Bitcoin is also attributed to its adoption as a preferred payment method by Silk Road, which was the biggest online marketplace for drugs and other illegal goods and services. It based its existence on Tor, a software that allows users to browse the Web without the possibility of being tracked, and Bitcoin, which allowed for anonymous payments. Christin (2012, p. 20) estimated that in 2013 between 4.5 and 9% of all Bitcoin exchange trades were related to Silk Road. In 2013, the website was shut down by the Federal Bureau of Investigations, but it is estimated that the sites that replaced it soon became larger than Silk Road (Soska and Christin, 2015). Bitcoin's popularity suffered when Mt. Gox, the first exchange for Bitcoin (that also became the largest one, handling around 80% of all the transactions), closed down and filed for bankruptcy protection in 2014 (Abrams and Popper, 2014). The company lost almost 850,000 bitcoins (which, at that time, amounted to around $450 million), and its CEO was arrested and charged with fraud and embezzlement.

Since 2014, the general perception of cryptocurrencies has become more positive. According to De Filippi and Loveluck (2016), this is mostly due to Bitcoin bringing a new opportunity for speculation. This increase in Bitcoin's popularity led to the creation of a new variety of cryptocurrencies that moved away from the political and ideological ideas behind Bitcoin. These new currencies are more likely to embrace the centralization of certain parts of their infrastructure and accept more conventional governance structures. These factors made financial institutions embrace cryptocurrencies on a larger scale: The New York Stock Exchange, Goldman Sachs and BBVA have invested in cryptocurrency start-ups (Shin, 2015) and both a Wall Street clearinghouse and the Australian Securities Exchange announced that they are planning on adopting blockchain technology (Popper, 2017; Yermack, 2017).

Financial institutions are not necessarily interested in cryptocurrencies but in the blockchain technology. For instance, Hyperledger — one of the largest consortia of companies that decided to invest in blockchain technology — made clear that they will never be interested in creating a new currency.[2] The prospect for an even bigger increase in the cryptocurrency market is given by the new funding mechanisms for innovations, called Initial Coin Offerings (ICOs). An ICO, which is a method that is somewhere between a traditional Initial Public Offering (IPO) and a crowd-funding initiative, gives investors early access to new coins in return for investment funds (Kaminska and Murphy, 2017).

Most of the new cryptocurrencies not only work as currencies but also fulfill other auxiliary roles. Ripple, for instance, is a cryptocurrency project that also creates a currency exchange and remittance network which is based on the blockchain technology. Another popular cryptocurrency project, Ethereum, with its own currency called Ether, realizes Szabo's idea of "smart contracts" (Szabo, 1997). These are self-enforcing contracts that work through blockchain technology.

The close links between conventional financial institutions and the cryptocurrency community have deepened the division that already existed in the latter between a core group of supporters of a more idealistic version of cryptocurrencies and a group of users that see cryptocurrencies as the sign of a new, emerging technology or just as an investment opportunity. This division can be seen in the various governance crises, when the inability of the community to reach a consensus puts currencies like Bitcoin (Popper, 2016), Ethereum (Coppola, 2016) or Litecoin at the risk of breaking apart.

[2] http://www.eweek.com/cloud/hyperledger-blockchain-project-is-not-about-bitcoin.

2. The Mechanisms Behind Cryptocurrencies

The cryptographic nature of the underlying mechanism which enables the decentralization of cryptocurrencies is the main technological feature distinguishing them from other digital currencies. As a result, Bitcoin has become the first currency which allows the transfer of money without the mediation of a third party (Franco, 2014).

2.1 *Transaction Path and Wallets*

We define cryptocurrency as *a fixed-value cryptographic object represented as a chain of digital signatures over the transactions in which the coin was used* (Kroll *et al.*, 2013). A chain of digital signatures is a data pattern the digital value is assigned to. What distinguishes it from any other worthless stream of data is the fact that its system prevents *double spending* without the involvement of a central counterparty. This is possible thanks to the introduction of the *blockchain*, a public ledger that is the common element of different cryptocurrency systems.

In contrast to a central authority system, information about the balance of the user's account is available to everyone. Users are identified by large strings of characters known as *addresses*. These are the public part of the public–private cryptographic keys. The private piece, a *signature*, is controlled only by the user. As a result of excluding any third party from the system and identifying participants only by their addresses, their pseudo-anonymity is preserved.

When one participant sends some tokens to another user, she advertises the message stating that a given amount of coins is supposed to be subtracted from her address and added to another one. The new transaction generates a hash, which provides the details of the message and points to the previous transaction the coin was used in.

As a result, every token can be traced back to its inception. Subsequently, a user signs the message with a *digital signature* — a code that is cryptographically derived from the message and private key. Such a transaction is sent to the network. Upon receiving the message, there are three steps that must be completed before the transaction is finalized (Franco, 2014). Firstly, the signature is verified. Next, the balance of the sending address account is checked in order to determine whether there are sufficient funds to honor the transaction. If both tests are passed, the database is updated with new account balances. In the case when the value of the output exceeds the preliminary input, the difference constitutes a *transaction fee* (Kroll *et al.*, 2013), which is paid to the participant who successfully appends the transaction to the blockchain. The transaction can be treated as finalized when it achieves multiple confirmations. There is no fixed number for that, but six is a commonly accepted heuristic (Narayanan *et al*., 2016).

For a majority of cryptocurrencies, all participants are given equal rights. Everyone can join the network by downloading a *wallet* software, which generates addresses and private keys. The user starts connecting with other nodes by sending her *seed node* message to the address she knows. The message asks the recipient to share all the other addresses in the network that this node knows about.

The aim is to build the network in order to publish, confirm and complete the transactions. When the user sends a transaction, her node distributes the message to all the nodes it is peered with. Each recipient individually checks and determines if it accepts the transaction. The process includes transaction validation with the current blockchain, checking if the outputs have not been already spent, rejecting already seen transactions, and checking the validity of the script.[3] If approved, the message is further distributed in the same way.

This process is called a *flooding* algorithm. Each node that receives the message puts it in the pool of transactions not attached to the blockchain. The transactions in the pool are not further broadcast by the nodes in order to prevent the creation of the indefinite loop. It is estimated that there are approximately 10,000 permanently connected nodes which fully validate every transaction and (as of Q1 2019) 35 million Blockchain wallet users (Statista, 2019). Such an outcome is possible because the majority of them are *lightweight* wallets (Narayanan *et al*., 2016).

Fully validating nodes must be permanently connected to the Internet to receive new transactions and they must also store the entire blockchain and unspent transactions pool, which is out of reach for the average desktop computer. The lightweight nodes, on the other hand, do not store the entire blockchain, but only pieces which are necessary for validation of

---

[3] There is no obligation for the node to comply with all checks. A majority comply with the rules in order to protect the smooth operation of the network. Some may deter from this strategy and try to forward double spends, or similarly invalid transactions. The attempt ultimately fails, because only one transaction can be added to the block, and when it happens, the other nodes will drop the invalid transaction from their memory pool.

the transaction that concerns them. They rely on the *miners*, the owners of fully validating nodes who append transactions into the blockchain. They made a significant investment in the mining process and therefore must be certain that the transactions they are processing are valid.

The wallet is a comprehensive tool helping the user to manage their account. Besides generating keys, the software also creates transactions that are sent to the network, collects incoming and outgoing transactions to show the balance of available funds, and securely stores the user's private keys. If a private key is lost, there is no possibility to sign any transaction or access the funds in the ledger. Coins are not stored in the wallet or in the device where the software is installed but recorded in the ledger, which holds the balance of funds for each address.

Franco (2014) distinguishes two major groups of wallets: offline and web wallets. They differ by their connection to the Internet and the fact that the offline wallets are predominantly managed by the user itself, while in the case of web wallets, funds are transferred to the third party which manages them on behalf of the user. Both of these leaves web wallets at greater risk of being compromised. Web wallets are a subgroup of the larger category called online or *hot wallets*, which are any device holding a wallet and being connected to the Internet at the same time.

Offline wallets sign transactions offline. Before it takes place, the private key should be imported from a cold storage (USB, a piece of paper known as a *paper wallet*[4] or any other storage medium which cannot be accessed from the Internet). We can find a physical cryptocurrency in the form of a coin or paper, with the private key hidden behind a tamper-proof mechanism. Among offline wallets, there are also independent *hardware wallets*; the devices both store private keys and receive, sign, and return the transaction.

Web-based wallets are online accounts provided by a third party where users deposit their funds (Franco, 2014). The transaction cost will be lower if the operator decides to pool many transactions before sending them into the blockchain, and the outsourcing of account management makes Web wallets more accessible to the first-time users.

Approximately three-quarters of the providers do not store private keys (Hileman and Rauchs, 2017), which means that they do not have a control over users' funds. These are named *hybrid web wallets*. For the

---

[4]Although it is an accepted name, a paper wallet is not technically a wallet, because it is not able to perform all the other tasks that the software named *wallet* does.

remaining minority, there is a risk if a provider is fraudulent and aims to steal the clients' funds. Web wallets are also exposed to hacking attacks. For this reason, their use is predominantly limited to day-to-day financial operations, which matches the fact that the mobile format is the most popular one among wallet providers.

Among the alternatives, we find the *brain wallets* (Franco, 2014) that has a long password which is supposed to be remembered by a user. We also distinguish *deterministic wallets*, which generate many addresses and their associated private keys from a common private key. Finally, there are also *multi-signature wallets* which increase security by requiring several signatures to unlock funds and *vault wallets* that provide custody solutions for enhanced security management.

As described above, users can make the transactions in cryptocurrency using wallets. However, because of the fact that the cryptocurrencies are currently not a widely accepted payment method, we can expect that for the majority of users, the aim is to exchange them into the national currencies. In order to do that, the agent must approach the currency exchanges. They are the first sector that emerged in the cryptocurrency industry, have the highest number of operating entities and employees (Hileman and Rauchs, 2017) and remain the biggest driver of industry growth (Rauchs *et al.*, 2018). The first one appeared in 2010, and today, there are over 500 exchanges in operation.

The exchanges function similar to the traditional bourses by matching the demand and supply orders. Such transactions are not updated in the blockchain. The exchange registrar updates its contracts with the users involved in the exchange, and no money movement actually takes place. Alternatively, a person can access selected cryptocurrencies using ATMs, at private meetings or trading events. They can exchange real cash for the physical cryptocurrency or use *payment providers*.

The role of payment providers can be placed in between wallets and exchanges. Their primary function is being a payment link between the cryptographic and real worlds. They are used by the merchants who accept cryptocurrency payments (Narayanan *et al.*, 2016), for business-to-business transactions and individual money transfers such as bill payments (Hileman and Rauchs, 2017).

In summary, the key crypto-asset industry segments are Storage, Payments, Exchange and Mining (Rauchs *et al.*, 2018). Over the years, the provision of multiple crypto-assets expanded and, as of the end of 2018, Bitcoin (92%), Ether (79%), Litecoin (61%), Bitcoin Cash (47%)

and Ripple (41%) were supported by the largest share of providers (excluding miners).

2.2 *Blockchain*

The blockchain derives its name from a chain of *blocks*, in which the data (ordered transactions) are grouped. Once the information is added to the blockchain, it cannot be altered, and its security relies on the verification mechanism used. The cryptographic links between the blocks create the record of all past transactions. It is a peer-to-peer network, where a node is any computer system with the software installed in it.

Each block stores the data of the transactions (Nian and Chuen, 2015) whose size is determined by the number of inputs and outputs. Every block is built from a body, where transactions are stored, and a header. The header includes identifiers, such as the hash value of the previous block of the chain, the hash of all the transaction hashes in the block, and the bit field of the current target value. When the block is validated, a computer must solve a mathematical puzzle of finding the hash of a block's header lower than or equal to the current target.

All blocks combined together result in a complete history of all transactions ever made, which can be viewed by accessing the cryptocurrency software. They are grouped by order, where the most recent blocks are chained to the former ones, up to the genesis block. The *Hashcash* function transforms the input message into the bit digest. The computer must solve the aforementioned mathematical problem in order to add the next block into the blockchain, and the solution can be found only by random guessing. The first one which succeeds broadcasts it to the network and it is accepted as the next block in the chain.

The validation process is called *mining*. The goal of the system is to add a block to the chain in a timeframe specified in the code (Dwyer, 2016). Therefore, the difficulty of finding a solution is dynamically adjusted. If two miners find the solutions at the same time and broadcast them to the system, it is the longest block (the one which all miners will switch to and start adding the additional blocks) which is preserved. The other one is abandoned and becomes an *orphan block* (Franco, 2014). The agreement on the longest blockchain is named a *consensus* (Dwyer, 2016). Other miners express their approval of the block by including its hash in the next block they create (Narayanan *et al.*, 2016). In order to be accepted, all the transactions in the block must be signed by valid signatures.

Bitcoin is a proof-of-work system, which means that the selection of a random node is approximated by choosing nodes in proportion to a resource, i.e., computing power (Dwyer, 2016). Because of concerns regarding the efficiency of the system, alternative mechanisms for reaching consensus have been developed, such as the proof-of-stake or proof-of-importance.

Blockchain as a data structure has found multiple applications beyond the cryptocurrencies market (Swan, 2015). The new cryptocurrencies proposed additional solutions, such as smart contracts software *that codifies legal procedures with decentralized autonomous execution* (Williams, 2016). Its possible applications include the property market, (Dwyer, 2016), finance industry, voting mechanisms, supply chain and IoT projects (Pilkington, 2015). Visa, Nasdaq, IBM, Microsoft and other institutions invested in the development of this technology (Frost & Sullivan, 2016).

There is a small group of cryptocurrencies which does not have a blockchain. The most widely used one is Ripple, which operates with a *global consensus ledger* as an alternative (Hileman and Rauchs, 2017). It requires no mining, but instead verifies transactions with an algorithmic consensus. Therefore, as opposed to Bitcoin, the verification is instantaneous. On the other hand, it uses a centralized ledger instead of a decentralized blockchain.

2.3 *Mining*

In the absence of a central authority, the community is responsible for adding the data to the blockchain. Miners carry out this task. The source of income for them is the *block reward*, i.e., the newly generated coins and/or transaction fees (if any).

The miner receives a block reward only if it is appended into the blockchain. This mechanism incentivizes the nodes to behave in the way that is accepted by the majority of the miners and penalizes those that are trying to act dishonestly. As a result, the creators of the invalid blocks never get paid. On the other hand, the transaction fee is purely voluntary and variable. It is determined by the creator of the transaction who may choose to make the total value of the outputs less than the value of the inputs. The miner who first puts such a transaction to the blockchain collects the difference. When block rewards disappear completely, we may speculate that fees will become mandatory in order to ensure the smooth processing of the transactions.

By looking into proof-of-work mechanism, Kroll *et al.* (2013) estimate that the equilibrium situation would imply small, but non-zero, transaction fees. The miners can benefit from cooperation. However, because each miner has an incentive to include every transaction whatever be the fee, any other outcome is not stable. As a result, they are trapped in the classic prisoner's dilemma. The miners ensure currency survival by confirming the validity of transactions, and their dedicated computer power is the guarantee of system security. When the system starts to rely solely on the transaction fees, Houy (2014) suggests that the only way to correct this market inefficiency is by integrating into the protocol the block size constraint or a built-in transaction fee.

Similar to any other user, the miner joins the network and connects with other nodes (Narayanan *et al.*, 2016). She subsequently starts to listen to the transactions on the network and validates them. At the same time, the miner needs to maintain the blockchain and wait for the new blocks. She must first ask other nodes to provide her with the historical blocks already included in the chain. Next, the miner starts validating each block she receives by examining each transaction it contains and checking if the block has a valid *nonce*. As soon as the miner has the updated blockchain, she can start the ultimate task of building her own block. In order to do that, she groups the transactions from the waiting pool, confirms that each of them is valid, and clusters them into the new block. When completed, the miner must find a nonce which makes the block valid, meaning that she must solve the hash function matching current prerequisites. If she manages to do it before the other users, she messages the block to other nodes. Only if other miners accept the block and start mining on top of it, the miner receives the reward. It may happen that two miners distribute the block at the same time. In such a case, even if the block contains all valid transactions, only one block becomes appended to the blockchain and the other one remains orphaned.

We now look at how the miners' community is structured. *Solo mining* lets the owner of the device compute solutions to the hashing function individually. If successful, one is paid the entire reward. The probability of success is low and variability high. Bhaskar *et al.* (2015) estimate that a well-equipped miner earns a reward on average every three months. Because of the random nature of the process, the lags can take too long a time to make an investment profitable. Alternatively, players can get involved in *mining contracts* or *mining pools*. Mining contracts offer the possibility of investment in the mining process without managing hardware or software. Contracts provide mining services or mining shares in the large-scale mining centers. This includes cloud mining, i.e., using shared processing power run from remote data centers.

The mining pools are the groups of miners who contribute their resources into joint mining which generates higher hashing power. The probability of mining the block increases with the amount of resources dedicated to the process, but the reward is split between participants based on their individual contributions. Such organized groups of miners have also a higher influence on protocol content. In 2017, five mining pools controlled 79% of the market, with three-quarters of all mining pools being based in China and the USA.

2.4 *Vulnerability to Cyber Attacks*

The attacks on the system can be grouped into two categories. The first includes the attacks on a single user attempted by trying to find out the person's private key or misleading her into sending funds to the wrong address. These are performed either virtually by *address tampering* (Franco, 2014) (largely impossible as most of the cryptocurrency codes have protections against it), or physically by substituting a physical QR code sticker with the illicit one in the places that accept Bitcoin payments.

The second category includes the attacks made on the blockchain itself. We do not describe all the possible attacks that may occur, nor we provide all their consequences. Our aim is to outline some possible vulnerabilities.

The most discussed one is called a *51% attack* (Franco, 2014). The attack is performed when a person commands a hash rate equal to or larger than the hash rate of the rest of the network. Such an individual may then try to perform a *double-spent attempt* or prevent other miners from mining the blocks, and ultimately destabilize the system.

If one would wish to change the blockchain at a certain point, she would have to mine again all the blocks from that point in time to the present. Additionally, she would need to surpass the pace of the current new block creation. In order to make it possible, the attacker would need to command a hash rate equal to the rate of the rest of the network. The probability of success decreases exponentially with the control rate smaller than 50% and the number of blocks required to outpace.

In the case of *race attack*, the attacker could double-spend by sending a *transaction to the nodes close to the vendor and a different transaction to many other nodes in the network* (Franco, 2014, p. 115). If the vendor accepts payment on an unconfirmed transaction by checking only a few nodes, the attack is successful.

A *Finney attack* was discovered in 2014 by Hal Finney. It happens when a miner secretly mines a block, including in it a transaction between two of her addresses, which has never been broadcast to the network. Before releasing the block, the attacker sends a double spend included in her transaction. If the victim accepts the payment, the miner releases a secret block. In contrast to the 51% attack, the action does not require a high hash rate. In order to defend themselves against such a situation, the users should require at least two conformations for their transactions.

Lastly, we face attacks on the infrastructures where blockchain is hosted or the surrounding institutions such as cryptocurrency exchanges. During the attack on the Ethereum blockchain, hackers sent the spam that used up *gas*, the network's computational power, in order to slow down activity in the network (Hertig, 2017a). In another instance, 3.8 million worth of Ether has been drained from the DAO, the autonomous organization supporting the operations of the Ethereum network, which led to a fork and the currency split.

3. The Governance of Cryptocurrencies

In the previous section, we used Bitcoin as a case study to show the technological innovations behind cryptocurrencies and how they can be employed by regular users. Still, there is a consensus in the academic literature on the fact that what makes cryptocurrencies unique is not only the technology that powers them, but the way in which the technology is used to govern over the currency — the fact that the blockchain is distributed among a network of peer-to-peer users in a non-hierarchical fashion (Hsieh *et al.*, 2017; Evans, 2014; Swanson, 2015).

Apart from being a distinctive feature of cryptocurrencies, their governance is also considered to be a significant factor that affects their performance. For this reason, in this section, we synthesize the views present in the academic literature on the different approaches that can be taken in governing a cryptocurrency. We divide the section into two parts. Since the blockchain is a defining feature for most cryptocurrencies, the first part focuses on governance within the blockchain. The second part analyzes the governance of institutions that manage the blockchain.

3.1 *Governance within the Blockchain*

One of the innovative aspects behind cryptocurrencies is that they were the first organizations to use the blockchain technology. As explained in the first section, digital currencies that used cryptography to secure their operations and assure anonymity existed before Bitcoin, but it was Nakamoto (2008) who first put into practice the idea of a ledger that can be operated without a central authority. Since users do not require a third party to centralize the management of the system, blockchain-based organizations are usually assumed to manage transactions without the need for an intermediary. This description is misleading, however, because the blockchain in itself is the intermediary and its operability and economic efficiency depend on its ability to attract the workforce to work for it (Evans, 2014), which means that the design of the blockchain itself bears an important role in the success of a cryptocurrency.

Moreover, the novelty of a blockchain-based organization does not reside in its capacity to remove people from the operation of the blockchain, but rather in its ability to put software at the core of the organization, leaving human actors on the margins (Hsieh *et al.*, 2017). It is these actors that we are concerned with in this section. More specifically, we first look at actors that can bring modifications to the blockchain, *given a certain blockchain protocol,* and then we survey different approaches to structure a blockchain and how they impact the authority and incentives of these actors.

In the literature, the actors mentioned above are usually labeled as *miners*. This term comes from the fact that cryptocurrencies use cryptography by asking agents that operate in the blockchain to solve costly tasks. These tasks — meant to verify and record transactions into the blockchain — are probabilistically impossible to deconstruct, thus preventing malevolent agents from tampering with the system, and also require significant technological resources from the miners.

Hsieh *et al.* (2017, p. 8) describe miners as having two roles: Firstly, they act as "employees" by following the rules imposed through a software-embedded protocol in order to accomplish certain tasks. The protocol sets the timing and priority of transactions, which Yermack (2017, p. 26) compares to the rules of a regular stock exchange. Secondly, they act as *decision makers*, as they can decide which transactions to accept in the blockchain or not. By doing this, they have the agency to say which is the correct version of the blockchain. It is this second role that can affect the stability of cryptocurrencies, if small groups of users can exert outsized power over the network (Kroll *et al.*, 2013).

3.1.1 *The centralization of the blockchain*

Having defined the actors that are relevant for governing within the blockchain, we now look at the relations between them. When analyzing the networks formed by miners, the academic literature usually focuses on one feature of these networks — their level of decentralization. For a few years after Bitcoin was invented, the academic literature ignored the governance of cryptocurrencies (Yermack, 2017), and this gave birth to a dichotomous view of currencies, where at one end there was the fully decentralized Bitcoin, and at the other end the centralized models on which traditional currencies operated. In fact, blockchain-based organizations rather lie on a spectrum of decentralization, which can be divided into three broad categories: centralized, decentralized and distributed networks.

Centralized networks have a central node and a set of peripheral nodes which are only connected to the central node through which all communication is conducted. From a governance perspective, there is nothing innovative in these networks and indeed most cryptocurrencies do not want to replicate this model. Still, the technology employed by blockchains can be of interest for the redesign of centralized networks, and there have been suggestions that central banks could create their own centralized cryptocurrencies (Piscini, 2015; Broadbent, 2016).

Distributed networks lie at the other end of the spectrum and consist of a set of nodes that are all connected to each other. This is an idealistic design of a network, where all nodes have equal authority and there is no need for intermediaries when a transaction is added to the ledger, as the ledger is distributed among users who compete to add information to it (Weber, 2016). The currency that resembles the most this kind of network is Bitcoin. Bitcoin was envisioned by Nakamoto as an egalitarian network and it was assumed to be self-governing. Still, Bitcoin moved away from this network structure over time for reasons that we explore below.

Decentralized networks exist somewhere in between the distributed and the centralized models. These networks do not have a central node that has full authority over the blockchain, but there are some nodes in the network that can act as intermediaries for transactions. Moreover, these networks differentiate themselves from distributed networks by the fact that nodes do not have equal authority in the blockchain. Most of the cryptocurrencies today operate on a model like this.

Lo and Wang (2014) suggest three reasons why Bitcoin moved away from the fully decentralized network model. The first reason is the apparition of intermediaries outside of the blockchain protocol. These intermediaries facilitate certain types of financial transactions with cryptocurrencies (such as exchanging cryptocurrencies with legal tender) and can gain a lot of influence over the cryptocurrency ecosystem (such was the case of the Mt. Gox exchange). The second reason is the apparition of intermediaries whose purpose is to connect end-users to the network in an easier manner, such as electronic wallets.

The third reason why cryptocurrencies that employ proof-of-work (like Bitcoin) become more centralized is the collusion of groups of miners into mining pools that do the "mining" operations in a centralized fashion. Out of the three reasons, this is the most important one for the stability of the system and also the one that is related to the operability of the blockchain protocol. Mining pools arise for two reasons. The first reason is that the rewards from mining are highly volatile. Miners gain a return from the process of mining when they solve the cryptographic puzzle embedded in the verification mechanism.

Since the puzzle is a complex computational task, with its difficulty increasing over time, the probability of solving the puzzle is small, which makes the rewards from mining uncertain. If we assume that a mining pool can harness the same technology as a solo miner, joining a mining pool does not increase the expected value of the return from mining, but reduces the variance of the reward, since all the computing power in a pool is used aggregately and rewards are shared among users (Eyal, 2015).

But mining pools can also harness better technology, and this is the second reason why miners are incentivized to join mining pools — this is especially relevant as rewards from mining become smaller as the currency approaches its cap, thus making mining become exponentially harder over time (Eyal, 2015). This increase in difficulty can be offset only by acquiring more complex equipment to mine. As Tindell (2013) points out, whilst in the early stages of Bitcoin a regular PC was powerful enough to make mining a profitable endeavor, in 2013 specialized equipment was already necessary. Nakamoto did not foresee this development, as the stability of the blockchain was based on the idea that all nodes in the network are equally powerful (hence, the idea of *one-CPU-one-vote*).

Currently, mining technology becomes increasingly more expensive, in what certain authors have qualified as an arms race (Tarasiewicz and Newman, 2015). Mining pools turn into large-scale businesses that exhibit economies of scale and require specific conditions in order to operate efficiently, which impose significant barriers to entry for newcomers — an article from *The Economist* describes how, currently, mining pools are relocating to areas that have low temperatures and can provide cheap energy in order to cut costs (The Economist, 2017).

3.1.2 *Verification mechanisms*

The literature has also focused on another aspect of cryptocurrencies that is significant in determining the governance of blockchains: the verification mechanism. The verification mechanism lies at the core of the blockchain and it is instrumental in establishing the level of centralization in the network and the authority relationships between miners.

Verification mechanisms represent the technology that enables cryptocurrencies to have an innovative governance structure. There are significant differences between various mechanisms, but what all of them have in common is that they ask miners to dedicate significant resources to add valid transactions to the blockchain. The vast amount of resources spent creates a structure that is hard to tamper with and thus it makes it highly improbable for a user to fraud the system. Verification mechanisms can be classified based on two criteria: the nature of the task miners are asked to solve, and the distribution of power among miners. Verification mechanisms can prioritize the decision of some miners and thus determine the level of centralization within the blockchain.

The most common verification mechanism is called proof-of-work and it is the one employed by Bitcoin and by almost all of the alternative currencies that copied the source code of Bitcoin (Bonneau *et al*., 2015). Proof-of-work is a system with significant disadvantages and there are multiple verification mechanisms that have been created in the recent years in order to address the deficiencies. We dedicate the rest of this section to an overview of some of the most common verification mechanisms.

Proof-of-work

Proof-of-work was first used in a cryptocurrency by Nakamoto (2008) and it is based on Adam Back's Hashcash algorithm (Back, 2002). The distinctive feature of this algorithm is that it allows users to add elements to the blockchain based *solely* on their ability to solve a computationally intensive puzzle. Proof-of-work users do not have to own currency in order to mine it. Mining power is proportional to the computing power that each user has, which means that currencies that use proof-of-work are usually associated with a high degree of decentralization (Hsieh *et al.*, 2017). If there are no significant differences in the computing power of agents, this mechanism does not only facilitate the validation of individual transactions, but also creates a credible commitment against attacks on the blockchain, since it becomes increasingly more difficult for a malevolent actor to tamper with the structure of the ledger, as the effort required for an attack increases proportionally with the number of blocks that the user wants removed (Catalini and Gans, 2016).

Lee (2016) points out that proof-of-work is considered to have three disadvantages: The first disadvantage is the high amount of computational power that is required. Computational power is an issue, in particular for proof-of-work algorithms because they are egalitarian in nature, meaning that all users have roughly the same incentive to compete (adjusted to their available CPU), but only one of the users actually solves the puzzle, which means that large amounts of computational effort and electricity are wasted (Papadopoulos, 2015, p. 159). This problem is aggravated by the fact that the difficulty level of the puzzles increases over time.

The second disadvantage comes from the fact that in a proof-of-work system, miners are incentivized to bear the costs of mining by being rewarded with new coins and transaction fees, but the rate of new coin creation is usually set to decrease over time. This can disincentivize miners from investing resources into mining, which is detrimental for regular users of Bitcoin (Davarpanah *et al.*, 2015).

Finally, the decentralized nature of proof-of-work algorithms does not prevent attacks that can modify the components of the blockchain. Attacks can still be conducted by an agent that amasses more than half of the computing power of the whole network. The risks of such “51% attacks” has increased with the apparition of mining pools, and some authors argue that the centralization of the mining process is inevitable for these cryptocurrencies, as the increasing costs and volatility of returns incentivize users to cooperate (Davarpanah *et al.*, 2015).

Proof-of-stake

The main difference between proof-of-work and proof-of-stake mechanisms lies in the way voting power is distributed among users.

In proof-of-work, the voting power is proportional to the computational power of each user. In proof-of-stake, the voting power depends on some posted collateral that each user has, which usually is the number of the coins they own (Mazieres, 2015). Since computational power is not required, this means that the operating costs are smaller, which also reduces the necessary values of transaction fees (Davarpanah *et al.*, 2015). The reward is also not fixed, as in the case of proof-of-work, and miners receive a rate of return akin to a regular interest rate (Davarpanah *et al.*, 2015, p.13). Moreover, because each miner has a vote proportional to their stake, 51% attacks are not expected from a rational user as this would also involve losing their stake in the currency. Still, a disadvantage of proof-of-stake mechanisms is that they create more centralized networks compared to proof-of-work, as users that own more resources also have more power (Lee, 2016). Examples of cryptocurrencies that use proof-of-stake are Nxt and NeuCoin (Davarpanah *et al.*, 2015). Ether, the currency associated with the Ethereum project, is functioning on a proof-of-work mechanism, but it is planning on transitioning to proof-of-stake (Hertig, 2017b).

Another addition to a verification mechanism that needs to be mention here, although it is also compatible with proof-of-work-based currencies, is the introduction of a checkpointing mechanism, which aims to prevent 51% attacks. Checkpoints are hard-coded blocks that cannot be rewritten. This means that even if a group of users gains the necessary power to attack a blockchain, their attack would not be able to go past certain blocks in the ledger (Tarasiewicz and Newman, 2015). Feathercoin and Peercoin are examples of currencies that adopted this mechanism (Davarpanah *et al.*, 2015). Even if this measure clearly secures a cryptocurrency, it is criticized for the fact that it is a form of centralization and it implies putting trust in a user that creates the checkpoints.

Alternatives to proof-of-stake

All proofing mechanisms involve imposing a cost on mining (forwarded by a reward) in order to secure a cryptocurrency. What proof-of-stake does is that it replaces the operational cost required in proof-of-stake with a capital cost — the financial stake that one has in a currency.

Many new cryptocurrencies try to harness the benefits of both proof-of-work and proof-of-stake by employing mixed verification mechanisms. Peercoin is such a currency, which employs proof-of-stake in order to offset the negative impact of mining diminishing returns generated by proof-of-work. The system accomplishes this by creating a steady inflation rate of 1% through proof-of-stake mining.

Since the apparition of proof-of-stake, multiple new algorithms have emerged. Among these algorithms, we can mention the following: proof-of-burn (P4Titan, 2014) (which asks miners to destroy some coins at each verification), proof-of-luck (Milutinovic *et al.*, 2016) (which introduces a lottery in the mining process) or proof-of-time (Intel, 2015) (which uses a lottery and enforces a time frame on the mining process).

3.2 *Governance of the Blockchain*

Up until now, we described various ways in which the protocol of the blockchain can be organized. In this section, we look at the institutions that take decisions about the way the protocol is organized. Since the creation of Bitcoin, hundreds of cryptocurrencies have been launched, which came with numerous governance structures of these alternative currencies. There is no comprehensive overview of all these structures in the literature, and this section will not attempt to fill this gap. Instead, we first describe the governance structure that is embraced by most projects and that is also the focus of most academic research studies — the open-source-like organization — and then briefly present the alternative organizational structures that some of these currencies embrace.

One of the goals of cryptocurrencies is to create a currency that can function without its users having to trust a central authority. This ideal is reflected not only in the employment of blockchain, but also in the way the blockchain protocol is managed. Most early cryptocurrencies have a simple governance structure, with a group of core developers, usually overseen by a chief scientist, that implement all the necessary changes in the blockchain protocol. Changes to the source code can be proposed by anyone. The decision on what changes are to be made can be taken either by the group of core developers or through a democratic procedure where miners vote on proposed changes. Hsieh *et al.* (2017) classify these decision-making procedures by using a scale of decentralization, where at one end, core developers concentrate all power and implement changes with no external input, and at the other end, there is a formal voting mechanism. Bitcoin, for instance, lies somewhere in the middle of this scale, with non-controversial issues being decided by a group of core developers, whereas controversial issues are decided through informal voting procedures on online forums (Papadopoulos, 2015, p. 159). The open-source nature of the code and the fact that cryptocurrencies function because of a group of volunteer developers together with a decentralized group of supporters (the miners) made some authors compare cryptocurrencies with open-source projects (Kroll *et al.*, 2013).

Still, there are authors that point out that there are significant discrepancies between an open-source project and a cryptocurrency, discrepancies that can threaten the stability of these organizations. Evans points out how one of the significant differences is the divergence in interests between miners and developers. Whereas in an open source project like Wikipedia, the goals of the core developers are the same as the goals of the regular contributors (to create a repository of free articles), in a cryptocurrency miners have goals different from those of the developers. This happens because in an open-source project, contributors work for a non-pecuniary interest that also defines the existence of the project, but in the case of cryptocurrencies, miners work in order to obtain revenue (Evans, 2014).

Miners require an incentive scheme to work, and the existence of a group of core developers that can take decisions regarding it without their consultation can significantly destabilize a currency. Indeed, multiple currencies, such as Litecoin (Rizzo, 2017) or Ethereum, have been affected by such disagreements between groups of miners and the core developers, either because core developers took decisions without consulting miners or because of the lax voting procedures that do not incentivize stakeholders to reach a consensus. As a consequence, some authors have suggested that cryptocurrencies need stronger governance structures (Kroll *et al.*, 2013), while others have described the current institutional arrangements of most cryptocurrencies as going against the democratic ideals they propose.

Still, there are an increasing number of cryptocurrency projects that embrace more conventional governance frameworks. This is made possible, to an extent, by the existence of verification mechanisms that allow for more centralization, and it is motivated by the fact that some of these projects want to create stronger links with the financial sector instead of creating a system parallel to it. Such an example is Ripple, a cryptocurrency and blockchain-based payment protocol that embraces a regular corporate structure, which Evans (2014, p. 16) compares to Google's governance structure over Android.

The current state of cryptocurrencies does not offer a clear model of the way they should be governed, although there is an emerging consensus in the academic literature that organizations that retain the decentralized nature of the blockchain, which differentiates them from other financial institutions, while embracing a more complex and centralized governance structure, tend to perform better. This view is supported by the findings of Hsieh *et al.* (2017, p. 3) who analyzed the correlation between the return of investment in various cryptocurrencies and their governance structure, and observed that returns increase as the blockchain is more decentralized, but the decentralization of the organization negatively affects returns.

4. Conclusion

This chapter aims to familiarize the reader with the concept of cryptocurrencies and their current market structure. Based on the academic literature and on market news, we provide an overview of the basic features characterizing these alternative payments systems. In four sections, we introduce the economic origins of cryptocurrencies, provide an introduction to their technical architecture and supporting systems, explain their different forms of organizational structures, and finally provide examples of different cryptocurrency projects. We hope that this work is a useful contribution in synthesizing the present knowledge of the diversified world of cryptocurrencies and in providing an introduction to the subject for future research.

Acknowledgments

Financial support by the University of Manchester's FinTech Initiative is gratefully acknowledged.

References

Abrams, R., and N. Popper. 2014. "Trading Site Failure Stirs Ire and Hope for Bitcoin." *The New York Times*, 25th February. p. B1(L). *Gale Academic OneFile*, https://link.gale.com/apps/doc/A359788335/AONE?u=jrycal5&sid=AONE&xid=0cfb5c53.

Ametrano, F. M. 2016. "Hayek Money: The Cryptocurrency Price Stability Solution." Available at SSRN: https://ssrn.com/abstract=2425270.

Back, A. 2002. "Hashcash — A denial of service counter-measure." www.hashcash.org/papers/hashcash.pdf.

Bhaskar, N. D., L. P. Nian, and D. L. K. Chuen. 2015. "Bitcoin IPO, ETF, and Crowdfunding." In D. L. K. Chuen (ed.), *Handbook of Digital Currency*, Chapter 27, 529–557, Amsterdam: Elsevier.

Bonneau, J., A. Miller, J. Clark, A. Narayanan, J. A. Kroll, and E. W. Felten. 2015. "Research perspectives and challenges for bitcoin and cryptocurrencies." MIT Computer Science and Artificial Intelligence Laboratory.

Broadbent, B. 2016. "Central banks and digital currencies." *Speech at London School of Economics,* Bank of England.

Catalini, C., and J. S. Gans. 2016. "Some simple economics of the blockchain." *National Bureau of Economic Research (NBER) Working Paper No. 22952.*

Chaum, D. 1983. "Blind Signatures for Untraceable Payments." In D. Chaum, R. L. Rivest, and A. T. Sherman (eds.), *Advances in Cryptology: Proceedings of Crypto 82*, 199–203. Amsterdam: Elsevier.

——— 1982. "Computer systems established, maintained and trusted by mutually suspicious groups, PhD dissertation." *Electronics Research Laboratory*, University of California.

Christin, N. 2012. "Traveling the Silk Road: A Measurement Analysis of a Large Anonymous Online Marketplace." CyLab, Carnegie Mellon University.

Coppola, F. 2016. "Ethereum's Latest Hard Fork Shows it has a Very Long Way to Go," *Forbes*, 16th November.

Davarpanah, K., D. Kaufman, and O. Pubellier. 2015. "NeuCoin: The First Secure, Cost-Efficient and Decentralized Cryptocurrency." Available at https://arxiv.org/abs/1503.07768.

De Filippi, P., and B. Loveluck. 2016. "The invisible politics of bitcoin: Governance crisis of a decentralized infrastructure." *Internet Policy Review* 5(3). https://doi.org/10.14763/2016.3.427.

Dwork, C. 2006. "Pricing Via Processing or Combating Junk Mail," In: *Advances in Cryptology — CRYPTO 2006: 26th Annual International Cryptology Conference*, 139–147.

Dwyer, G. P. 2016. "Blockchain: A Primer." Available at SSRN: https://ssrn.com/abstract=2900450.

Evans, D. S. 2014. "Economic aspects of bitcoin and other decentralized public-ledger currency platforms." *Coase-Sandor Institute for Law & Economics* Working Paper No. 685.

Eyal, I. 2015. "The Miner's Dilemma," paper presented at the 2015 *IEEE Symposium on Security and Privacy*. https://ieeexplore.ieee.org/document/7163020.

Franco, P. 2014. *Understanding Bitcoin: Cryptography, Engineering and Economics.* Hoboken, NJ: Wiley.

Frost & Sullivan. 2016. "The Definitive Blockchain Conference — Consensus." Available at http://www.frost.com/sublib/display-report.do?id=9B06-00-15-00-00.

Golumbia, D. 2016. *Politics of Bitcoin: Software as Right-Wing Extremism.* Minneapolis, MN: University of Minnesota Press.

Haber, S., and W. Scott Stornetta. 1991. How to Time-Stamp a Digital Document." In A. J. Menezes and S. A. Vanstone (eds.), *Advances in Cryptology-Crypto '90: Proceedings*, 437–455. Springer. Berlin.

Hertig, A. 2017a. "Ethereum Developers Stymie Blockchain Spammer's New Attack, CoinDesk, 1st June." Available at https://www.coindesk.com/ethereum-developers-stymie-blockchain-spammers-latest-attack/.

——— 2017b. "Ethereum's Big Switch: The New Roadmap to Proof-of-Stake." Coindesk, 5th May, Available at https://www.coindesk.com/ethereums-big-switch-the-new-roadmap-to-proof-of-stake/.

Hileman, G. 2014. "From bitcoin to the brixton pound: History and prospects for alternative currencies." paper presented at the *International Conference on Financial Cryptography and Data Security 2014.*

Hileman, G., and M. Rauchs. 2017. "Global Cryptocurrency Benchmarking Study." Working Paper, Cambridge Centre for Alternative Finance.

Houy, N. 2014. "The economics of bitcoin transaction fees." *Working Paper GATE 2014–07.*

Hsieh, Y.-Y., J.-P. Vergne, and S. Wang. 2017. "The Internal and External Governance of Blockchain-Based Organizations: Evidence from Cryptocurrencies." Available at SSRN: https://ssrn.com/abstract=2966973.

Huckle, S., and M. White 2016. "Socialism and the Blockchain." *Future Internet* 8:4, 49.

Intel. "Introduction to Sawtooth." 2015. https://intelledger.github.io/introduction.html.

Kaminska, I., and P. Murphy. 2017. "Crypto currency offerings spur speculation frenzy." *Financial Times 14th May.*

Kroll, J. A., I. C. Davey, and E. W. Felten. 2013. "The Economics of Bitcoin Mining, or Bitcoin in the Presence of Adversaries," paper presented at the Proceedings of WEIS.

Lee, L. 2016. "New Kids on the Blockchain: How Bitcoin's Technology Could Reinvent the Stock Market," *Hastings Business Law Journal* 12:2, 81–132.

Lo, S., and J. C. Wang. 2014. "Bitcoin as Money?" *Current Policy Perspectives*: Federal Reserve Bank of Boston.

Lustig, C., and B. Nardi. 2015. "Algorithmic Authority: The Case of Bitcoin." In: *HICSS 2015, 48*th *Hawaii International Conference on System Sciences,* 743–752.

Mazieres, D. 2015. "The stellar consensus protocol: A federated model for internet-level consensus." *Stellar Development Foundation.* http://www.scs.stanford.edu/17au-cs244b/notes/scp.pdf.

Milutinovic, M., W. He, H. Wu, and M. Kanwal. 2016. "Proof of luck: An efficient blockchain consensus protocol." paper presented at the Proceedings of the 1st Workshop on System Software for Trusted Execution.

Nakamoto, S. 2009. "Bitcoin Open Source Implementation of P2p Currency." Available at http://p2pfoundation.ning.com/forum/topics/bitcoin-open-source.

——— 2008. "Bitcoin: A Peer-to-Peer Electronic Cash System."

Narayanan, A., J. Bonneau, E. Felten, A. Miller, and S. Goldfeder. 2016. *Bitcoin and cryptocurrency technologies: A comprehensive introduction*. Princeton, NJ: Princeton University Press.

Nian, L. P., and D. L. K. Chuen. 2015. "Introduction to Bitcoin." In D. L. K. Chuen (ed.), *Handbook of Digital Currency*, Chapter 1, 5–30, Elsevier.

P4Titan 2014. "Slimcoin a Peer-to-Peer Crypto-Currency with Proof-of-Burn." Available at www.slimcoin.club/whitepaper.pdf.

Papadopoulos, G. 2015. "Blockchain and Digital Payments: An Institutionalist Analysis of Cryptocurrencies." In D. L. K. Chuen (ed.), *Handbook of Digital Currency*, Chapter 7, 153–172, Amsterdam: Elsevier.

Pilkington, M. 2015. "Blockchain Technology: Principles and Applications." In F. X. Olleros and M. Zhegu (eds.), *Research Handbook on Digital Transformations*, Cheltenham: Elgar.

Piscini, E. 2015. "State-Sponsored Cryptocurrency, Deloitte." Available at https://www2.deloitte.com/content/dam/Deloitte/us/Documents/strategy/us-cons-state-sponsored-cryptocurrency.pdf. Accessed 31st August 2017.

Popper, N. 2016. "A bitcoin believer's crisis of faith." The New York Times, 17th January, p. 1(L). Gale Academic OneFile, https://link.gale.com/apps/doc/A440094953/AONE?u=jrycal5&sid=AONE&xid=dce66479.

Popper, N. 2017. "Bitcoin Technology to Power Database Used by World's Largest Banks." The New York Times, 10th January, p. B4(L). Gale Academic OneFile, https://link.gale.com/apps/doc/A476905245/AONE?u=jrycal5&sid=AONE&xid=dcefd440.

Rauchs, M., A. Blandin, K. Klein, G. C. Pieters, M. Recanatini, and B. Z. Zhang. 2018. "2nd Global Cryptoasset Benchmarking Study." Available at SSRN 3306125.

Rizzo, P. 2017. "8-Hour Miner Meeting Ends with Litecoin Scaling Agreement." Coindesk, 21st April.

Shin, L. 2015. Bitcoin's Shared Ledger Technology: Money's New Operating System." Forbes, September 28. Available at: https://www.forbes.com/sites/laurashin/2015/09/09/bitcoins-shared-ledger-technology-moneys-new-operating-system.

Soska, K., and N. Christin 2015. "Measuring the Longitudinal Evolution of the Online Anonymous Marketplace Ecosystem." Paper presented at the USENIX Security Symposium 2015.

Statista 2019. "Worldwide Blockchain Users." https://www.statista.com/statistics/647374/worldwide-blockchain-wallet-users/.

Swan, M. 2015. *Blockchain: Blueprint for a New Economy*. Sebastopol, CA: O'Reilly.

Swanson, T. 2015. "Consensus-as-a-Service: A brief report on the emergence of permissioned." Distributed Ledger Systems. https://www.ofnumbers.com/2015/04/06/consensus-as-a-service-a-brief-report-on-the-emergence-of-permissioned-distributed-ledger-systems/.

Szabo, N. 2008. "Bit Gold." *Website/Blog*.

——— 1997. "The God Protocols, Satoshi Nakamoto Institute." Available at https://nakamotoinstitute.org/the-god-protocols/.

——— 1998. "Secure Property Titles with Owner Authority, Satoshi Nakamoto Institute." Available at http://nakamotoinstitute.org/secure-property-titles/.

——— 2002. "Shelling Out: The Origins of Money." Altruists.Org/F40. http://nakamotoinstitute.org/the-god-protocols/.

Tarasiewicz, M., and A. Newman. 2015. "Cryptocurrencies as distributed community experiments." In D. L. K. Chuen (ed.), *Handbook of Digital Currency*, Elsevier, Chapter 10, 201–222.

The Economist 2017. "The Magic of Mining," 8th January.

Tindell, K. 2013. "Geeks Love the Bitcoin Phenomenon Like They Loved the Internet in 1995." 5th April, Available at http://www.businessinsider.com/how-bitcoins-are-mined-and-used-2013-4?IR=T.

Weber, B. 2016. "Bitcoin and the legitimacy crisis of money." *Cambridge Journal of Economics* 40:1, 17–41.

Williams, S. 2016. "Decentralization is Disrupting Vertical Industries, Digital Finance News." 19th January, Available at https://digitalfinancenews.com/index.php/2016/01/19/decentralization-is-disrupting-vertical-industries/.

Wood, G., and A. Buchanan. 2015. "Advancing Egalitarianism." In D. L. K. Chuen (ed.), *Handbook of Digital Currency*, Elsevier, Chapter 19, 385–402.

Yermack, D. 2015. "Is Bitcoin a Real Currency? An Economic Appraisal." In D. L. K. Chuen (ed.), *Handbook of Digital Currency*, Amsterdam: Elsevier. Chapter 2, 31–43.

——— 2017. "Corporate governance and blockchains." *Review of Finance* 21, 7–31.

https://doi.org/10.1142/9789811239670_0002

Chapter 2

The Impact of Coronavirus Pandemic on Bitcoin: A Literary Overview

Devinder Gandhi*, Shaista Jaffer†, and Sahar Shabani‡

Telfer School of Management, University of Ottawa, Canada

**gandhi@telfer.uOttawa.ca*

†shaistajaffer@hotmail.com

‡sshab007@uottawa.ca

Abstract

Bitcoin has several features that set it aside from traditional currencies. Digital convenience ensures the safety and convenience of Bitcoin users, while decentralization also poses as a primary benefit. Not only does this specific type of cryptocurrency portray many advantages, it also positions several disadvantages as well. Extreme volatility and the impact of negative externalities on the value of Bitcoin contribute to the assessment of Bitcoin trends in the market. The recent outbreak of the coronavirus (COVID-19) has shown evidence of influencing Bitcoin prices as the virus is spread across continents, leaving the global financial environment in turmoil. The classification of Bitcoin as either a portfolio diversifier, a hedge or a safe haven is dependent on various factors, including the global economic uncertainty. Analyzing the literature on the influence of the crisis on the Bitcoin movement will provide an explanation as to why COVID-19 has had such a significant impact on the global financial markets, especially that of cryptocurrencies.

Keywords: coronavirus, bitcoin, hedge, economic uncertainty, safe haven, cryptocurrency

1. Introduction

Cryptocurrencies are being positioned in the highest ranking of importance in global financial markets. This form of currency exists only in the digital world as a medium of exchange; cryptocurrencies are available over the Internet, the most popular one being Bitcoin.

Being the first ever type of cryptocurrency declared in 2009, Bitcoin has become exceptionally popular over the years due to its unique properties. Not only is it the first form of a decentralized peer-to-peer payment network in existence, but it is also solely controlled by Bitcoin users all over the world. Without having any central authority monitoring the transactions, Bitcoin allows its users to be in full control, while maintaining identity protection. More explicitly, there is no connection between a bitcoin and the owner of the bitcoin beyond possession. The identity of the individuals involved in a Bitcoin transaction is virtually anonymous (Brito and Castillo, 2013). Thus, security is identified as an essential advantage to Bitcoin, alongside many other positive features, such as the ease to use and transfer the currency, as well as the speed of the transfer.

Aside from the several advantages of Bitcoin, several disadvantages also exist. Extreme volatility is a key identifying feature of Bitcoin. The volatility of this type of cryptocurrency can be significant in any given hour of the day (Franklin, 2016). The risk–return trade-off theory of finance states that high volatility comes with high expected returns. For this reason, many have chosen to invest in cryptocurrencies. The current debate in this area of research investigates whether the investment in Bitcoin is merely for portfolio diversification or does it also act as a hedge or a safe haven. The global economic uncertainty is found to have an effect on the way Bitcoin is classified into three categories. In fact, several negative externalities can affect the role and value of Bitcoin.

One of the most recent economic uncertainties has been caused by the Novel Coronavirus, also termed COVID-19. This pneumonia-type virus was officially declared in 2019, and by January 23, 2020, Wuhan, China, the source of coronavirus, was placed under quarantine as the virus uncontrollably spread to several countries and continents (Bouoiyour and Selmi, 2020). As COVID-19 spread rapidly across the whole country, it turned into a national crisis leading to major shutdowns of industries and businesses. Since China's share of global trade is as high as 14%

(Bouoiyour and Selmi, 2020), the impact on the global scale of financial markets is much more significant than any past economic uncertainties. During the SARS outbreak in 2003, also sourced from China, its share of global trade was only 5% (Bouoiyour and Selmi, 2020). Therefore, the effect of COVID-19 on the financial markets is significant. Stock markets have experienced an unprecedented decline in share prices; cryptocurrencies have also experienced severe volatility. As such, the global implications of COVID-19 have become a topic of interest not only in the health sector but also in the fields of economics and finance.

The goal of this chapter is to explain the reaction to the coronavirus pandemic, depending on Bitcoin's classification as a portfolio diversifier, a hedge or a safe haven. This particular analysis allows for the foundations of cryptocurrency and Bitcoin to be laid out. The unique advantages and disadvantages to Bitcoin users and Bitcoin issuers will also be compared to understand the dynamics of the network. The framework of the coronavirus outbreak of 2019 will be established, using it as an asset in determining the classification and role of Bitcoin during the global pandemic.

2. Theoretical Framework

2.1 *Cryptocurrency*

Cryptocurrencies were introduced as a new form of currency and over time, and they grew into a billion-dollar market. The exclusion of financial institutions and other third parties served as an advantage of these digital currencies, allowing their users to control their transactions (Shahzad *et al.*, 2019b). In fact, a concise definition of the digital currency states as follows:

> *Cryptocurrencies are peer-to-peer electronic cash systems which allow online payments to be sent directly from one party to another without going through a financial institution.* (Corbet *et al.*, 2019)

In general, cryptocurrency is considered to have emerged in 2008 in response to the Global Financial Crisis (GFC) (Vojtko and Cisár, 2020).

2.2 *Bitcoin*

The design of Bitcoin was developed by Satoshi Nakamoto, an alleged pseudonym of one person or a group of persons (Kliber *et al.*, 2019). The purpose of this particular cryptocurrency was to work as a medium of exchange in order to buy and sell goods and services. What is important to note is that Nakamoto did not control Bitcoin; he was simply another user in the network that established this particular form of cryptocurrency. The smallest denomination of bitcoin is called a "satoshi," which represents 0.0000001 of a bitcoin (Grant and Hogan, 2015). The total number of bitcoins that can be mined is 21 million, with the last satoshi expected to be mined in the year 2140 (Brito and Castillo, 2013). Nakamoto is expected to hold approximately 1 million bitcoins, which is approximately 5% of the total possible bitcoins. As of April 2020, 18,310,825 bitcoins have been mined (*How Many Bitcoins Are There? How Many Left to Mine?*, 2020).

> *Bitcoin is a virtual currency that began as a white paper in November 2008 and transitioned from an idea to reality in 2009 with the mining of the first bitcoin.* (Grant and Hogan, 2015)

Bitcoin has gained traction over the years for several reasons. Bitcoin, as an asset, enables complete transactions, and also acts as an investment opportunity. Investors are attracted to the Bitcoin network because of its exclusive properties. The properties of Bitcoin lead to its advantages and disadvantages, which can further be classified to distinguish between Bitcoin issuers and Bitcoin users.

2.3 *Advantages of Bitcoin*

Digital convenience serves as one of the main advantages of Bitcoin. Although Bitcoin may not be able to perform as a dominant global currency, it can still play a significant role due to its ease of use and ability to work in developing markets (Franklin, 2016). Bitcoin has witnessed a great deal of acceptance because it is a network run on computer programs, which are more commonly used nowadays than in the past (Grant and Hogan, 2015).

Furthermore, the extraordinarily quick speed of bitcoin transfers protects the users from chargeback fraud (Dumitrescu, 2017). Because transfers are instantaneous, once they are complete, they are final. There are no boundaries for bitcoin transfers in the sense that international and domestic transfers are not subject to foreign currency exchange rates and fees.

The absence of a central authority poses yet another key identifying property of Bitcoin (Franklin, 2016). Decentralization allows for cryptography to control bitcoin creation and management, rather than having a central bank, or any other form of authority, do so (Kliber *et al.*, 2019). This implies that Bitcoin is independent of the possibility of the central authority devaluing the currency through arbitrary currency creation (Grant and Hogan, 2015), and of inflation (Shahzad *et al.*, 2019b).

Also, Dumitrescu (2017) identified personal data protection as one of the primary advantages of Bitcoin. It was stated that the anonymity of the users is better ensured through encrypted mathematical algorithms, thus firewalling security breaches. This result is similar to that of Kayal and Rohilla (2019) in that payments are protected and verified through electronic transfer and that the privacy of the user is delinked from the actual transaction.

Furthermore, the low transaction costs as a result of decentralization is another incentive for joining the Bitcoin network. Symitsi and Chalvatzis (2019) estimate the economic gains of the transaction costs associated with Bitcoin transfers. They study the effect of these gains both with and without transaction costs and find that economic gains are not reduced after introducing transaction costs. This suggests that the costs of Bitcoin transactions are reasonably priced. Dumitrescu (2017) finds that on average, the transaction costs are over five times lower than those of credit cards. Transaction costs are also unrelated to the amount transferred, implying that the transaction cost is constant for sending 1 bitcoin or any number of bitcoins. Thus, transaction costs serve as another key advantage of Bitcoin.

3. Bitcoin Classification: Advantages for the Investor

There are several reasons for investors to accept Bitcoin trading as an attractive business. These reasons are more broadly defined as the roles or classifications of the Bitcoin asset itself. While some investors will participate in the crypto market because bitcoins are considered to be an asset that is useful for portfolio diversification, others partake of the market activities because they consider Bitcoin either as a hedge or as a safe haven. Several recent studies consider the classification of Bitcoin to be dependent on several factors and impacts.

3.1 *Hedge*

This classification of Bitcoin is defined by Jana and Das (2020) as an investible asset that is either uncorrelated or negatively correlated with another investible portfolio instrument on average. The risk return mechanism allows for the maximization of expected profits. Several past studies have evaluated the role of Bitcoin under different circumstances to determine whether it acts as a hedge or has any other role.

Bitcoin was found to act as a weak hedge for both Bitcoin-friendly economies and all other markets included in the study by Kliber *et al.* (2019). This result is similar to that of Jana and Das (2020), where they found Bitcoin to be a weak hedge for all markets. Stensås *et al.* (2019) observe that Bitcoin acts as a hedge for investors in most of the developing countries like Brazil, Russia, India and South Korea but as a diversifier for other countries and commodities, while Urquhart and Zhang (2019) conclude that Bitcoin can be an intraday hedge for some currencies, while it can be a diversifier for others. Because these results are theoretically accepted, when Bitcoin behaves differently, several questions arise.

Bitcoin is commonly compared with different commodities, like oil and gold, and its behavior is tested by comparing it to the behavior of these other commodities. Shahzad *et al.* (2019a) and Bouoiyour and Selmi (2020) find that Bitcoin and gold do not move in the same direction. These two assets are generally viewed as a hedge and a safe haven in times of economic turmoil; however, the factors driving the price of Bitcoin and the price of gold may be different. This result implies that Bitcoin can act as an effective hedge for energy commodities but not for non-energy commodities. Shahzad *et al.* (2019a) conclude that gold is a better hedge than Bitcoin, similar to the conclusion of Pal and Mitra (2019) that gold is found to provide a better hedge against Bitcoin when compared to wheat, a non-energy commodity. Das *et al.* (2020) study the comparison of Bitcoin with oil and find that Bitcoin is not superior to other assets when hedging oil-related uncertainties. Investors may prefer different investment instruments to hedge the downside risk in different economic situations and market states. In fact, Bitcoin is found to better hedge the demand-side shocks than the supply-side shocks.

The classification of Bitcoin as a hedge is also dependent on the economic uncertainty. Fang *et al.* (2019) find that global economic policy uncertainty has a significantly negative impact on the Bitcoin–bonds correlation and a positive impact on both Bitcoin–equities and Bitcoin–commodities correlations, suggesting the possibility of Bitcoin acting as a hedge under specific economic uncertainty conditions. Kayal and Rohilla (2019) and Al Mamun *et al.* (2020) conclude that during the period of high policy uncertainty and worsening economic conditions, Bitcoin investors are better off to hedge their portfolio with gold and not with other financial assets. The identification of Bitcoin as a hedge is complex in its foundations, depending on several underlying factors and situations that need to be assessed.

3.2 *Portfolio Diversification*

Portfolio diversification is one of the primary reasons why investors invest in any sort of asset. It is defined as an investible instrument that is positively, but imperfectly correlated with another instrument in the portfolio (Jana and Das, 2020). Diversification is commonly practiced in order to moderate the risk that one investment type may perform poorly when multiple assets are invested in. Vojtko and Cisár (2020), Al-Yahyaee *et al.* (2019), Shahzad *et al.* (2019b) and Kayal and Rohilla (2019) conclude that Bitcoin is classified as an asset used for portfolio diversification. Further, Jana and Das (2020) and Klein *et al.* (2018) discuss the differences of Bitcoin impacts on equity and on other assets and find that the results are consistent. Bitcoin is found to be an effective diversifier of the downside risk in equity markets in a study conducted by Shahzad *et al.* (2019b).

Further analyzes were conducted to better understand the classification of Bitcoin under various circumstances and across different countries. Bouoiyour and Selmi (2020) studied the role of Bitcoin and concluded that it could act as an effective diversifier against movements in energy commodities but not for non-energy commodities. On the other hand, Stensås *et al.* (2019) evaluated the difference in the role of Bitcoin in major developed and developing countries and found that Bitcoin acted as a diversifier not only for investors in developed countries but also for all commodities. While Ji *et al.* (2019) and Shahzad *et al.* (2019a) also found that the diversification role of Bitcoin was not necessarily as strong as commonly believed, Symitsi and Chalvatzis (2019) concluded that their results were statistically significant for the diversification benefits of Bitcoin. In fact, Urquhart and Zhang (2019) took one step further and evaluated the role of Bitcoin against world currencies at an intraday level, due to the extreme volatility of the asset. They concluded that Bitcoin acted as an intraday hedge for some currencies, while it acted as a diversifier for others.

An increasing number of analyzes find that the presence of Bitcoin in a portfolio enhances its performance by improving the risk-return profile of the portfolio. While Vojtko and Cisár (2020), Al-Yahyaee *et al.* (2019), Shahzad *et al.* (2019b) and Kayal and Rohilla (2019), along with several others, found that Bitcoin acted as both a hedge and a diversifier, and consequently as the next digital gold, Jana and Das (2020), Klein *et al.* (2018) and others found that Bitcoin behaves quite the opposite. They found that Bitcoin and stock market returns were positively correlated during the periods of downward markets. Therefore, the evidence on the classification of Bitcoin as a portfolio diversifier is still under investigation.

3.3 *Safe Haven*

Bitcoin is often considered a safe haven asset for many investors. A safe haven is an investible asset that is negatively correlated with other instruments in the portfolio, as defined by Jana and Das (2020). It is a financial instrument that is expected to retain or gain value during periods of economic uncertainty. Recent studies have aimed to classify this role of Bitcoin by comparing it to different commodities and by analyzing the network under several conditions and in various locations.

Some researchers, such as Bouoiyour and Selmi (2020) and Al Mamun *et al.* (2020), say that Bitcoin is classified as a safe haven. Bouoiyour and Selmi (2020) examined whether Bitcoin exhibited a safe haven property during global uncertainty. The results found using a 20-day time span indicated that Bitcoin was considered a crypto safe haven and that Bitcoin reinforced its status as a digital gold. On the other hand, Al Mamun *et al.* (2020) found that Bitcoin is not necessarily a safe haven investment like gold but the correlation between the two is positive and significant during a deteriorating economic situation This suggests that when investors look for a safe haven, Bitcoin performs as good as gold. Given the global economic uncertainty observed in 2020, researchers were able to capture the classification of Bitcoin as a safe haven based on its market behavior.

Several other studies have been performed to determine whether or not Bitcoin should be classified as a diversifier, a hedge or a safe haven. Vojtko and Cisár (2020), Luis *et al.* (2019), and Stensås *et al.* (2019) find that Bitcoin is not a safe haven for investors in their analyzes. Evidently, Vojtko and Cisár (2020) concluded that Bitcoin is not a preferred asset to hold during times of stress because its price behaves like the price of the stock market index, which is volatile during financial crises. Similarly, Luis *et al.* (2019) find that Bitcoin behaves as a speculative asset in the short term but in the long term, speculation does not seem to influence Bitcoin behavior. Rather, the demand for Bitcoin may be driven by its future capabilities as a medium of exchange and, therefore, it is not regarded as a safe haven or a means of payment.

To continue this analysis further, several studies consider the comparison of Bitcoin to other commodities, such as gold or oil, to determine Bitcoin's classification as a safe haven, similar to when evaluating the asset's role as a hedge or a diversifier. Jana and Das (2020), *Stensås et al.* (2019), Klein *et al.* (2018) and Shahzad *et al.* (2019a, 2019b), along with several other researchers, conclude that Bitcoin is not the new gold. Bitcoin and gold have distinct characteristics and, generally, one of the main properties of gold is being a safe haven. Therefore, in terms of protection during global uncertainty, gold outperforms Bitcoin.

Shahzad *et al.* (2019a) investigate the behavior of gold and Bitcoin for the G7 countries and find that gold is an indisputable safe haven and hedge for several G7 stock indices, whereas Bitcoin takes these two roles only in the case of Canada. Comparatively, *Shahzad et al.* (2019b) find that each of Bitcoin, gold, and the commodity index can be considered as a weak safe haven asset in some cases. The roles of these commodities vary across time and also differ between economies. Developed markets find gold as the only weak safe haven asset, while gold and commodities play the same role in emerging markets, and Bitcoin serves as a diversifier. Therefore, it can be stated that gold and Bitcoin may perform similarly at a given time but vary due to other features such as geographical differences. Kliber *et al.* (2019) study the difference in Bitcoin performance for energy and non-energy commodities and find that Bitcoin was considered a safe haven only in the case of Venezuela. Bitcoin may also serve as a safe haven in emerging financial markets, similar to the findings of Shahzad *et al.* (2019b). Again, it becomes evident that Bitcoin classification is dependent on the time of the study and the market status in the country of analysis, developed or emerging.

When comparing the classification of Bitcoin, gold and other commodities to the Oil Implied Volatility Index (OVX), Das *et al.* (2020) find that the US Dollar (USD) is a better alternative to hedge the OVX than Bitcoin. The cryptocurrency is found to outperform gold and other commodities in hedging the OVX, while gold acts as a better safe haven to the OVX when compared to Bitcoin. Stensås *et al.* (2019) find that Bitcoin acts as a safe haven for only a few national equity indices, regional indices and commodities but that in most cases, Bitcoin is not found to be a strong safe haven. Klein *et al.* (2018) explicitly announce that Bitcoin is not the new gold because although its volatility dynamics share some aspects with gold and silver from a diversification perspective, it differs in that Bitcoin does not serve as a safe haven, which is a prominent feature of gold.

3.4 *Externalities: Historical Incidences*

While these classifications of Bitcoin may serve as an advantage, there are several disadvantages as well. Bitcoin is known to experience extreme volatility both during times of economic uncertainty and times of economic stability. The impact of externalities, such as SARS and the Novel Coronavirus, on Bitcoin is a major concern that greatly influences the financial markets. Studying the efficiency of Bitcoin by considering the Efficient Market Hypothesis (EMH) and reviewing the results generated from previous studies with regard to externalities and market uncertainties contributes to a more comprehensive understanding.

The Efficient Market Hypothesis suggests that once information is recognized, it spreads rapidly and is incorporated into the price of the securities without delay (Malkiel, 2003). The EMH is a theoretical model with a strong foundational history of development and is currently evolving and being applied to many situations on a daily basis. Gronwald (2019) conducts a number of non-linearity tests in his study and finds that Bitcoin markets are inefficient. Furthermore, Urquhart (2016) conducted a distinct report on the efficiency of Bitcoin and found that Bitcoin returns are not consistent with market efficiency over the full sample considered for the analysis. However, when the sample is split into two subsample periods, some tests indicate that Bitcoin is efficient in the latter period. Also, Bouoiyour and Selmi (2020) concluded that the adjustment of Bitcoin prices is inconsistent with EMH. Bitcoin is far from being closer to efficiency due to its speculative and volatile behavior. The returns do not respond immediately to coronavirus, and therefore, it would be reasonable to infer that Bitcoin is in an inefficient market but may be in the process of moving towards efficiency.

Externalities in the form of market uncertainty are also deemed as negative influencers of Bitcoin. Albulescu (2020) finds that financial volatility has different sources: economic conditions, institutional issues or market uncertainty. Fang *et al.* (2019) declare that for Bitcoin investors, the results suggest the ability to use evidence about the state of global economic uncertainty to improve the predictions of Bitcoin volatility. Comparably, *Al Mamun et al.* (2020) state that the geopolitical risk and global economic policy uncertainty command a risk premium, particularly in distressed market conditions. In fact, throughout the period of high policy uncertainty and deteriorating economic circumstances, Bitcoin investors can only hedge their portfolio with gold and not with other financial assets. The consequence of geopolitical risk and global and US economic uncertainty is far more significant during unfavorable economic conditions. Geopolitical risk is the most significant feature that contributes to the volatility and risk premia of Bitcoin. The effect of the US economic policy uncertainty is insignificant while global economic policy uncertainty is significant in explaining Bitcoin risk premia.

Considering historical events that have greatly impacted the value of Bitcoin in the past will contribute to a concrete understanding of the behavior of Bitcoin as a result of its classification. Stensås *et al.* (2019) consider past global externalities, such as the burst of the Chinese market bubble in 2015, the US election in 2016, and the Brexit referendum in 2016. Bitcoin has acted as a safe haven asset for both the US and non-US investors in these situations, but the volatility observed in response to these events was extreme. Bouoiyour and Selmi (2020) also discuss that the recent Bitcoin rally associated with the 2020 global pandemic can be due to heightened global economic uncertainties consisting of increasing worries over the US–China war, US–Iran tensions, Brexit concerns as well as tensions between Japan and South Korea. All of these factors have boosted Bitcoin prices, but the coronavirus is clearly the most important catalyst as of yet.

The impact of the negative externalities and the volatile movement of Bitcoin values together identify the fundamentals of the network. While the behavior of Bitcoin depends on time-varying measures, as well as market developments, the externalities suggest a strong impact on the observed volatility and price behavior of Bitcoin. The coronavirus of 2020 is found to have the most significant impact as of yet.

4. Coronavirus (COVID-19)

Recently, a flu-like virus had affected several residents in the city of Wuhan severely. Within days, the virus spread across the whole world as a cataclysmic event. The Novel Coronavirus, known as COVID-19, has infected over 1.5 million people across the world as of April 2020, claiming the lives of almost 90,000 individuals (*Coronavirus Update (Live): 1,518,719 Cases and 88,502 Deaths from COVID-19 Virus Pandemic — Worldometer*, 2020).

As with past crises, the consequences of the coronavirus can also be felt in the global economy as well as in the financial markets. Many analysts such as Bouoiyour and Selmi (2020), Kayal and Rohilla (2019) and Yue *et al.* (2020) compare the coronavirus to the 2003 SARS outbreak. While this can provide useful information, there are several dissimilarities between the two periods to account for. China currently has a much larger share of the global economy and markets than it did 17 years ago. China's share of global trade increased to almost 14% in 2019 compared to 5% in 2003 (Bouoiyour and Selmi, 2020). Furthermore, its share of the Morgan Stanley Capital International (MSCI) Emerging Markets Index has risen to almost 35% in 2019 from 8% in 2003 (Bouoiyour and Selmi, 2020).

Bouoiyour and Selmi (2020), Kayal and Rohilla (2019) and Yue *et al.* (2020) report that when past disease outbreaks occurred, they were quickly contained. The economic consequences were relatively moderate, and the equities were modestly affected. For example, the outbreak of SARS in 2003 killed 774 people, but it was contained and the stock market rose by more than 20% that year (Bouoiyour and Selmi, 2020). However, things are likely to be much different with the coronavirus. The global economy currently appears to be very precarious and an extended disease outbreak might tip the aging business cycle into a global recession. This outbreak aggravates the uncertainty surrounding the global economic outlook.

Current news reports consistently discuss the decline in value of the global stock markets as a result of the COVID-19 outbreak, leading to an increase in the number of investors that are in search of a safe haven for their investments. Bouoiyour and Selmi (2020) find that the Bitcoin price has witnessed a rapid increase from January 23 to February 9, 2020. Albulescu (2020) points out that the Bitcoin price has not experienced such an increase in almost 3 months. In this context, Bitcoin is regarded as a safe haven asset within the timeframe considered, as observed by Jana and Das (2020). Even though there may be various important factors driving it, the emergence of the coronavirus as a determining factor cannot be overlooked, as mentioned by Kayal and Rohilla (2019). Much significant research has been conducted to investigate the responses of Bitcoin to uncertainty over different externalities including the US presidential elections, the Brexit Referendum, the oil market crash, the Asian financial crisis and many more such events.

The financial volatility that has resulted from the coronavirus until now shows to be significant and may be the possible source for a new financial crisis, as investigated by Albulescu (2020). Market uncertainty is found to be a determining factor of financial volatility through the results obtained from a regression on the infection ratios and death ratios performed with data within China, outside of China and overall on a global scale. The higher the number of affected countries, the higher the financial volatility. While the effects within China on financial volatility were negative, those outside of China were positive. Therefore, the global effect remains inconclusive. Yue *et al.* (2020) discuss the implications of risk management on the coronavirus and offer suggestions on how to mitigate the risk felt on a global level. It is important to acknowledge that COVID-19 is continuously spreading at rapid speeds while this paper is being developed and, therefore, once the virus has stabilized, the classification role of Bitcoin may differ.

The information about the coronavirus takes time to be reflected in the Bitcoin prices, which highlights the inefficiencies it implies. Bouoiyour and Selmi (2020) find that the adjustment of Bitcoin prices is inconsistent with the EMH. In fact, Bitcoin is far from being close to efficiency due to its speculative and volatile behavior. They find that the returns do not respond immediately to coronavirus, similar to the findings of Jana and Das (2020), Albulescu (2020), Kayal and Rohilla (2019) and Urquhart (2016).

Bouoiyour and Selmi (2020) mention that one of the reasons that the Bitcoin price may be increasing as the new virus spreads is because 65% of Bitcoin mining takes place in China. More accurately, coronavirus exerts a significant influence on mining activity, which may thereafter be driving up the Bitcoin price. Kayal and Rohilla (2019) discuss this reasoning in their literary study.

The implications of COVID-19 are found to significantly affect not only the economic markets but also the financial markets. Bitcoin has witnessed a great deal of volatility over the past few months because of the virus. The investor attention in response to the search for a safe haven asset is one of the main reasons for the extreme volatility observed by Bitcoin. The behavior of this cryptocurrency is dependent on several underlying factors that appear as the advantages and disadvantages of the asset, as well as the economic uncertainties that are faced on the national and international levels.

4.1 *Coronavirus and Financial Markets' Volatility*

Albulescu (2020) examines the impact of the virus on financial market volatility and its potential to emerge as a new financial crisis. The author hypothesizes that good and bad macroeconomic announcements impact the volatility index (VIX) asymmetrically. The findings indicate that the death ratio positively influences the VIX, mostly contributed to by the countries aside from China, and that the higher the number of affected countries, the higher the financial volatility.

Furthermore, new reported cases have a marginally negative effect on volatility in China, whereas outside of China, coronavirus contributes to an increase in volatility. The overall situation reveals inconclusive results about the total number of new coronavirus cases on the VIX.

Therefore, the increasing spread of the coronavirus accelerates the volatility, and the persistence of COVID-19 might generate a new episode of international financial stress.

4.2 *Hedging and Safe haven Potentials of Bitcoin during the Coronavirus Outbreak*

The global economy appears fragile; therefore, an extended outbreak of the disease might tip the contemporaneous aging business cycle into a global recession. The risk to investors may be much more pronounced. There is an onset of anxiety in the financial markets about the virus. If an effective remedy is not found promptly, it can spell disaster for the global market.

Jana and Das (2020) investigate the following questions: Does Bitcoin provide diversification benefits when the Chinese equity portfolio investors do not? Given this, does Bitcoin outperform gold? Is the price increase in altcoins due to the quivering equity markets in China or a mere spillover from Bitcoin? Could Bitcoin have been used to diversify oil and commodity investments? They show that Bitcoin is a weak hedge during the overall period studied and a weak safe haven upon the onset of the crisis. Bitcoin is a weak hedge, diversifier and a weak safe haven for the sectoral equity indexes, while gold outperforms Bitcoin in its hedging and safe haven roles. These results parallel those of Bouoiyour and Selmi (2020). Altcoin price increments are mainly due to the spillover from Bitcoin prices.

In another study, Bouoiyour and Selmi (2020) analyze the following questions: Does Bitcoin exhibit a safe-haven property against heightened uncertainty? Did the initial news of the coronavirus outbreak lead to the increased volatility of Bitcoin? Does Bitcoin immediately react to publicly announced information (Efficient Market Hypothesis (EMH))? They find Bitcoin to be a crypto safe haven during the time span of January 1 to February 15, 2020, right before the major decline in the value of the cryptocurrency. The virus is found to intensify the volatility of Bitcoin due to a search by investors for alternative asset classes amid concerns about the coronavirus, also discussed by Kayal and Rohilla (2019).

Since the global markets fell due to fears of a coronavirus outbreak, it is naturally expected that investors will look for a safe haven. The Bitcoin price has witnessed a rapid rise from January 23, 2020 to February 9, 2020 which means that Bitcoin can act as a safe haven. If Bitcoin follows the EMH, its prices would adjust with the emergence of unforeseen events, but these price adjustments would become less pronounced after the announcement day. The results show that Bitcoin prices react positively to coronavirus, reinforcing its status as a digital gold or safe haven.

The money velocity of bitcoins in circulation exerts a negative impact on the Bitcoin price. The exchange-trace ratio is positively and strongly correlated with the price of Bitcoin. Bitcoin and gold do not move in the same direction. A negative effect of the hash rate on the Bitcoin price is observed, which means that the higher the number of miners that join the Bitcoin network, the more important the network hash rate is. Mining could be seen as a type of Bitcoin investment.

Using the theoretical foundations of the Bitcoin literature and the idea of hedging, Harvey (2020) discusses the financial implication of the coronavirus and compares the situation to that of the global financial crisis. Due to the pandemic, many individuals have lost their income and wealth and have gone into debt. Therefore, they are likely to turn to another avenue to source income. Interest rates currently being very low, it is difficult to convince individuals to consider bond-based financing. This is where cryptocurrencies have an opportunity to be analyzed in the modern setting. Harvey (2020) concludes that while gold has a long history and is volatile, it is an unreliable hedge due to the fact that it has a long holding time, of almost centuries. During COVID-19, it also does not serve as an effective hedge.

Harvey (2020) also addresses cryptocurrencies that too are not a hedge because they are not linked to any fundamental; cryptocurrencies are essentially computer programs. Since cryptocurrencies are fairly new, there is no history that would guarantee the hedging capabilities of the digital currency. Therefore, due to its extreme volatility and classification as a risky asset, Bitcoin is not considered to be an effective hedge, especially during times of economic turmoil.

5. Conclusion

There are several properties underlying the foundation of Bitcoin's existence. These properties are generalized into advantages and disadvantages and are useful when examining Bitcoin behavior and responses to macroeconomic uncertainty. Bitcoin properties extend beyond its transactional roles, such as digital convenience, ease of use and quick speed. The decentralization of the cryptocurrency encourages safe and secure transactions because of the anonymity of the Bitcoin users through encryption. The classification of Bitcoin as a portfolio diversifier, a hedge or a safe haven is considered when discussing the reaction of Bitcoin under various situations. While Bitcoin can be defined as a hedging asset, termed as an investible asset that is either uncorrelated or negatively correlated with other financial instruments in the investor's portfolio, a portfolio diversifier is expressed as an investible instrument that is positively but imperfectly correlated with the other assets, as defined by Jana and Das (2020). They also define a safe haven as an investible asset that is negatively correlated with other instruments in the portfolio.

Considering these definitions, the impact of the disadvantages of Bitcoin have numerous implications for the cryptocurrency. The extreme volatility of the digital currency can be viewed as a disadvantage under risk aversion. Most of these externalities include historical events with uncontrollable effects on the global and financial markets. The main externality considered is the Novel Coronavirus of 2019. This global pandemic has caused great economic uncertainty and financial discomfort. Developing a cure for COVID-19 is found to be the only way to reduce the anxiety of this uncertainty.

The Efficient Market Hypothesis is used to examine the severity of the coronavirus. The inefficiency that is inferred from recent empirical studies suggests that the time span of the analysis is the key in determining the long-term effects: When the entire time span is considered in the analysis, inefficiency is recorded, whereas when the sample time is split into two, the latter subsample is found to show efficiency. Without conducting a thorough investigation of the entire time span of the virus, beginning with the onset of the crisis and ending with the development of a successful remedy, the results remain inconclusive. Therefore, the impact of Bitcoin's reaction to the coronavirus pandemic is essentially dependent on its classification.

References

Al Mamun, M., G. S. Uddin, M. T. Suleman, and S. H. Kang. 2020. "Geopolitical risk, uncertainty and Bitcoin investment." *Physica A: Statistical Mechanics and Its Applications* 540, 123107.

Albulescu, C. (2020). "Coronavirus and financial volatility: 40 days of fasting and fear." *ArXiv Preprint ArXiv:2003.04005*.

Al-Yahyaee, K. H., W. Mensi, I. M. W. Al-Jarrah, A. Hamdi, and S. H. Kang (2019). "Volatility forecasting, downside risk, and diversification benefits of Bitcoin and oil and international commodity markets: A comparative analysis with yellow metal." *The North American Journal of Economics and Finance* 49, 104–120.

Bouoiyour, J., and R. Selmi. 2020. "Coronavirus spreads and Bitcoin's 2020 rally: Is there a link?" Working Papers hal-02493309, HAL.

Brito, J., and A. Castillo. 2013. *Bitcoin: A Primer for Policymakers*. Mercatus Center at George Mason University.

Corbet, S., B. Lucey, A. Urquhart, and L. Yarovaya. 2019. "Cryptocurrencies as a financial asset: A systematic analysis." *International Review of Financial Analysis* 62, 182–199. https://doi.org/10.1016/j.irfa.2018.09.003.

Coronavirus Update (Live): 1,518,719 Cases and 88,502 Deaths from COVID-19 Virus Pandemic — Worldometer (n.d.). Retrieved April 8, 2020, from https://www.worldometers.info/coronavirus/?utm_campaign=home Advegas1?.

Das, D., C. L. Le Roux, R. K. Jana, and A. Dutta. 2020. "Does Bitcoin hedge crude oil implied volatility and structural shocks?" A comparison with gold, commodity and the US Dollar. *Finance Research Letters* 36:C, p. 101335.

Dumitrescu, G. C. 2017. "Bitcoin — A brief analysis of the advantages and disadvantages." *Global Economic Observer* 5:2, 63–71.

Fang, L., E. Bouri, R. Gupta, and D. Roubaud. 2019. "Does global economic uncertainty matter for the volatility and hedging effectiveness of Bitcoin?" *International Review of Financial Analysis* 61, 29–36.

Franklin, M. 2016. "A profile of Bitcoin currency: An exploratory study." *International Journal of Business & Economics Perspectives* 11:1, 80–92.

Grant, G., and R. Hogan. 2015. "Bitcoin: Risks and controls." *Journal of Corporate Accounting & Finance* 26:5, 29–35.

Gronwald, M. 2019. "Is Bitcoin a Commodity? On price jumps, demand shocks, and certainty of supply." *Journal of International Money and Finance* 97, 86–92.

Harvey, C. 2020. "The Economic and Financial Implications of COVID-19." https://www.darden.virginia.edu/mayo-center/events/virtual-speaker-series.

How Many Bitcoins Are There? How Many Left to Mine? 2020. Retrieved April 7, 2020, from https://www.buybitcoinworldwide.com/how-many-bitcoins-are-there/.

Jana, R. K., and D. Das, 2020. "Did Bitcoin act as an antidote to the Chinese equity market and booster to Altcoins during the Novel Coronavirus outbreak?" Available at SSRN 3544794.

Ji, Q., E. Bouri, D. Roubaud, and L. Kristoufek. 2019. "Information interdependence among energy, cryptocurrency and major commodity markets." *Energy Economics* 81, 1042–1055.

Kayal, P., and P. Rohilla. 2019. "Bitcoin in the Literature of Economics and Finance: A Survey." Available at SSRN 3441652.

Klein, T., H. P. Thu, and T. Walther. 2018. "Bitcoin is not the New Gold — A comparison of volatility, correlation, and portfolio performance." *International Review of Financial Analysis* 59, 105–116.

Kliber, A., P. Marszałek, I. Musiałkowska, and K. Świerczyńska. 2019. "Bitcoin: Safe haven, hedge or diversifier? Perception of bitcoin in the context of a country's economic situation — A stochastic volatility approach." *Physica A: Statistical Mechanics and Its Applications* 524, 246–257.

Luis, P., G. de la Fuente, and J. Perote. 2019. "The drivers of Bitcoin demand: A short and long-run analysis." *International Review of Financial Analysis* 62, 21–34.

Malkiel, B. G. 2003. The Efficient Market Hypothesis and Its Critics. *Journal of Economic Perspectives* 17:1, 59–82.

Pal, D., and S. K. Mitra. 2019. "Hedging bitcoin with other financial assets." *Finance Research Letters* 30, 30–36.

Shahzad, S. J. H., E. Bouri, D. Roubaud, and L. Kristoufek. 2019a. "Safe haven, hedge and diversification for G7 stock markets: Gold versus bitcoin." *Economic Modelling* 87, 212–224.

Shahzad, S. J. H., E. Bouri, D. Roubaud, L. Kristoufek, and B. Lucey. 2019b. "Is Bitcoin a better safe-haven investment than gold and commodities?" *International Review of Financial Analysis* 63, 322–330.

Stensås, A., M. F. Nygaard, K. Kyaw, and S. Treepongkaruna. 2019. "Can Bitcoin be a diversifier, hedge or safe haven tool?" *Cogent Economics & Finance* 7:1, 1593072.

Symitsi, E., and K. J. Chalvatzis, 2019. "The economic value of Bitcoin: A portfolio analysis of currencies, gold, oil and stocks." *Research in International Business and Finance* 48, 97–110.

Urquhart, A. 2016. "The inefficiency of Bitcoin." *Economics Letters* 148, 80–82.

Urquhart, A., and H. Zhang. 2019. "Is Bitcoin a hedge or safe haven for currencies? An intraday analysis." *International Review of Financial Analysis* 63, 49–57.

Vojtko, R., and D. Cisár, 2020. "Bitcoin in a Time of Financial Crisis." Available at SSRN 3557575.

Yue, X.-G., X.-F. Shao, R. Y. M. Li, M. J. C. Crabbe, L. Mi, S. Hu, J. S. Baker, and G. Liang. 2020. *Risk Management Analysis for Novel Coronavirus in Wuhan, China*. Multidisciplinary Digital Publishing Institute.

https://doi.org/10.1142/9789811239670_0003

Chapter 3

Cryptocurrencies and Inequality

Usman W. Chohan

Economics and National Affairs,
Centre for Aerospace and Security Studies, Islamabad, Pakistan
uchohan2@gmail.com

Abstract

This chapter seeks to contextualize the nature of cryptocurrencies as an alternate form of capital that, while being inspired by cryptoanarchist thought, has come to embody extreme forms of inequality among its owners. The concentration of wealth produces a "whale effect" that, as the chapter argues, in fact reflects the forms of inequalities that are found in the ownership of traditional forms of capital. The chapter thus alludes to the mismatch between the professed cryptoanarchist philosophical bent of cryptocurrency owners and the reality of capital ownership in the cryptocurrency domain; while cryptoanarchism postulates autonomy, decentralization, and the spread of ownership, the whale effect suggests that cryptocurrencies are insufficiently different from traditional forms of capital in this regard. This challenges the degree to which the praxis of cryptocurrencies coheres with the philosophy of cryptoanarchism.

Keywords: cryptocurrencies, inequality, whale effect, Bitcoin, capitalism anarchism

1. Introduction: Cryptoanarchism's Shadow

The inequalities in the ownership of capital within and between societies have been the subject of intense and prolonged debate (Piketty, 2015), and form both a cornerstone of political economy as a contemporary discipline (Law and Gill, 1988) as well as the Marxian critique of social theories (Carling, 2006). At the root of both earlier political–economy literature and contemporary "new gilded age" critiques of capital ownership (see Bartels, 2018) is the observation of glaring inequalities among social classes. A rich literature has emerged in the past decade, or more precisely since the Global Financial Crisis of 2008 (see Chohan, 2019a), that has sought to proactively offer solutions with perspectives from across the political spectrum, including the following: a political restructuring (see democratic critique in Bartels, 2018), institutional reformism (see extractive institutions in Acemoglu and Robinson, 2012; budget reform in Chohan, 2017a), Marxian approaches (Carling, 2006), ecological stimulus (see Green New Deal in Barbier, 2010), or centrist accommodation (see public value theory in Chohan, 2019a), among others.

One attempt to wrest power away from traditional forms of government-regulated monetary structures (see "new anarchists" in Graeber, 2002) has emerged from the philosophy of *cryptoanarchism* (see review in Chohan, 2017b), which has served as a guiding philosophy for many adherents of cryptocurrencies. In fact, cryptocurrencies can be thought of as a materialization of the principles of cryptoanarchism (Narayanan, 2013; Chohan 2017b). For this reason, it serves to discuss some elements of cryptoanarchism as made manifest by cryptocurrencies. At its essence, cryptoanarchism is a form of anarchist philosophy (see review on anarchism in Marshall, 2009), transposed onto the digital realm, with the concomitant reverence for a virtual utopia founded on anarchist principles (see Ludlow, 2001). The seminal work on cryptoanarchism is Timothy C. May's *The Crypto Anarchist Manifesto* (1992), which delineated the context in which the cryptoanarchist movement would become increasingly potent and necessary. In May's words:

> *Just as a seemingly minor invention like barbed wire made possible the fencing-off of vast ranches and farms, thus altering forever the concepts of land and property rights in the frontier West, so too will the seemingly minor discovery out of an arcane branch of mathematics come to be the wire clippers which dismantle the barbed wire around intellectual*

> *property. Arise, you have nothing to lose but your barbed wire fences!* (May 1992, p. 2)

In this vein, cryptocurrencies would serve as a metaphorical "wire clipper" of liberation for individuals from the exploitative structures of property concentration (particularly digital property). The arcane branch of mathematics which May referred to is cryptography, from which cryptocurrencies are derived as forms of code that are structured to be ostensibly less tamperable, more immutable, more robust, and less trust-dependent (see Chohan, 2019b). In a subsequent work, May argued that "the combination of strong, unbreakable public key cryptography and virtual network communities in cyberspace will produce interesting and profound changes in the nature of economic and social systems" (May, 1994). Cryptocurrencies did not exist at the time that May presciently conceived of the need for anarchist protection of the individual from the state's power in the digital realm, and cryptoanarchism finds itself at odds with the typical structures of power in the "info-national order" (Bennett, 2003). Cryptoanarchists are in fact broadly mobilized against the coercive "surveillance state," attempting to protect against government mass surveillance programmes, such as PRISM, Tempora, telecommunications data retention, the NSA warrantless surveillance controversy, Room 641A, the FRA and other "police state methods" (Greenwald, 2014). In terms of their penchant for hacking and for working outside the regularized zones of cyberspace, the modes of cryptoanarchists may or may not violate national laws (Bratich, 2007), and this has created unease for structures of the state (Bennett 2003), which is why the legality of Bitcoin, as an example, differs significantly across national jurisdictions (see Law Library of Congress, 2019; Chohan, 2017c).

For its part, the largest cryptocurrency, Bitcoin, has garnered significant interest not just from avant-garde investors, but also from adherents of cryptoanarchism (see the history of Bitcoin in Chohan, 2017d) whose perception of cryptocurrencies rests on a belief that it can serve as a monetary instrument liberated from the clutches of centralized power (see Vigna and Casey, 2016; Vidan and Lehdonvirta, 2019). As May put it, "Crypto anarchy is liberating individuals from coercion by their physical neighbors — who cannot know who they are on the Net — and from governments. For libertarians, strong crypto provides the means by which government will be avoided" (1994). For such adherents, they have maintained this belief even as evidence has arisen of manipulations, thefts, shutdowns, and other malpractices in the domain of cryptocurrencies (see malpractices in Gandal *et al.*, 2018; Chohan, 2018).

For such adherents, the liberation that cryptocurrencies offer also includes an element of anarchist dissemination in the ownership of wealth with greater equality (the "crypto dream," see Narayanan, 2013), no longer concentrated within or manipulated by a central authority (May, 1992, 1994; Ludlow, 2001; Chohan, 2017b; Vigna and Casey, 2016). It is thus assumed and inferred that, over time, cryptocurrencies will expand the ownership of new capital across users who can engage in "voluntary, uncoerced economic transactions" (May, 1994). Indeed, it is generalizable to state that the "cryptocurrency was created to encourage decentralization" (Chainalysis, 2019). They are disintermediated from traditional chains of monetary domination, and so an anarchocapitalist model (see Friedman, 1973) might be achieved in the digital realm (Ludlow, 2001). But given the dissemination of cryptocurrencies over the past decade, and the hype that was generated around their rise (Vigna and Casey, 2016; Chohan, 2017d), is the claim of greater anarchocapitalist empowerment in the digital realm really true? More specifically, has the cryptoanarchist assumption of wider egalitarian digital disintermediation of the ownership of capital truly materialized? This chapter seeks to test this claim and cryptoanarchist inference more rigorously and shall discuss the methods of approaching this problem in the next section.

2. Testing for Inequality in Cryptocurrencies

To test the cryptoanarchist inference about the wider, freer, and more anarchically inclined egalitarian disposition of cryptocurrency as capital, this chapter draws upon an open source and public domain database known as Bitinfocharts (2020). This database breaks out the distribution of Bitcoin, the most circulated and celebrated cryptocurrency, according to the amount of coins held by each wallet/address. If the cryptoanarchist vision is reflected in the distribution of cryptocurrencies across many addresses, we might hypothesize that the spread across the largest and smallest Bitcoin wallets may not be very large, and that the ownership among the highest deciles would not be *too* disproportionate or exaggerated compared to that of the lower deciles of Bitcoin wallets. Conversely, if the cryptoanarchist inference about freer and more equal ownership of cryptocurrencies is not found to manifest in the actual proportions of Bitcoin ownership among addresses/wallets, then the distribution may be skewed to varying degrees: perhaps as badly unequal as with traditional forms of capital, perhaps worse. This is the nuance that an empirical assessment of Bitcoin ownership by wallet will seek to glean.

The approach towards examining the distribution of Bitcoins by wallets/addresses does mirror a more general corpus of income inequality assessments in economics, which include the Gini coefficient, the 20/20 ratio, and the Palma ratio, among various others (see Cobham *et al.*, 2016; Equality Trust, 2018). The purpose in all of these is to measure the *degree* of inequality (see Bartels, 2018; Piketty, 2015), but they frame it along different points of reference: the top 10%, the top 20%, the infamous "1%", etc. Alternatively, some measures try to assess the amount of redress that would be required to make all members within the set equal (see Equality Trust, 2018). To be sure, there is a growing international movement militating against the current levels of inequality in ownership of traditional capital (Carling, 2006; Payne, 2017; Saez and Zucman, 2019), labeling it as the "triumph of injustice" (Saez and Zucman, 2019) and a "broken ladder" (Payne, 2017). Whether cryptocurrencies are in any significant way reflective of such inequality, or perhaps even a replica of it, is the question at hand. Ergo, if the ownership of Bitcoins reflects a very narrow concentration in the hands of but a few wallets, some degree of questioning about the adherence of Bitcoin's (and other cryptocurrencies') reality to the ideals of cryptoanarchism will be necessary. There are approximately 30 million addresses, and Bitcoin is indeed the most owned and traded of cryptocurrencies; hence, its large sample size of addresses ensures some statistical generalizability. Table 1 presents the distribution in graphical form across ownership, sourced from the public database Bitinfocharts and titled by them as "The Bitcoin Rich List."

What the Bitcoin Rich List suggests is a degree of massive inequality. The top 0.01% of addresses, a mere basis point worth of the total quantity

Table 1: Bitcoin Rich List.

	Addresses	**Coins Held**
Top %	0.01%	42%
	0.05%	62%
	0.50%	86%
	2.10%	95%
	9.70%	99%

Source: Bitinfocharts.(2020). Bitcoin Rich List. https://bitinfocharts.com/top-100-richest-bitcoin-addresses.html.

of 30 million odd addresses, account for nearly half (42%) of the value of Bitcoins held in wallets. Extending this to a mere 0.05% of top addresses covers nearly two-thirds of the value of Bitcoins outstanding (65%). Taking this to half of 1% would cover a large majority (86%) of the value of Bitcoins held, and extending this to the top 2% would cover the vast majority (95%) of Bitcoins. Tapering it off from there, and for statistical income inequality reference, less than one-tenth of all Bitcoin addresses (9.7%) hold 99% of all Bitcoins in circulation. The bottom 90% owns less than 1% of Bitcoins in circulation, thereby hinting at a staggering level of inequality, surprising even in comparison with traditional forms of capital.

The long-tail of Bitcoin ownership, as gleaned from further Bitinfocharts data, is also worth noting in this regard. There are three wallet addresses with a particularly high concentration of ownership that own a combined 540,000 BTC (Bitcoin units), which is equivalent to $5 billion (at the time of this writing), while there are 102 addresses that own a combined 2.2 million BTC or the equivalent of $20 billion. To arrive at the top 0.01%, we might add the next 2000 wallets/addresses, which collectively own 4.8 million BTC or the equivalent of $45 billion. By contrast, the bottom 50% of addresses (roughly 15 million wallet addresses) own 0.02% of the total BTC outstanding, worth a paltry $27 million combined. To see all of this another way, it may be noted that only 1,570 wallets have a dollar value greater than $10 million, while only 13,000 exceed $ 1 million, and hardly 135,000 exceed $100,000. By contrast, 21 million addresses are worth less than $100 USD and 7 million are worth less than $1,000. After all, the total market value for Bitcoin, as of this writing, is approximately $150 billion.

3. Discussion: Wherefore Cryptoanarchism?

Based on the aforementioned data from a public domain database (Bitinfocharts, 2020), it is in no uncertain terms, then, that the following may be stated: Bitcoin faces a problem of rampant inequality that would put traditional forms of capital to shame. It is in fact quite instructive to compare the Bitcoin ownership distribution to that of traditional measures of capital. Piketty's (2015) monumental study of wealth inequality in the United States for the period 1810–2010 illustrates that, even in the worst (most unequal) of times, the top decile held only 80% of the assets (circa, 1910), and this dropped progressively to 65% by 1970, before edging upwards. In addition, the top 1% held only 45% of the assets of the total wealth of the United States in 1910 (most unequal), and this fell to 30%

by 1970, before edging back towards 40% by 2010. A work by Saez and Zucman (2019) indicates that the ratio of total household wealth to national income in the United States for the top 0.1% was a mere 4% in the most unequal years on record (in 1912 and in 1930), and in even our "new gilded age" (Bartels, 2018), the ratio of total household wealth to national income for the top 0.1% is edging towards 5% (Saez and Zucman, 2019). Conversely, their work also illustrates how the bottom 90%'s ratio of total household wealth to national income is now falling to 4%, similar to levels in the 1930's and falling from a high of 8%.

An important point to delineate here is that national-level inequality is different from the global level of inequality in the traditional terms of wealth — with global inequality being much starker. As various authors have pointed out in contemporary "new gilded age" critiques of capital ownership (see Bartels, 2018), the standards are quite frightening, perhaps best framed by the work of Chan in *Public Good or Private Wealth?* (see Chan, 2019). In a rigorous comparative study, Chan indicated that 26 billionaires owned as much as half of the world's entire population, and that a 1% tax on their wealth would raise enough to solve a host of problems ranging from illiteracy to malnutrition (Chan, 2019). At the same time, their measurements showed that billionaire fortunes increased by 12% in 2018 — or $2.5 billion a day — while the bottom half of 3.8 billion saw their wealth decline by 11%. World inequality, therefore, resonates quite closely with the yawning gaps of Bitcoin ownership discussed earlier. However, the aim is not to set *cryptocurrencies* as a standard for wealth maldistribution in traditional assets, but rather to gauge how closely the uneven ownership of traditional capital is also reflected in cryptocurrencies. For the purposes of comparison, the second most sought after currency, Ethereum (ETH) has one-third of its ownership in just 376 addresses (Chainalysis, 2019), a similarly glaring amount of inequality. According to a work by Chainalysis, out of the top 500 holders of ETH, 124 were organizations/services and 376 were individuals; while they held 33% of outstanding ETH as of 2019, this proportion was in fact lower than that in earlier years (e.g., 46% in 2016; Chainalysis, 2019). As such, the issue of the levels of inequalities in ownership is not relegated to Bitcoin per se but to cryptocurrencies as a wider asset class.

What are the effects of this on cryptocurrencies themselves? A common practitioner term for large holdings of cryptocurrencies is the *whale effect,* alluding to the large waves that the marine beasts create through their aquatic movements, akin to the intraday volatility and price effects that large holders have on markets. The whales create a *concentration risk* in this asset class (see also Brands *et al.*, 2005), and make it very risky for smaller entrants in the market. Market manipulation is in fact a grave element in the (mis)pricing of Bitcoin (see Gandal *et al.*, 2018; Chen *et al.*, 2019; Chohan, 2018). The whale effect generates pump-and-dump schemes (see Xu and Livshits, 2019), where prices are artificially inflated and then quickly sold off, leaving later entrants high-and-dry with the losses. Initial coin offerings (ICOs), which are the primary mechanism for raising capital through the issuance of new cryptocoins, and are similar to the traditional initial public offering (IPO) model, also struggle with regulatory and governance issues due to manipulations (see Chohan, 2019c). In fact, the publicity of ICOs is expressly banned by social media platforms such as Facebook and Twitter for this very reason (Chohan, 2019c). That said, the degree to which whales impact the prices of cryptocurrencies is contested. Some ETH analysis suggests that whales might not impact the price of cryptocurrencies over time as much as they increase the intraday volatility (Chainalysis, 2019). More rigorous *herding behavior* finance studies have pointed towards whale effects (see an example in Bouri *et al.*, 2019). The mere presence of whales, however, signals that there is an underlying problem of inequality in the ownership of cryptocurrencies. Corroborating the aforementioned analysis of BTC ownership, the notion of whales highlights the reality of cryptocurrencies as divergent from the implications of cryptoanarchist rhetoric. Whereas cryptoanarchist ideals sought to promote a decentralized ownership of capital that would empower participants as free individuals, the reality is that all cryptocurrency market trading occurs in the shadow of large and powerful holders of capital that can move the market at their every whim due to information asymmetries.

Such spikes and drops have indeed occurred in the past five years of BTC trading, the most noticeable being in the weeks following Christmas Day, 2017 and known in practitioner circles as the *Great Crypto Crash*. Between January 6 and February 6, 2018, the price of Bitcoin fell by 65%. It continued to slump such that by September 2018, the 9-month price decline was equivalent to an 80% fall from the peak of January 2018 (Chohan, 2018). This was the time when the metaphor of large leviathans and their whale effect on the markets sunk into the public mind. Yet, given the cryptoanarchist underpinnings of cryptocurrencies, as instruments outside of the traditional modes of finance (Chohan, 2017c–d, 2019b–c), there was scarce recourse for the smaller participants who lost the most in crypto-crashes. Yet, their resentment and rancor at such dismal investment outcomes led to an outcry for greater oversight of cryptocurrencies through traditional regulatory institutions (Chohan, 2017c, 2019b). This was particularly true in the United States, whose Securities and Exchange Commission (SEC) is both a bellwether and leader in the field of international securities regulation. In conjunction with the Commodities and Futures Trading Commission (CFTC), the chairman of the SEC Jay Clayton issued statements with regard to the need for striking a regulatory balance between fostering the innovation of cryptocurrencies and maintaining some degree of oversight to mitigate criminality and predatory behavior (see Clayton, 2017; Clayton and Giancarlo, 2018). Such intervention by formalized regulatory authorities was welcomed by many disenchanted investors, but it harks back to the question of freedom that cryptocurrencies were meant to embody.

If cryptocurrencies fall into the regularized oversight architecture of financial authorities, how well can they really cohere with the aspirations of cryptoanarchists who seek to spearhead a revolution in autonomous and individually powered finance? Evidently, the greater the mainstreaming of cryptocurrencies under the mandates of monetary authorities and regulators, the less the individual empowerment is possible, leading ultimately to cryptocurrencies accounting for just another alternative asset class in the wider mainstream investment universe. The SEC and various other international regulatory bodies have exercised a lighter hand with Bitcoin than with other smaller cryptocurrencies, arguing that the wider investor base of BTC allows for sufficient market depth and diversification for a semi-normal market to function (Clayton, 2017; Clayton and Giancarlo, 2018). However, the problem of whales and unequal ownership of cryptocurrencies continues to loom large, even if the asset classes fall under traditional oversight and even if the semblance of a market exists, the disparities that are present in BTC ownership nonetheless pose a risk. On the one hand, this chapter draws attention to the practical problems of concentration, such as market manipulation and the whale effect. On the other hand, it highlights a mismatch between the aspirations of cryptoanarchists for autonomous and decentralized financial empowerment with the contrast of a highly unequal ownership distribution among even the largest cryptocurrencies (BTC and ETH).

4. Conclusion

To bring anarchist thought into practical action through human agency within amorphous structures has been an ideal of many revolutionary thinkers and civil society groups (Graeber, 2002), even as its idealism "demands the impossible" (Marshall, 2009). For digital activists too, there was a prescient discourse that alluded to the need for the individual to protect herself in the era of the surveillance state (Greenwald, 2014), and for her to seek the "wire clippers" of liberation to exercise her personal and financial autonomy in cyberspace (May, 1992). Cryptoanarchism brought anarchocapitalist values to wrestle with the challenge of cyberactivity (Ludlow, 2001), and foresaw that "the combination of strong, unbreakable public key cryptography and virtual network communities in cyberspace will produce interesting and profound changes in the nature of economic and social systems" (May, 1994). Cryptocurrencies derived ideological inspiration from this anarchist bent, and reflected it in the praxis of their cryptographic methods to shape and transact with digital assets (Chohan, 2017b). But an important inference about digital autonomy and self-determination lay in the equalization and decentralization of digital wealth. Only if participants had some semblance of even tolerable levels of inequality in their ownership of digital capital could they do justice to a free and autonomous exercise of financial transactions in cyberspace.

In that light, the aim of this paper was to test what sorts of inequalities were present in the ownership of digital cryptoassets. It drew upon an open source public domain database (Bitinfocharts, 2020) to examine the "rich list" distribution of BTC ownership. As its data indicated, the very top 0.01% of addresses held nearly half (42%) of the value of BTC outstanding, while a paltry 0.05% of top addresses covered nearly two-thirds of the value of Bitcoins (65%), and further that the scarce top 2% would cover the vast majority (95%) of value of Bitcoins in wallets. This was compared to national-level inequalities, particularly with the ratio of total household wealth to national income for the top 0.1%, which at its worst (most unequal) veered towards 5% (Saez and Zucman, 2019). A comparison with a similar work by Piketty in the United States showed that the top 1% held only 45% of the assets of the total wealth of the United States during the most unequal period of the 1910's (Piketty, 2015) and the closely trailing 2010's. This suggested that Bitcoin ownership inequalities were greater than national-level ones which today rule the political discourse as a "triumph of injustice" (Saez and Zucman, 2019) in a "new gilded age" (Bartels, 2018). However, some perspective was then infused with the stark global levels of inequality, which are indeed far more grotesque than national-level inequities (Chan, 2019). The instance of BTC, given its size of 30 million wallets/addresses, was made more generalizable by drawing upon a similar analysis on Ethereum (ETH), which suggested similarly unequal patterns of ownership (Chainalysis, 2019).

The practical effects of such glaring disparities in cryptocurrency ownership were framed in terms of the *whale effect* and the concentration risk that this entailed. Even the slightest of trades at such levels of market domination would rattle the space and leave smaller investors vulnerable to shocks. Like the small fish swept by the roaring waves that emanated from submerging whales, investors could not really exercise digital–financial independence and autonomy even if the whales themselves remained largely benign. The events of the Great Crypto Crash were mentioned in this regard, since the long-tail of small investors buried under the waves of such a massive decline sought recourse for their losses from traditional institutions of financial regulatory oversight. But the need for recourse from government jars with the very ethos of anarchism to which cryptocurrencies adhere ideologically. The SEC and CFTC have been proactive in responding to the collective calls of investors for some degree of oversight, and they have insisted on striking an appropriate balance between fostering innovation and promoting accountability. Yet, the mainstreaming of cryptocurrencies in this manner does not just distance them from cryptoanarchist ideals, it also fails to solve the problem of inequalities in the ownership of BTC. Better oversight does not automatically translate into better equality outcomes, neither with traditional capital (Bartels, 2018; Acemoglu and Robinson, 2012) nor with cryptoassets. So long as a handful of Bitcoin wallets/addresses hold nearly half of all outstanding BTCs, the realm of cryptocurrencies cannot be seen to cohere with the decentralized, trustless, autonomous, and free principles that help comprise cryptoanarchism.

Indeed, the conundrums that have forced anarchism to "demand the impossible" in historical experience (Marshall, 2009; Graeber, 2002) are also demanding the impossible of cryptocurrency investors. If cryptocurrencies are regulated and properly overseen by traditional financial authorities, they are nothing more than a minor alternative asset class within a larger mainstream investment universe. However, if they are the avenues for financial autonomy of the individual in the digital realm, then they have to contend with the various problems, manipulations, schemes, dangers, and threats (see Gandal *et al.*, 2018; Xu and Livshits, 2020; Chohan, 2018) that actually lurk in the cryptocurrency domain more specifically and in cyberspace more broadly. In the meantime, cryptocurrencies reflect the inequalities found in traditional forms of capital, and can thus not be considered the panacea or the tool of liberation that the staunchest ideological proponents still claim to be its guiding moral contribution to wrest power away from the structures of government that would impose themselves as ruthlessly in the realm of the virtual as they would in the realm of the real. As such, those who yearn for less egregious economic inequalities in the world are unlikely to find their solace in the world of cryptocurrencies just yet.

References

Acemoglu, D., and J. A. Robinson. 2012. *Why nations fail: The origins of power, prosperity, and poverty*. London: Crown Books.

Barbier, E. 2010. "How is the global green new deal going?" *Nature* 464:7290, 832–833.

Bartels, L. M. 2018. *Unequal democracy: The political economy of the new gilded age*. Princeton, NJ: Princeton University Press.

Bennett, J. C. 2003. "Networking nation-states: The coming info-national order." *The National Interest*, 74:2, 17–30.

Bitinfocharts. 2020. "Bitcoin Rich List." https://bitinfocharts.com/top-100-richest-bitcoin-addresses.html.

Bouri, E., R. Gupta, and D. Roubaud. 2019. "Herding behaviour in cryptocurrencies." *Finance Research Letters* 29:2, 216–221.

Brands, S., S. J. Brown, and D. Gallagher. 2005. "Portfolio concentration and investment manager performance." *International Review of Finance* 5:3-4, 149–174.

Bratich, J. 2007. "Popular secrecy and occultural studies." *Cultural Studies* 21:1, 42–58.

Carling, A. 2006. "Karl Marx's Theory of History and the recovery of the Marxian tradition." *Science & Society* 70:2, 275–297.

Chainalysis. 2019. "The Economic Impact of Ether Whales on the Market." *Chainalysis Reports*. May 15.

Chan, M.-K. 2019. "Public Good or Private Wealth?" *Oxfam Briefing Papers*. Oxfam.

Chen, W., W., Jun, Z., Zibin, C., Chuan, and Y. Zhou. 2019. "Market manipulation of bitcoin: Evidence from mining the Mt. Gox transaction network." *IEEE INFOCOM 2019-IEEE Conference on Computer Communications*, 964–972. IEEE.

Chohan, U. W. 2017a. "Budget Reform and Political Reform." In Ali Farazmand (ed.), *Global Encyclopedia of Public Administration, Public Policy, and Governance*. New York: Springer.

Chohan, U. W. 2017b. "Cryptoanarchism and cryptocurrencies." *Philosophy & Methodology of Economics eJournal.* Social Science Research Network, SSRN.

Chohan, U. W. 2017c. "Assessing the differences in bitcoin & other cryptocurrency legality across national jurisdictions." *International Political Economy: Monetary Relations eJournal.* Social Science Research Network, SSRN.

Chohan, U. W. 2017d. "A history of bitcoin." *Monetary Economics: Financial System & Institutions eJournal.* Social Science Research Network, SSRN.

Chohan, U. W. 2018. "The problems of cryptocurrency thefts and exchange shutdowns." *Information Systems & Economics eJournal.* SSRN.

Chohan, U. W. 2019a. *Public value and budgeting: International perspectives.* London: Routledge.

Chohan, U. W. 2019b. "Are Cryptocurrencies Truly Trustless?" In Gouette *et al.* (eds.), *Cryptofinance and Mechanisms of Exchange: The Making of Virtual Currency,* 77–89. Cham: Springer.

Chohan, U. W. 2019c. "Initial coin offerings (ICOs): Risks, regulation, and accountability." In Gouette *et al.* (eds.), *Cryptofinance and Mechanisms of Exchange: The Making of Virtual Currency*, 165–177. Cham: Springer.

Clayton, J. 2017. Statement on Cryptocurrencies and Initial Coin Offerings [Press release]. Securities and Exchange Commission [SEC], Washington, DC.

Clayton, J., and J. C. Giancarlo. 2018. Statement by SEC Chairman Jay Clayton and CFTC Chairman J. C. Giancarlo: Regulators are Looking at Cryptocurrency [Press release]. Securities and Exchange Commission [SEC], Washington, DC.

Cobham, A., L. Schlögl, and A. Sumner. 2016. "Inequality and the tails: The Palma proposition and ratio." *Global Policy* 7:1, 25–36.

Equality Trust, 2018. How is Inequality Defined? London: Equality Trust. https://www.equalitytrust.org.uk/how-economic-inequality-defined

Friedman, D. 1973. *The Machinery of Freedom: Guide to a Radical Capitalism.* Open Court Publishing.

Gandal, N., J. T. Hamrick, T. Moore, and T. Oberman. (2018). "Price manipulation in the Bitcoin ecosystem." *Journal of Monetary Economics* 95, 86–96.

Graeber, D. 2002. "The new anarchists." *New Left Review* 13:6, 61–73.

Greenwald, G. 2014. *No Place to Hide: Edward Snowden, the NSA, and the US surveillance state.* New York: Macmillan.

Law, D., and S. Gill. 1988. *The Global Political Economy: Perspectives, Problems, and Policies*. London: Harvester.

Law Library of Congress. 2019. "*Regulation of Cryptocurrency Around the World.* Law Library of Congress, Global Legal Research Center." Washington DC.

Ludlow, P. 2001. *Crypto Anarchy, Cyberstates, and Pirate Utopias*. Boston: MIT Press.

Marshall, P. 2009. *Demanding the Impossible: A History of Anarchism*. London: PM Press.

May, T. C. 1992. "The crypto anarchist manifesto." *High Noon on the Electronic Frontier: Conceptual Issues in Cyberspace.*

May, T. C. 1994. *Crypto anarchy and virtual communities.* Timothy C. May.

Narayanan, A. 2013. "What happened to the crypto dream?" *IEEE Security & Privacy* 11:2, 75–76.

Payne, K. B. 2017. *The broken ladder: How inequality affects the way we think, live, and die*. London: Penguin.

Piketty, T. 2015. "About capital in the twenty-first century." *American Economic Review* 105:5, 48–53.

Saez, E., and G. Zucman. 2019. *The Triumph of Injustice: How the Rich Dodge Taxes and How to Make them Pay*. London: WW Norton & Company.

Vidan, G., and V. Lehdonvirta. 2019. "Mine the gap: Bitcoin and the maintenance of trustlessness." *New Media & Society* 21:1, 42–59.

Vigna, P., and M. J. Casey. 2016. *The age of cryptocurrency: How bitcoin and the blockchain are challenging the global economic order*. New York: Macmillan.

Xu, J., and B. Livshits. 2019. "The anatomy of a cryptocurrency pump-and-dump scheme." In *28th (USENIX) Security Symposium ({USENIX} Security 19)* (pp. 1609–1625).

https://doi.org/10.1142/9789811239670_0004

Chapter 4

Towards a Better Understanding of the Resistance Factors of Cryptocurrency Spread

Sihem Ben Saad[*,‡], Aida Allaya[*,§], Fayda Taârit[*,¶], and Rafla Hchaichi[*,†,||]

[*]*Carthage Business School, University of Tunis Carthage Tunis, Tunisia*

[†]*ESCTRA Lab IHEC Carthage Tunis, Tunisia*

[‡]*Sihem.bensaad@utctunisie.com*

[§]*Aida.allaya@utctunsie.com*

[¶]*faydataarit@utctunsie.com*

[||]*Rafla.hchaichi@utctunsie.com*

Abstract

A cryptocurrency is a digital medium of exchange that operates independent of the central bank. It relies on cryptography to secure financial transactions and to check asset transfer. Several studies have shown that several factors play a role in inhibiting cryptocurrency spread, such as national culture, variables related to consumer psychology as well as factors related to regulation and monetary policy. Despite all the technological innovations, the inclusion of cryptocurrencies has become a challenge to governments and central banks since cryptocurrencies are often disfavored by rigorous regulation and monetary policy. On the other hand, psychological levels such as the need for human interaction, the organizational and functional barriers and many other variables related to power distance and uncertainty avoidance are the hindering factors for cryptocurrency adoption. In this chapter, we study the phenomenon of resistance to the spread of cryptocurrency. This study aims to explain how economic and psychological factors could discourage the consumer to use cryptocurrency.

Keywords: individual factors, collective and organizational factors, functional barriers and perceived difficulty, need for human interaction, perceived risk, national culture, monetary policy, regulation of cryptocurrency

1. Introduction

Today, digital currency has spread in several territories and more specifically in "online services." It is in this context that financial transaction modes are at the heart of today and tomorrow's issues. Advances in information and communication technologies have favored new modes of financial transaction. With these advances, several virtual currencies such as cryptocurrency have appeared. Cryptocurrency is a virtual reality technology that uses cryptographic functions to make financial transactions.

Cryptocurrency gained the attention of the public during its first years of existence (Gervais *et al.*, 2014; Giaglis and Kypriotaki, 2014; Alghamdi and Beloff, 2015; Gil-Saura *et al.*, 2011; Mendoza-Tello *et al.*, 2019). The interest has rapidly increased since 2011. A second generation of cryptocurrency appeared in 2014 with technological innovations allowing new functions. In 2017, the third generation appeared. It presents new limits, such as security and capacity.

Despite this development, several statistics show that, for some contexts, today's consumer is becoming resistant to this digital change. According to Statista's (2019)[1] results, the total number of Bitcoin wallet users in the world between the first quarter of 2015 and the third quarter of 2019 has been steadily increasing worldwide since the introduction of bitcoin cryptocurrency. In 2019, there were more than 42.3 million users of Blockchain electronic wallets as of September 30, 2019.

---

[1] https://fr.statista.com/statistiques/665756/nombre-detenteurs-portefeuille-bitcoin-sur-blockchain-monde/.

Similarly, results from the same source show that the share of virtual money users is 38% in Asia-Pacific and 27% in Europe, compared to 17% in North America, 14% in Latin America and 4% in Middle East. For instance, in Europe, the share of consumers using cryptocurrencies as a method of daily payment is 4% in France and 11% in Eastern Europe, as against 2% in Germany, 2% in Spain, 2% in Benelux, 2% in Switzerland and 1% in the United Kingdom (Statista, 2019). The same source showed that nearly 40% of bitcoin users were between 25 and 34 years old. Therefore, men are more averse to change than women and therefore are more resilient (56% for men). In addition, the Figaro (2019)[2] stipulates that as of 2020, more than 25,000 points of sale in France could accept cryptocurrencies. France does not want, however, Facebook's Libra because it is very expensive.

Despite the development of cryptocurrency, it remains relative in some contexts. In the US context, we can see that the number of Bitcoin wallet users has been decreasing worldwide since the introduction of bitcoin cryptocurrency in 2009. This resistance is explained by the fact that bitcoin was the most expensive virtual currency in recent years, a bitcoin worth nearly $7099.18, as against Thorecoin (1,042.02); 611.41 (Maker); 347.93 (Bitcoin Cash); 230.21 (Ethereum), 167.8 (Mixin); 132.1 (Dash); 86.39 (Litecoin); 78 (Monero); 67.9 (Zcash). Thus, several cryptocurrencies present risks related to their uses. Let's mention the case of Facebook, which launched the cryptocurrency Libra.

The growth of digital financial services has been phenomenal and has been stimulating social and economic growth by facilitating access to capital and financial services. Besides, cryptocurrency has been created to break free from government control, and therefore it has generated concerns for money laundering, criminal activity, tax evasion (Slattery, 2014), and the government's inability to regulate the economy or conduct monetary policy as they were not familiar with blockchain technology. The openness and cross-border nature of cryptocurrency transactions and wallets present, also, a problem in terms of jurisdiction and regulation. The crucial concern of governments and central banks remains to be guaranteeing the safety of its users and ensuring financial integrity; more particularly, it is a question of fighting financial crime (Gruber, 2013). So, cryptocurrency regulation is becoming a top priority. Unfortunately, restrictive regulation could harm cryptocurrency and could inhibit

---

[2] https://www.lefigaro.fr.

its spread. Hence, many risks related to regulation have emerged as resistance factors against cryptocurrency use.

Storage, conversion, transfer and securing of data are the other types of risks that are related to operations. These potential losses are induced by the instability of the sector, which has not yet had time to mature. If consumer resistance to the introduction and insertion of information and communication technologies is a central theme in the field of information systems, it does not seem to be always treated to the height of its scientific interest.

Resistance is generally defined as the behavior of an individual (Markus, 1983) in response to a present or future situation, perceived as negative (Ang and Pavri, 1994), to a feeling of inequity (Joshi, 1991), fear or stress (Marakas and Hornik, 1996; Ciaian and Rajcaniova, 2016). It is within this framework that we seek to further understand the facets of consumer resistance to the adoption of cryptocurrency. This chapter aims to provide an in-depth understanding of the advanced problem.

No studies have to date investigated the simultaneous impact of individual and economic factors on cryptocurrency use. To fill this gap in the literature, we are interested in factors of resistance towards the adoption of cryptocurrency. Our contribution lies in the treatment of variables related to consumer psychology, culture, monetary policy, and regulation.

Extensive research on the determinants of resistance to digital change, specifically the adoption of cryptocurrency, distinguishes between several types of explanatory factors of this issue, including individual factors, collective and organizational factors, functional barriers, the need for human interaction, the perceived risk, culture, and economic variables related to regulation risk and monetary policy. The remainder of the chapter is organized as follows. Firstly, we examine the variables related to consumer psychology. Then, we debate the variables related to culture. Finally, we develop the variables related to monetary policy and regulation that harm cryptocurrency spread.

2. What is Cryptocurrency?

Today, the rise of cryptocurrency is not perceived as just a simple feat; it is a real technology that has disrupted the monetary system and it has prompted a new approach to how a new currency works in a new economy. This technology has spread in all afferent areas, such as management, national culture, and marketing (Glenski *et al.*, 2019). As with any unprecedented innovation, the qualification of this phenomenon keeps attracting the attention of everyone.

The cryptocurrency breaks from the classical definition of money and is defined according to Stevenson (2010) as a digital currency in which encryption techniques are used to regulate the generation of units of currency and verify the transfer of funds, operating independent of a central bank. In other words, cryptocurrency is a method of constituting a virtual "coin" and is perceived as a digital medium of exchange that relies on cryptography instead of the monetary authority.

The first and the most popular cryptocurrency was Bitcoin, which was launched in 2008. Bitcoin is considered a peer-to-peer cash system (Nakamoto, 2008). So, Bitcoin's transactions made by users will be stored in a huge database called blockchain technology. Since 2011, the field of cryptocurrencies has expanded dramatically and various cryptocurrencies have appeared, such as Ethereum, Ripple, Litecoin, and Monero (Sovbetov, 2018).

As we know, cryptocurrencies are virtual funds without a paper trail that identifies transactional parties. The cross-border nature of cryptocurrency transactions has now become a concern. The legislators are skeptical that cryptocurrencies are used for funding illegal activities and criminal organizations. Unfortunately, cryptocurrency spread is confronted with major obstacles.

The awareness, adoption, and use of cryptocurrencies are correlated with various factors related to consumer psychology, culture, regulation, and monetary policy. The factors that inhibit cryptocurrency use are shown in Figure 1.

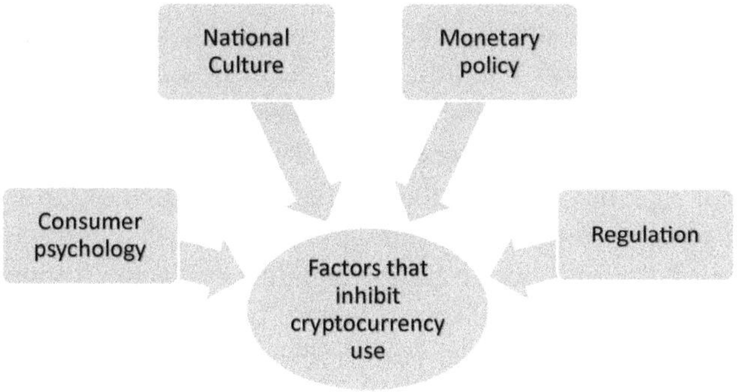

Figure 1: Factors that Inhibit Cryptocurrency Use.

2.1 *Consumer Psychology*

Psychological factors have aroused the interest of many researchers (Ijaz and Vitalis, 2011; Kunze *et al.*, 2013; Michel *et al.*, 2013; Oreg and Berson, 2011; Sargent *et al.*, 2012; Durand and Vanheems, 2015; Ciaian and Rajcaniova, 2016). These highlight the importance of taking into account certain psychological variables such as perceived risk, individual and collective factors, perceived difficulty, and the need for human interaction when studying mediated environments. These key factors are considered the main causes of resistance to the adoption of information and communication technologies.

2.1.1 *Individual factors*

Individual factors refer to factors that are directly related to the individual and his personal characteristics. Several studies suggest that these factors are the main cause that can lead to resistance to digital change, including the adoption of ICTs such as cryptocurrency (Bareil, 2008; Oreg, 2003; Ijaz and Vitalis, 2011).

The literature identifies six potential sources of resistance associated with the consumer's personality: fear of losing control, cognitive rigidity, insufficient psychological resilience, intolerance to the adjustment period linked to change, the non-preference of new things and reluctance to abandon old habits (Oreg, 2003; Kunze *et al.*, 2013; Michel *et al.*, 2013; Oreg and Berson, 2011; Sargent *et al.*, 2012).

Furthermore, researchers have discussed other factors that may influence consumer resistance to the adoption of cryptocurrency. Namely, anxiety, depression, emotional instability, worry, nervousness, insecurity and fear can impact the user's behavior towards the adoption of cryptocurrency (Ayadi and Daoud Elleuch, 2009, etc.). In fact, the mistrust makes consumers more likely to view cryptocurrency as a threat, thus reducing their use of technologies (Devaraj *et al.*, 2008).

Although age has been tested by several studies as an explanatory variable for resistance to digital change, few studies have treated the gender variable of the individual as an explanatory factor. Indeed, age can influence the resistance to adopting technology. Some researchers find a negative impact of age on the consumer's degree of resistance. Older consumers generally have more belief in losing than winning over the intended change. In addition, older individuals are generally associated with high levels of stability seeking and therefore are more resistant to change (De Bernadis *et al.*, 2011). In addition, Charneau (2015) indicated that resistance to change is inherent in humans. Men are more averse to change than women and therefore are more resistant. Several authors have explained this result by the fact that men have more cognitive rigidity than women (Van Dam *et al.*, 2008; De Bernadis *et al.*, 2011). As a result, individual factors may have a negative impact on the intention to adopt cryptocurrency.

2.1.2 *The collective and organizational factors*

These factors can be defined as factors that may impact the behavior of consumers who belong to the same organization. Research shows that social influences are determinants of resistance to change (Oreg, 2006; Ciaian and Rajcaniova, 2016). Authors defined these factors as the degree of importance that the consumer places on the opinions of others (Venkatesh *et al.*, 2003). The influence of others is defined as the perception that individuals have of what others expect of them, and their degree of motivation to comply with these expectations (Venkatesh *et al.*, 2003).

It is considered a subjective norm because it influences the behavior. The influence is social because it reflects environmental factors such as the opinions of family members, friends, colleagues and media on the behavior of users. Indeed, there will be mimicry behavior when the consumer is influenced by others and share their opinions. The opinions of others can determine the attitude of the consumer. According to Sargent *et al.* (2012), the influence of others has a significant impact on the intention to adopt a technology. The authors add the idea that the collectivist dimensions associated with consumer values, rites and symbols can cause resistance to digital change. Similarly, Bareil (2008) points out that the value of the consumer is one of the causes of resistance to change. In other words, resistance to digital changes is driven by individuals' conservatism and rooting of their values. Therefore, organizational culture is expected to have a negative impact on the intention to adopt cryptocurrency.

2.1.3 *Functional barriers and perceived difficulty*

Functional barriers include use barriers and value barriers. Value barriers are based on the monetary value of innovation. If technological innovation does not offer a strong performance at the price level, there is no motivation to adopt it (Ciaian and Rajcaniova, 2016). Indeed, Folkinshteyn and Lennon (2016) state that value barriers are the most intense barriers to adopting technology.

As for use barriers, they are related to the divergence of innovation with past practices, habits and experiences. As a result, consumers need time to accept it. Gerrard and Cunningham (2003) believe that consumers do not adopt technology because it is complex and difficult to use.

Folkinshteyn and Lennon (2016) state that the concept of "perceived complexity" has a negative impact on the perception of the usability of a technology.

Indeed, perceived difficulty can have a direct influence on attitude. That is, the more consumers perceive difficulty in using technology, the more their attitude towards this technology will be unfavorable. Consequently, perceived difficulty is expected to have a negative impact on the intention to adopt cryptocurrency.

As a conclusion, we expect use and value barriers to have a negative impact on the intention to adopt cryptocurrency.

2.1.4 *The need for human interaction*

The concept of "need for social interaction" is valued by several researchers (Langeard *et al.*, 1981; Bateson, 1985; Curran and Meuter, 2005; Dabholkar, 1996). This concept means that some people express the need to interact with someone to perform a service. Langeard *et al.* (1981) and Bateson (1985) put forward the idea that human contact is important for some people to provide a service.

Some customers are convinced that online services dehumanize human interpersonal interaction (Curran and Meuter, 2005).

These researchers add the idea that it is possible that these customers attach paramount importance to the use of personal computers, but that they do not like the idea of using them in a service situation.

Also, Dabholkar (1996) defines the need for human interaction as "the desire to maintain personal contact" (Dabholkar, 1996). The service encounter involves interpersonal interactions between the customer and the provider. This interaction takes into account the development of interpersonal relationships. Currently, the use of technology removes this interpersonal interaction. Research indicates that consumers value human interaction, which drives their assessment of the service experience (Bateson, 1985; Dabholkar, 1996; Zhou, 2012). As a result, the use of technology may be less attractive to consumers. Thus, we expect the need for human interaction to have a negative impact on the intention to adopt cryptocurrency.

2.1.5 *The perceived risk*

Bauer (1960) states that any behavior may involve a risk, which represents a key concept in consumer decision-making (Volle, 1995). Indeed, a consumer perceives a risk when he cannot anticipate with certainty the potentially negative consequences of his behavior (Luo *et al.*, 2010). Based on the work of Bauer (1960), the concept of perceived risk was presented as a two-dimensional concept: the risk of loss (i.e., anticipating the consequences of potential failure) and the risk of uncertainty (i.e., probability of occurrence of potentially negative consequences). In the field of information and communication technologies, the concept of perceived risk has been presented as the uncertainty the consumer faces when he cannot predict the consequences of his decisions (Luo *et al.*, 2010; Giovanis *et al.*, 2012).

Uncertainty includes several factors such as the value of services, Internet reliability, as well as spatial and temporal separation (Giovanis *et al.*, 2012). These factors can cause the consumer to lose time, financial and psychological security, confidentiality and performance. Doolin and Corner (2005) state that risk is one of the main factors of consumer resistance to the adoption of new technologies (Doolin and Corner, 2005; Lee *et al.*, 2007; Luo *et al.*, 2010). Rieunier (2000) highlights the importance of considering certain variables such as the perceived risk when studying media environments. Perceived risk is one of the main causes of technology development (Durand and Vanheems, 2015). Indeed, the consumer has difficulties in evaluating the technology before its adoption. This concept has been studied in e-banking (Lee, 2009; Bauer and Hein, 2006). The latter authors have incorporated the concept of perceived risk as an antecedent of behavioral intentions.

Perceived risk has been shown to have a negative effect on perceived usability as well as perceived usefulness. Consequently, perceived risk negatively affects the attitude towards the use of electronic banking and the intention of its adoption (Lee and Chung, 2009; Bettman, 1973). The perceived risk by Internet users in the use of a new technology increases (Durand and Vanheems, 2015).

Several studies show that perceived risk is a multidimensional construct that includes a physical dimension (i.e., risk incurred by the use of the product), a psychological dimension (i.e., the image that the consumer has of himself), a social dimension (i.e., the image that others have of the consumer), a financial dimension (i.e., the feeling of loss of money in case of defection of the product), a performance dimension (i.e., the functional aspects of the product) and a time loss dimension (i.e., the product does not fulfill its function, the consumer loses time) (Jacoby and Kaplan, 1972; Durand and Vanheems, 2015).

Consequently, we expect that the perceived risk will further prevent people from adopting cryptocurrency. It is therefore possible to confirm that the perceived risk has a negative impact on the intention to adopt cryptocurrency. In addition to psychological factors, another stream of research advances the idea that cultural variables are considered a determinant of resistance to change (Hofstede, 1994; Frias and Castenada, 2012). Indeed, the individual is influenced by others; the more he shares their opinions the more there will be mimicry behavior. The social environment or social system in which an individual operates has a primary role in determining an individual's attitude. In this perspective, cultural variables can influence the adoption of a new technology. This is the subject of the following section.

2.2 *National Culture*

Regarding cryptocurrency penetration, and attention to use it, national culture factors can predict the perceived value of cryptocurrency. In this section, we will use the definition of national culture according to Hofstede (1994). The authors define that "Culture is the collective programming of the mind that distinguishes the members of one group or category of people from others." The authors have succeeded in developing a model of comparative analysis of national specificities articulated around four main factors that represent the fundamental sociological elements of society: the power distance, Individualism/Collectivism, Masculinity/Femininity, and the avoidance of uncertainty.

2.2.1 *Power distance*

This dimension measures "the degree of acceptance of an unequal distribution of power for those who have the least. Members of a high-level distance society accept the dominance of some high power members. The latter will concentrate power by centralizing their level of decision-making. In such a context, information is considered as the primary source of personal power. As a result, those in power have control over access to information. In countries with strong hierarchical distance, we usually find authorities of constraint and reference" (Hofstede, 1994, p. 74).

Regarding cryptocurrency, in countries with high power distance, individuals don't use cryptocurrency (Tarhini *et al.*, 2017). In fact, irreversibility, public networks and cryptographic are the features of Bitcoin. In other words, the bitcoin network is decentralized and doesn't need hierarchy because it is not controlled by any institution.

In contrast, in countries with a low hierarchical distance, the individuals are more autonomous and they give a lot of importance to their status. In this context, the individuals are more innovative and adopt new ideas. In particular, the individuals will be more curious about adopting new technologies (Criscotti, 2013). These individuals make decisions alone and they adopt the use of new technologies easily.

As mentioned before, power distance has an impact on cryptocurrency adoption. The research of Juneman *et al.* (2019) has demonstrated that "the higher the power distance of a country, the lower the bitcoin penetration in the country. This hypothesis is the result of the control level of regulation. Therefore, the country with high power distance has a level control regulation.

2.2.2 *Uncertainty avoidance*

Uncertainty avoidance is a cultural dimension that measures the degree of tolerance acceptable to a culture in the face of disturbing events. If tolerance is low, control is strong and vice versa (Bollinger and Hofstede, 1987). In societies with strong control of uncertainty, the institutions try to avoid vagueness and informal procedures. On the other hand, in countries with weak control of uncertainty, individuals develop relationships of trust.

The management of uncertainty by society; if uncertainty is accepted as a normal thing in life, society accommodates it and integrates it into its functioning. If, on the other hand, uncertainty is perceived as a threat, society tries to control and reduce it by structuring and institutionalizing social relations and valuing the beliefs and institutions that produce certainty and conformity.

Using new technology involves the exposure to a very high level of risk. To cope with unknown situations, individuals with a strong culture of uncertainty avoidance place a high value on service quality and usefulness (Frias and Castenada, 2012). Ladhari *et al.* (2011) showed that quality is important for these individuals because it represents an assurance. So, the instability and the volatility value of bitcoin doesn't encourage the penetration on a country with high uncertainty avoidance.

However, countries with low uncertainty avoidance tolerate the ambiguity of bitcoin and don't ban bitcoin. As an example, Singapore is a country with a low level of uncertainty avoidance and has not applied rigid laws for using bitcoin but informed individuals to be more vigilant in using cryptocurrency.

2.2.3 *Collectivism versus individualism*

This dimension refers to the degree of independence and freedom among the members of a nation. It reflects, thus, the degree of cohesion of the group (strong or weak). According to Arthur Koestler individuals have two basic needs that differ from one culture to another: the need to belong to a group such as the homeland, the family, the religious community or the enterprise, and at the same time the need to be an independent individual and to have a unique identity. Collectivism is the tendency of people who give priority to belonging to groups and control each other for the purpose of loyalty.

The system of payment to bitcoin needs a collective network between citizens and the government. Trust is a necessity to perform cost transactions between parties.

So, using bitcoin and blockchain technology needs collectivism values. First, social relations are established to facilitate technological processes, such as creating code and text. Second, collectivism is necessary for creating discussion from mailing and WhatsApp.

2.2.4 *Masculinity versus feminity*

In societies with a female culture, individuals show solidarity. They help each other and support each other in difficult situations. The collective interest takes precedence over the individual interest and the ideal is to render service. Interpersonal trust will be developed in a feminine culture. On the other hand, in male cultures, individuals are rather independent. They attach great importance to achieving personal ambitions. Personal success takes precedence over solidarity and mutual aid. Thus, this dimension presents the valuation in society of gender roles. Just as an individual, male or female, can be more masculine than feminine in his personality, a society may rather have masculine values (separation of gender roles, valorization of self-fulfillment, material success, etc.) than feminine (undifferentiated gender roles, valuing interpersonal harmony, modesty, etc.).

2.2.5 *Long-term versus short-term orientation*

Long-term and short-term orientation is also called Confucian dynamism. In the long run, values are future oriented. On the other hand, in the short term, cultural values focus on the past and the present, giving more respect to tradition and social commitments. This dimension defines the time horizon in a country. Countries with a short-term culture give importance to traditional methods, while taking considerable time to create relationships, and perceive time as circular. This culture means that the past and the present are interconnected. On the other hand, the long-term orientation perceives time as linear and aims at the future rather than the present.

Bitcoin and blockchain are very volatile, are not stable and are developing continuously. The work of Tasca *et al.* (2018) showed that the evolution of the use of Bitcoin is the result of the implantation of technological culture. Therefore, the evolution of bitcoins is long term.

Kim's work (2015) has shown that price volatility decreases following a long maturation of Bitcoin. The author has shown that bitcoin speculation is entirely related to the country's economic indicators. Therefore, "the higher the long-term orientation of a country, the higher the penetration of Bitcoin in this country."

To obtain more adequate explanation regarding the factors that inhibit cryptocurrency, analysis of economic factors such as monetary policy and regulation is very important.

2.3 *Monetary Policy*

The rigidity of monetary policy is an obstacle to the use of cryptocurrencies, which threaten financial stability and economic objectives. If cryptocurrencies reach a sufficiently high level of stability, central banks may consider it appropriate to add them to their asset portfolio. Some have gone so far as to consider Bitcoin as money and regard it as an improvement over the current system (Rogoff, 2014).

For a prudent monetary policy, cryptocurrencies can be a good alternative in times of financial crisis. However, not all central banks agree with the use of cryptocurrencies even within the Fed. Cryptocurrency risks are creating serious financial stability problems. The existence of this form of money constitutes an obstacle to monetary policy which aims at price stability and credit risk (Sumner, 1995). Central banks could even flip over to a Bitcoin-based reserve system just like gold and other assets. However, there is not much chance that a central bank can adopt a state-managed digital currency; this would not allow it to control the money supply. Discretionary applications of monetary policy to the money supply would no longer be possible (Dowd, 1999).

In the future, this digital currency could constitute an obstacle to the management of monetary policy and thus limit discretionary monetary policy. The management of money supply is the basis of monetary policy. The demand for cryptocurrency continues to grow since the use of the latter continues to increase; however, the supply of this currency cannot adapt, since it is unfluctuating and fixed at a predetermined rate (Dowd, 2014).

In trying to get rid of all monetary authority, bitcoin has chosen to have a deterministic and inelastic monetary policy, referring to the bitcoin protocol. A good currency aims at price stability and does not lead to inflation (Nakamoto, 2008).

Cryptocurrencies also facilitate tax evasion and criminal activity (European Department, International Monetary Fund). However, government-supported public sector cryptocurrencies could better perform the three functions of money, and tax evasion and criminal activity could be controlled.

Monetary policy adapted to the fixed and inelastic supply of bitcoins is fully elastic. The aim is to avoid any upward or downward trend in the purchasing power of the monetary unit and to control the elastic supply of cryptocurrency. This can be done automatically and without the use of discretionary intervention by a central authority (McLeavy *et al.*, 2014). Because of its inelastic offer, cryptocurrency has not been a good unit of account (Schlichter, 2011). The major problem with cryptocurrencies is price instability. Changing from money to good money means a currency that reflects price stability. In other words, a stable cryptocurrency (Hayek, 1986).

2.4 *Regulation as an Inhibitory Factor to Cryptocurrency Use*

Cryptocurrencies are a challenge for central banks and governments. Indeed, virtual money can compete with fiat money, causing capital flight from banks and governments that could weaken them (Peters *et al.*, 2016).

2.4.1 *The need for regulation*

The cryptocurrency is a decentralized peer-to-peer network whose digital currency payment does not require an intermediary (Alberts and Fry, 2015). There is currently no centralized organization, no monetary authority, and no legal or regulatory framework applicable to cryptocurrencies. Cryptocurrencies do not depend on any authority and escape from financial institutions and are considered as a fully independent currency, so it is impossible to devalue it (Hughes and Middlebrook, 2015). However, this virtual currency is not exempt from certain rules; its price is determined by the supply and demand; the price is so volatile that it makes it possible to reap colossal gains in a few hours. Hence, the cryptocurrency market has been extremely volatile as investors are eager to participate in speculation. Such a volatility would seriously undermine the function of transactional cryptocurrency as a medium to store value (Xie, 2019).

With the rise of cryptocurrency as an investment, the world of cryptocurrencies has grown in popularity in recent years, due in particular to the spectacular surge in the price. Despite all of the technological innovation, the inclusion of cryptocurrencies has become a challenge to governments and central banks since cryptocurrencies are extremely volatile assets and represent a high liquidity risk (Dabrowski and Janikowski, 2018). Therefore, cryptocurrency can lead to a speculative bubble that can decrease the number of users. According to the classical approach of regulation, government and central banks intervene in the virtual market as soon as the market fails (Nabilou and Prum, 2019).

The anonymity and the cross-border reach of virtual currencies lead to money laundering (Gruber, 2013), illegal activities, mafia, and terrorist financing risk, so the cryptocurrency is used to evade taxation (Slattery, 2014). Hence, the opacity of cryptocurrency networks generates a significant risk of hacking because they lack the security that explains the currency thefts. As an example, we mention the hacking of the exchange platform Mt. Gox, during which more than 800,000 bitcoins were stolen, and the hack of the Japanese exchange platform Coincheck, with the theft of more than $500 million in cryptos. Since the launch of the Initial Coin Offerings (ICOs), it has been estimated that several hundred million dollars have been stolen or misappropriated by malicious people. The last scam concerns the ICO Bee Token during which hackers embezzled several million dollars.

Since then, several countries have instigated a plan to regulate cryptocurrencies. The worries about scams, terrorism, anti-money laundering laws, and the concern about investor protection drive these regulations (Schaupp and Festa, 2018). For these reasons, institutions have to protect investors and ensure trade security; besides, public authorities have to be responsible for prosecuting and convicting crooks and scammers. The cryptocurrency regulatory body excludes, thus, bad players, ensures the certainty of the user, lets better control the source of funds to avoid scams and makes sure that the cryptocurrency is used to boost the economy and to promote the job market. Unfortunately, many projects become useless; the objective is to easily raise funds in ethers and bitcoins. Since cryptocurrencies are not under the yoke of stock market legislation, pump and dump operations are frequently found to pluck investors (Motsi-Omoijiade, 2018).

2.4.2 *Regulation's risk*

Many investors, institutional and individual, are investing in cryptocurrencies and many related risks have emerged (Zahudi and Amir, 2016). The major regulation risk is the "death" of cryptocurrency, even if it turned out impossible to block access to cryptocurrencies despite the Chinese government's attempts to do it. Each state wishes to launch its proper cryptocurrency. For example, China bans cryptocurrency transactions while denying cryptocurrency that is not a legal tender and attempts to create a state-initiated "centralized" crypto-fiat (Xie, 2019). Cryptocurrencies will then compete with each other that will eventually lead to the end of the monetary monopoly. Restrictive regulations could withdraw capital away from countries and consequently fuel the black market.

In the USA, a tax system more or less restrictive has emerged (Bal, 2015). This decision has received criticism from cryptocurrency supporters that confirm that it could harm cryptocurrency and it will become more difficult to use it as a currency because many transactions create a tax nightmare for users. They blame the need for the legislation and they state that "cryptocurrency is the future; we need to encourage it, not discourage it" (Wiseman, 2016). In contrast, Chinese regulators were less concerned with jurisdiction; they privileged direct control eliminating any likelihood that would undermine their existing regulatory efficiency. In 2017, China, explicitly, banned any exchange or financing activities between fiat money and bitcoin and has attempted to substitute the cryptocurrency market with state-led projects (Xie, 2019).

Finally, regulators must adopt a flexible attitude so as not to slow down the cryptocurrencies' development. The regulations should increase confidence in the cryptocurrency market. Investors should be protected and new projects should be more supported. Creating a legal framework should create new jobs and explore as much as possible cryptocurrency opportunities.

2.4.3 *The perceived regulation risks around the world*

Around the world, governments and financial regulators have taken steps to preserve consumer interests and to better prevent financial crime (McLeod, 2017). Since 2014, the New York State Department of Financial Services proposed BitLicense, the first comprehensive virtual currency regulatory regime. BitLicense will have an impact with a double-edged sword on the economy. It may promote investment and consumer trust, BitLicensed companies will establish banking relationships easier than the others (Hughes, 2017). However, BitLicense also generates barriers to entry and a huge application and compliance cost. Several regulatory mechanisms are possible such as the introduction of a closed-loop currency that would enable the regulator to pursue the end-to-end transaction process and manage issues related to price volatility, security, and reliability.

In 2017, the central banks of the United Arab Emirates (UAE) and Saudi Arabia announced a plan to test a new cryptocurrency for cross-border payments between each other. Besides regulations that are going to be mandatory and applicable by law, all cryptocurrency intermediaries must have an anti-money laundering program and report suspicious transactions (Hughes and Middlebrook, 2015). This law should allow third parties approved by central banks to verify that activities are up to the approved standards. Some governments, such as the United States, Germany, the United Kingdom, and Canada, have taken steps to clarify the applicability of anti-money laundering obligations and combating companies' financing of terrorism. Some others, such as Italy, have issued warnings to financial sectors on money laundering and terrorism financing risks, while China has barred transactions (Xie, 2019). It is better to adopt a holistic regulatory approach for a better international coordination between central banks and regulators to introduce global-standard regulations.

The cryptocurrencies and blockchain platforms have introduced cheaper and quicker ways to carry out transactions. It is time that the world embraces this technology and overcomes its constraints. While challenges remain on the jurisdiction in light of the borderless nature of transactions, regulating the points of access could be one way to overcome the related concerns.

In terms of fiscal policy in the USA, the decision to tax cryptocurrency as a property by subjecting it to general tax principles applicable to property transactions, real property, stocks, and bonds will lead to difficulties with reporting taxes. Besides, this decision disfavors those who use cryptocurrency to make a high volume of transactions, such as purchasing everyday goods, and incentivize its use as an investment. The US government is discouraging the use of cryptocurrency, particularly Bitcoin, by making tax policy a complex process with several requirements for users; consumers will be faced with the biggest tax reporting challenges and this is going to be a stumbling block for the wider adoption of Bitcoin and other virtual currencies (Wiseman, 2016). Worldwide, cryptocurrency regulation seems to oblige countries to choose between banning, tolerating, or adapting to this innovation. In a nutshell, it turns out that the effects of different regulatory approaches deserve a much more nuanced analysis.

3. Conclusion

Faced with globalization, ICT offers, for companies, new opportunities for development. ICTs recognize their importance as a factor for progress. This is why companies are quick to make large investments in the adoption of these technologies in order to become more competitive. For this purpose, the financial transaction modes offered by banks are at the heart of the current managerial challenges imposed by digitalization. To this end, cryptocurrency has been launched as a new form of financial delivery.

The potentialities offered by cryptocurrency make its application more and more important (Mendoza-Tello *et al.*, 2019). However, despite its many advantages, the adoption of cryptocurrency by customers is still limited. The way of offering the services as well as the very nature of the proposed services are modified (Gautam, 2015). Therefore, it seems important to take into consideration consumers' perception of these new services, as well as the antecedents for their resistance to adopt these new services.

The cryptocurrency faces different resistance factors that can hinder its adoption. We studied the main factors of resistance to the adoption of cryptocurrency. Individual factors, collective factors, functional barriers and perceived difficulty, the need for social interaction and perceived risk are the main variables used to explain consumer resistance to adopting cryptocurrency. Many other factors related to regulation and monetary policy have emerged as inhibitory factors to cryptocurrency use.

The worries about scams, terrorism and mafia financing, and money laundering drive rigorous regulation. Around the world, regulation obliges countries to choose between banning, tolerating or adapting to cryptocurrency. The US regulatory body is discouraging the use of cryptocurrency by making tax policy a complex process with several requirements for users, while China has barred transactions (Xie, 2019). Also, the adoption of BitLicense generates barriers to entry and a huge application and compliance cost. However, several states have restricted the spread of cryptocurrency. The central bank of Bolivia has banned the use of Bitcoin. Columbia does not authorize its use or investment and the use of cryptocurrency, in Ecuador, was banned by a majority vote in the national assembly. It turns out that the effects of different regulatory approaches deserve a much more nuanced analysis.

Although the resistance has been discussed in the literature through a reductionist view of a barrier to change, several studies recognize its positive role in the organization. To this end, Ford *et al.* (2009) consider resistance as a resource that could stimulate awareness, help to review and rethink the objectives set, encourage stakeholder participation and commitment and learn from past mistakes of changes made in the organization.

References

Alberts, J. E., and B. Fry. 2015. "Is bitcoin a security." *Boston University Journal of Science and Technology Law* 21:1.

Alghamdi, S., and N. Beloff. 2015. "Virtual currency concept its implementation, impacts and legislation." In Science and Information Conference (SAI). IEEE, London, 2:1, 175–183.

Ang, J., and F. Pavri. 1994. "A survey and critique of the impacts of information technology." *International Journal of Information Management* 14:2, 122–133.

Ayadi, F., and E. M. Daoud. 2009. "Les facteurs affectant la résistance des utilisateurs à l'adoption des TIC dans les établissements de santé privés." Actes du colloque AIM, Marrakech, Maroc.

Bal, A. 2015. "How to Tax Bitcoin?" In Handbook of Digital Currency, 267–282. Academic Press.

Bareil, C. 2008. "Démystifier la résistance au changement: Questions, constats et implications sur l'expérience du changement." Document de travail de l'Université de l'Administration Publique du Québec (ENAP), Canada.

Bateson, J. E. G. 1985. "Self-service consumer: An exploratory study." *Journal of Retailing* 61:2, 49–76.
Bauer, K., and S. E. Hein. 2006. "The effect of heterogeneous risk on the early adoption of Internet banking technologies." *Journal of Banking & Finance* 30:6, 1713.
Bettman, J. R. 1973. "Perceived risk and its components: A model and empirical test." *Journal of Marketing Research* 10:2, 184–90.
Bauer, R. 1960. "Consumer behavior as risk taking, in dynamic marketing for a changing world." *American Marketing Association* 3:12, 389–439.
Bollinger, D., and G. Hofstede (1987) "Les différences culturelles dans le management"éditions organization.
Charneau, P. 2015. *Libérer votre Grand Moi!* Paris: Editions Du Moment.
Ciaian, P., and M. Rajcaniova. 2016. "The digital agenda of virtual currencies: Can BitCoin become a global currency?" *Information Systems and e-Business Management* 14:883–919.
Crisioiti *et al.* 2013. "The impact of national culture on E-Commerce acceptance: The Italian case." *Knowledge Process Management* 20:2, 102–111.
Cryptocurrencies and monetary policy. Monetary Dialogue July 2018.
Curran, J. M., and M. L. Meuter. 2005. "Self-service technology adoption: Comparing three technologies." *Journal of Services Marketing* 19:2, 103–113.
Dabholkar, P. A. 1996. "Consumer evaluations of new technology-based self-service options: An investigation of alternative models of service quality." *International Journal of Research in Marketing* 13:1, 29–51.
Dabrowski, M., and L. Janikowski. (2018). "Virtual currencies and central banks monetary policy: Challenges ahead." Retrieved July 27, 2018.
De Bernadis, L., R. Maiolini, and A.-M. Braccini. 2011. "Does generation matter in strategic change implementation? Effects of the age on change propensity of managers after a privatization." Document de travail de l'Université LUISS, Italie.
Devaraj, S., M. Fan, and R. Kohli. 2008. "Antecedents of B2C channel satisfaction and preference: Validating e-Commerce metrics." *Information Systems Research* 3:3, 316–333.
Doolin, D., and J. L. Corner. 2005. "Perceived risk, the internet shopping experience and online purchasing behavior: A New Zealand Perspective." *Journal of Global Information Management* 13:2, 66–68.
Dowd, K. 1999. "An Almost Ideal Monetary Rule." *Greek Economic Review* 2:19, 53–62.
Dowd, K. 2014. New Private Monies: A Bit-Part Player? Institute of Economic Affairs, Electronic copy available at: https://ssrn.com/abstract=2535299.
Durand, E., and A. Vanheems. 2015. "Vers une nouvelle manière de concevoir la compétence et le risque perçu de l'acheteur à l'ère du numérique. Le cas de l'adolescent au sein de la famille." *Management et Avenir* 83, 33–49.

Folkinshteyn, D., and M. Lennon. 2016. "Braving Bitcoin: A technology acceptance model analysis." *Journal of Information Technology Case and Application* 18:2, 220–249.

Ford *et al.* 2009. "Resistance is futile: But it is slowing the pace of EHR adoption nonetheless." *Journal of the American Medical Informatics Association* 16:3, 274–281.

Frias, J., M. Carmen, and Castenada 2012. "The moderating effect of uncertainty avoidance on over all perceived value of a service purchased online" DOI: 10.1108/10662241211214557

Gautam, V. 2015. "Cryptocurrencies: Are disruptive financial innovations here?" *Model Economic* 6:816–832.

Gerrard, P., and J. B. Cunningham. 2003. "The diffusion of internet banking among Singapore consumers." *International Journal of Bank Marketing* 21:1, 16–28.

Gervais, A., G. Karame, V. Capkun, and S. Capkun. 2014. "Is Bitcoin a Decentralized Currency?" *SecurPriv* 12:1, 54–60.

Giaglis, G., and K. Kypriotaki. 2014. "Towards an agenda for information systems research on digital currencies and bitcoin." In W. Abramowicz and A. Kokkinaki (eds.), *Business information systems workshops. BIS2014. Lecture notes in business information processing*, 3–13. Cham: Springer.

Gil-Saura, I., M. Ruiz-Molina, and F. Arteaga-Moreno. 2011. "Value, supplier dependence and long-term orientation: Outcomes for B2B commerce in the travel industry." *Industrial Management & Data Systems* 111:2, 791–808.

Giovanis, A. N., S. Binioris, and G. Polychronopoulos. 2012. "An extension of TAM model with IDT and security/privacy risk in the adoption of internet banking services in Greece." *EuroMed Journal of Business* 7:1, 24–53.

Glenski, M., E. Saldanha, and S. Volkova. 2019. "Characterizing speed and scale of cryptocurrency discussion spread on reddit." In The World Wide Web Conference, 560–570.

Grégory C., M. Demertzis, and K. Efstathiou. 2018. "Cryptocurrencies and monetary policy Monetary Dialogue" Policy Department for Economic, Scientific and Quality of Life Policies, European Parliament.

Gruber, S. 2013. "Trust, identity and disclosure: Are bitcoin exchanges the next virtual havens for money laundering and tax evasion?" *Quinnipiac Law Review* 32:135.

Hayek, F. A. 1986. "Market standards for money." *Economic Affairs*, 6:4, 8–10.

Hofstede, G. 1994. *Cultures and Organizations. Software of the Mind*, Éditeur London: Harper Collins.

Hughes, S. D. 2017. "Cryptocurrency regulations and enforcement in the US." *Western State University Law Review* 45:1.

Hughes, S. J., and S. T. Middlebrook. 2015. "Advancing a framework for regulating cryptocurrency payments intermediaries." *Yale Journal on Regulation* 32:495.

Ijaz, S., and A. Vitalis. 2011. "Resistance to organizational change: Putting the Jigsaw Together." *International Review of Business Research Papers* 7:3, 112–121.

Jacoby, J., and L. Kaplan. 1972. The components of perceived risk. In M. Venkatesan (ed.), Proceedings, 3rd Annual Conference (pp. 382–393). Chicago: Association for Consumer Research. (it's a conference).

Joshi, K., 1991. "A model of users' perspective on change: The case of information systems technology implementation." *MIS Quarterly* 15:2, 229–242.

Juneman, A., D. U. Sutiksno, and K. Nuning. 2019. "Acceptance and penetration of Bitcoin: The role of psychological distance and national culture." *Sage Journal* 9:3, 1–14, https://doi.org/10.1177/2158244019865813.

Kim, J. H., Y. Steve. 2015. Yang bitcoin market return and volatility forecasting using transaction network follow proprieties Available at SSRN: https://ssrn.com/abstract=2633755 or http://dx.doi.org/10.2139/ssrn.2633755.

Kunze, F., S. Boehm, and H. Bruch. 2013. "Age, resistance to change, and job performance." *Journal of Managerial Psychology* 28:7/8, 741–760.

Ladhari, R., I. Ladhari, and N. Souiden. 2011. "Determinants of loyalty and recommendation: The role of perceived service quality, emotional satisfaction and image." *Journal of Financial Services Marketing* 16, 111–124.

Langeard, E., J. Bateson, C. Lovelock, and P. Eigler. 1981. "Marketing of Services: New Insights from Consumers and Managers." Report No. 81–104, Marketing Science Institute, Cambridge, MA.

Lee C., M. Mattila and J. Shim (2007), "An Exploratory Study of Information Systems Resistance: The Case of Mobile Banking Systems in Korea and Finland "Americas Conference on Information Systems" (AMCIS).

Lee, K. C., and N. Chung. 2009. "Understanding factors affecting trust in and satisfaction with mobile banking in Korea: A modified DeLone and McLean's model perspective instant messages in China." *Interacting with Computers* 21, 385–392.

Lee M., (2009), "Factors influencing the adoption of internet banking: An integration of TAM and TPB with perceived risk and perceived benefit," *Electronic Commerce Research and Applications* 8:3, 130–141.

Luo, X., H. Li, J. Zhang, and J. P. Shim. 2010. "Examining multi-dimensional trust and multi-faceted risk in initial acceptance of emerging technologies: An empirical study of mobile banking services," *Decision Support Systems* 49:2010, 222–234.

Marakas, G. M., and S. Hornik. 1996. "Passive resistance misuse: Overt support and covert recalcitrance in IS implementation." *European Journal of Information Systems* 5:3, 208–219.

Markus, M. L. 1983. "Power, politics, and MIS implementation." *Communications of the ACM* 26:6, 430–444.

McLeay, M., A. Radia, and R. Thomas. 2014. "Money creation in the modern economy." Bank of England Quarterly Bulletin 2014 Q1. bankofengland.co.uk/publications/Documents/quarterlybulletin/2014/qb14q102.pdf.

McLeod, S. 2017. "Bitcoin: The utopia or nightmare of regulation." *Elon Law Review* 9:553.

Mendoza-Tello *et al.* 2019. "Disruptive innovation of cryptocurrencies in consumer acceptance and trust." *Information Systems and e-Business Management* 52:1.

Michel, A., B.-R. Tondem, and B. Burnes. 2013. "The limitations of dispositional resistance in relation to organizational change." *Management Decision* 51:4, 761–780.

Motsi-Omoijiade, I. D. 2018. "Financial intermediation in cryptocurrency markets–regulation, gaps and bridges." In Handbook of Blockchain, Digital Finance, and Inclusion, Elsevier 1:207–223. Academic Press.

Nabilou, H., and A. Prüm. 2019. "Central banks and regulation of cryptocurrencies." Review of Banking and Financial Law, *Forthcoming*.

Nakamoto, S. 2008. "Bitcoin: A peer-to-peer electronic cash system." www.bitcoin.org/bitcoin.pdf.

Oreg, S. 2003. "Resistance to change: Developing an individual differences measure." *Journal of Applied Psychology* 88:4, 680–693.

Oreg, S. 2006. "Personality, context, and resistance to organizational change." *European Journal of Work and Organizational Psychology* 15:1, 73–101.

Oreg, S., and Y. Berson. 2011. "Leadership and employees' reactions to change: The role of leaders' personal attributes and transformational leadership style." *Personnel Psychology* 64:3, 627–659.

Paolo, T., H. Adam, and L. Shaowen. 2018. "The evolution of the Bitcoin economy: Extracting and analyzing the network of payment relationships." *The Journal of Risk Finance* 19:2, 94–126.

Peters, G. W., A. Chapelle, and E. Panayi. 2016. "Opening discussion on banking sector risk exposures and vulnerabilities from virtual currencies: An operational risk perspective." *Journal of Banking Regulation* 17:4, 239–272.

Rieunier, S. 2000. "L'influence de la musique d'ambiance sur le comportement des consommateurs sur le lieu de vente." Thèse de Sciences de Gestion, Université Paris IX.

Rogoff, K. 2014. "Costs and benefits to phasing out paper currency." Presented at NBER Macroeconomics Annual Conference.

Sargent, K., P. Hyland, and S. Sawang. 2012. "Factors influencing the adoption of information technology in a construction business." *Australian Journal of Construction Economics and Building* 12:2, 72–86.

Schaupp, L. C., and M. Festa. 2018. "Cryptocurrency adoption and the road to regulation." In Proceedings of the 19th Annual International Conference on Digital Government Research: Governance in the Data Age, 1–9.

Schlichter, D. S. 2011. *Paper money collapse: The folly of elastic money and the coming monetary breakdown.* New York: Wiley.

Slattery, T. 2014. "Taking a bit out of crime: Bitcoin and cross-border tax evasion." *Brooklyn Journal of International Law* 39, 829.

Sovbetov, Y. (2018). "Factors influencing cryptocurrency prices: Evidence from bitcoin, ethereum, dash, litcoin, and monero." *Journal of Economics and Financial Analysis* 2:2, 1–27.

Stevenson, A. 2010. *Oxford Dictionary of English.* USA: Oxford University Press.

Sumner, S. 1995. "The impact of futures price targeting on the precision and credibility of monetary policy." *Journal of Money, Credit, and Banking* 27, 89–106.

Tarhini, A., K. Hone, X. Liu, and T. Tarhini. 2017. "Examining the moderating effect of individual-level cultural values on users' acceptance of E-learning in developing countries: A structural equation modeling of an extended technology acceptance model." *Interactive Learning Environments* 25:3, 306–328. http://dx.doi.org/10.1080/10494820.2015.1122635

Tasca, P., S. Hayas, lui. 2018. "The evolution of the Bitcoin economy." *The Journal of Risk Finance* 19:2, 1–46.

Van Dam, K., S. Oreg, and B. Schyns. 2008. "Daily work contexts and resistance to organizational change: The role of Leader-Member Exchange, Development climate, and change process characteristics." *Applied Psychology: An International Review* 57:2, 313–334.

Venkatesh, V., M.-G. Morris, G.-B. Davis, and F.-D. Davis. 2003. "User acceptance of information technology: Toward a unified view." *MIS Quarterly* 27:3, 425–478.

Volle, P. 1995. "Le concept de risque perçu en psychologie du consommateur: Antécédents et statut théorique." *Recherche et Application Marketing* 24:2, 90–110.

Wiseman, S. A. 2016. "Property or currency: The tax dilemma behind bitcoin." *Utah Law Review* 417.

Xie, R. 2019. "Why China had to ban cryptocurrency but the US did not: A comparative analysis of regulations on crypto-markets between the US and China." *Washington University Global Studies Law Review* 18:457.

Zahudi, Z. M., and R. A. T. R. Amir. 2016. "Regulation of virtual currencies: Mitigating the risks and challenges involved." *Journal of Islamic Finance* 176:3446, 1–11.

Zhou, T. 2012. "Examining mobile banking user adoption from the perspectives of trust and flow experience." *Information Technology and Management* 13:1, 27–37.

https://doi.org/10.1142/9789811239670_0005

Chapter 5

Tokenization Disrupts ETFs

Ralf Wandmacher
Accadis University of Applied Sciences, Bad Homburg, Germany
ralf.wandmacher@edu.accadis.com

Abstract

The traditional asset management industry has grown substantially over the last decades with three main sectors: active asset management, passive asset management, and alternatives asset management. Crypto-assets as cryptocurrencies and tokens are a new asset growing from a small base and may move through the tokenization of individual assets into asset management.

The efficiency of the asset management industry may be substantially improved through the tokenization of existing assets. This research will discuss the implications of tokenization for passive asset management, in particular, for exchange-traded funds (ETFs) as one of the most efficient asset management products known so far.

ETFs are a success story in the asset management industry over the last two decades. The substantial growth in volume results from the low costs for clients and it's easy handling. ETFs create a picture of a no-risk, no-frills investment product. It seems to be easily understandable, easy to handle, and transparent with limited risks.

These "obvious" advantages are only partially congruent with the results of the exercised research. Risks of ETFs are in existence and are well documented in the selling prospectuses of the ETF providers. In addition, this research finds that fees are not fully transparent.

Furthermore, governance problems of passive asset management products such as ETFs do arise and have not been solved so far.

One solution to the research challenges of ETFs may be the usage of the latest technology, i.e., the tokenization of assets, which could lead to the abolition of ETFs by using crypto-asset management instead.

Keywords: ETF, passive asset management, crypto-assets, digital asset management, token, tokenization

1. The Old and New Worlds of Asset Management

Asset managers service clients as fiduciary agents by implementing a broad range of asset management models (Lopez, 2017). The size of the asset management industry is large with more than $84 trillion on a global basis in 2016 and an estimate of more than $145 trillion in 2025 (PWC, 2017).

Traditional asset management can be divided into active and passive management. Although the size of active asset management is forecasted to grow to $87.6 trillion in 2025, its relative part will sink from 71% to 60% as alternatives will grow from 12% to 15% and passive asset management will grow from 17% to 25%, i.e., from $14.2 trillion to $36.6 trillion in assets under management (PWC, 2017). Passive asset management can be defined as the management of ETFs and index-tracking strategies.

Exchange-traded funds (ETFs) and exchange-traded products (ETPs) enjoy increasing popularity. The volume of ETFs and ETPs under management is rising with more than $6.35 trillion under management (ETFGI, 2020), as they are an easy and cost-effective way of investing in different markets and thus diversifying the portfolio. Diversification is important to optimize the risk/return ratio in accordance with modern portfolio theory, which has been awarded the Nobel Prize (Nobel Media AB, 2020).

Over the last years, new assets have evolved into financial assets. These new assets are called crypto-assets as "digital instruments of economic value that are developed and traded on blockchain networks" (Stylianou and Carter, 2019). Crypto-assets can be cryptocurrencies, tokens, tokenized securities, and crypto-derivatives, and all assets fitting under the definition of a digital instrument of economic value, "there is no generally-accepted definition of what constitutes a crypto-asset"

(Houben and Snyers, 2020). The size of the assets under management in the crypto-asset world may be estimated by using the market capitalization of cryptocurrencies and tokens with 246 billion USD on CoinMarketCap (CoinMarketCap 25.5.2020 16:11 CET) and $249 billion on CoinGecko (CoinGecko 25.2.2020 16:11 CET) on 25 May 2020.

The tokenization of existing assets, i.e., the issuance of a token "that digitally represents a real tradable asset — in many ways similar to the traditional process of securitization" (Laurent *et al.*, 2019). The difference between securitization and tokenization lies in the introduction of smart contracts, i.e., programmability (Ho, 2018).

The new world of asset management may have already begun with the introduction of crypto-assets and, in particular, with the tokenization of existing assets. The asset management of crypto-assets is, in comparison to the traditional asset management industry, quite small today. However, crypto-asset management may solve fundamental challenges of the traditional asset management industry, e.g., in the strong, growing passive asset management in the case of ETFs.

1.1 *Exchange-traded Funds — Challenges of a Passive Investment*

ETFs are created on primary markets and they are traded on secondary markets. The creation and redemption process of ETFs in the primary market allows "authorized" market participants to exchange baskets of securities for shares in the ETF fund. Trading costs for the securities are paid by the authorized market participants (ETF.com n/a).

This creation and redemption process links the assets to the fund price per share. In addition, the liquidity of the ETF should be dependent on the liquidity of the securities in the fund.

This transparent setup is applied for so-called physical ETFs which are holding the securities in the fund according to the rules of the mirrored index. However, even physical ETFs may not hold all securities of an index if it is seen as too complicated or too expensive to buy each security. These kinds of ETFs are physically optimized ETFs.

ETFs can also be swap-based, i.e., the ETF supplies the performance of the mirrored index but holds other securities in its fund. The underlying swaps are collateralized to minimize the counterparty risk of the swaps (iShares n/a).

ETFs are usually based on indices, e.g., S&P 500. Investing in indices has the advantage for the investor that in the case of S&P 500, the investor can buy shares with just one trade and thus minimize the individual share risks.

The ETF with the highest investment amount is the SPDR S&P 500 ETF Trust on the US stock exchange index S&P 500 (Ticker: SPY US) with a net asset value of $261.8 billion on 22 May 2020 (State Street Global Advisors, 2020).

ETFs package the return of investment indices. They try to replicate these indices and make them tradable. Stock benchmark indices (such as S&P 500), ETFs on stock sector indices (such as car stocks), factor ETFs (such as dividend stocks) and ETFs on bond indices, commodities or alternative investments (such as hedge funds and private equity funds) are just a selection of the many underlying instruments for ETFs.

1.2 *Costs of ETFs*

ETFs try to track the benchmark as closely as possible, which is possible with an average deviation of 0.06% (Petajisto, 2017) or for large and broad indices from 0.016% for the SPDR S&P 500 ETF Trust to 0.06% for iShares FTSE MIB UCITS ETF EUR (Tsalikis and Papadopoulos, 2019). International benchmarks or illiquid securities may show pricing bands for premiums of over 2% at a 95% level (Petajisto, 2017), and the entire US ETF market results in premiums traded of almost $20 billion (Petajisto, 2017).

In addition, the costs for the ETF itself are low for liquid underlyings such as S&P 500, e.g., the SPDR® S&P 500® ETF has a gross cost ratio of 0.0945% per year. The average for American listed ETFs is 0.56% per year (Petajisto, 2017).

Bid–ask spreads are paid by investors to buy or sell ETFs. The research found a median ETF closing bid–ask spread of 0.15% depending on the liquidity of the fund (Petajisto, 2017).

Commissions of the investors can vary on an individual basis.

Two more costs are important for ETFs. ETFs may lend out securities and do receive fees. Some part of these fees will not remain in the fund but will go to the fund's company itself. Furthermore, ETFs must rebalance their underlying portfolio whenever there is a rebalancing of the index itself. The rebalancing will result in transaction costs and rebalancing risks with potential costs.

ETFs are not fully transparent about their fees. The published total expense ratio does not include all relevant fees, for example, the trading costs of "authorized" market participants for the creation of baskets of securities for shares in the ETF fund are not included (Riedl, 2015).

Costs of an ETF investment can be divided into six parts for investors:

1. Commission to trade
2. Operating expenses of the ETF
3. Bid–ask spread
4. Discounts and premium to NAV
5. Securities lending fees
6. Transaction and rebalancing costs.

1.3 *Issues of ETFs*

Low costs as well as the simple and fast possibility to acquire large portfolios make ETFs interesting for many investor classes. Nevertheless, the following aspects should be discussed critically:

1. The indices on which ETFs are based must be viewed critically in some cases, e.g., when a few stocks are overweight in them. Until recently, the Swiss SMI was exemplary, with Nestlé, Hoffmann-La Roche, and Novartis accounting for over 60% of the index weighting. This overweighting endangers diversification. Index regulations must take such problems into account, e.g., the Swiss Exchange (SIX Swiss Exchange, 2018) limiting the weighting of stocks in the SMI to 18%, still a quite high weighting.
2. The indices do change according to certain criteria on defined dates, e.g., following a merger or a reduction in market capitalization. Professional investors have been using these dates to their advantage for years. In 2006, it was estimated that investors in the S&P 500 would suffer losses of 0.12% per year due to the predictability of index changes and timing (Chen *et al.*, 2006). In 2017, this was estimated at 0.09% and was no longer considered significant (Kappou, 2017), however, it was totaling $225 million based on the SPDR S&P 500 ETF alone.
3. A continued strong increase in passive investments may have an impact on the selection of shares in the index and may possibly impair

the control function of the capital market if companies are bought based on their index membership but not on their profitability.

Initial research has shown that the growth of ETF investment amounts leads to the parallelism of equity returns and, at the same time, the reaction to future equity returns is reduced (Israeli *et al.*, 2017). However, the authors point out with some justification that ETFs have brought many benefits and they do not weigh up these benefits against their results. Further research is needed here.

4. ETFs use securities lending to generate income while keeping costs low. However, the breakdown of the substantial revenues of 0.23% to 0.28% per annum is hardly transparent, e.g., two of the three largest ETF providers in the US, BlackRock and State Street, receive between 10% and 20% of these revenues as agents (Blocher and Whaley, 2016). In this respect, further investigations into the transparency and distribution of revenues are also appropriate here.
5. The corporate governance function of passive index investors is still unclear. For example, the proxy fight for Procter & Gamble proved that passive investors are not aligned and showed their decisive influence according to media reports (Hirsch, 2017): State Street Global Advisors and BlackRock voted against the management of Procter & Gamble, and Vanguard voted for it.

   Transparent decisions and accountability are essential for the healthy development of capital markets. Similarly, the corporate governance function of fiduciary assets must not be overlooked.

ETFs are a far more complex subject than it might seem at first glance. In particular, there are governance, transparency, and costs issues of ETFs.

Crypto-asset management may help to solve the discussed issues of traditional passive asset management.

1.4 *Crypto-asset Management*

Crypto-asset management is substantially different from traditional asset management. The trading of assets may be direct, via an exchange or even via a broker through an exchange. Another difference is the custody function of the crypto-assets, i.e., assets can be held directly or via a custodian.

The trading and custody changes have implications for the index tracking, corporate governance, and the distribution of returns from tokenized assets lending.

1.5 *Tokenization of Existing Assets*

Tokenization is defined as a digital representation of a tradable asset (Stylianou and Carter, 2019). The tokenization of underlyings for index-tracking strategies and ETFs would result in tokenized assets which are digital twins of the underlyings with the advantage of fractionalization. Fractionalization means underlying assets begin to be tradable as fractions of their originals, i.e., a share of Amazon with a price of $2,446.74 (Closing Price on 22 May 2020 at Nasdaq) could be traded as a token on the Ethereum blockchain in fractions of $\$2{,}446.74 \times 10^{-18}$.

This fractionalization leads to a situation where each investor could buy the exact number of shares required for the index tracking of each available index. However, the investor needs the required weighting of each underlying with respect to an index.

The index weightings are provided by independent entities as Standard & Poor's for the S&P 500, Deutsche Boerse for the DAX, MSCI for the MSCI World, or by independent index boutiques, e.g., Solactive AG.

The investor would be able to buy for any amount according to the index weighting the individual tokens of S&P 500, i.e., 500 tokens with each token standing for an individual company. The purchase itself could be executed as 500 individual trades or as a basket trade with the basket holding the individual tokens.

1.6 *Trading of Token*

A trade can be executed via an exchange or directly as peer-to-peer trading. Trading via an exchange would execute the transfer of private keys from one to another wallet, i.e., the transfer of payment and tokens between the investor and the seller.

The wallet is centrally administered by the exchange. In Figure 1, the example of hybrid crypto- or token exchange is illustrated.

The buy and sell orders do flow via the exchange. The exchange itself provides a custody service by administering the private keys for the investor and seller through the private key custody.

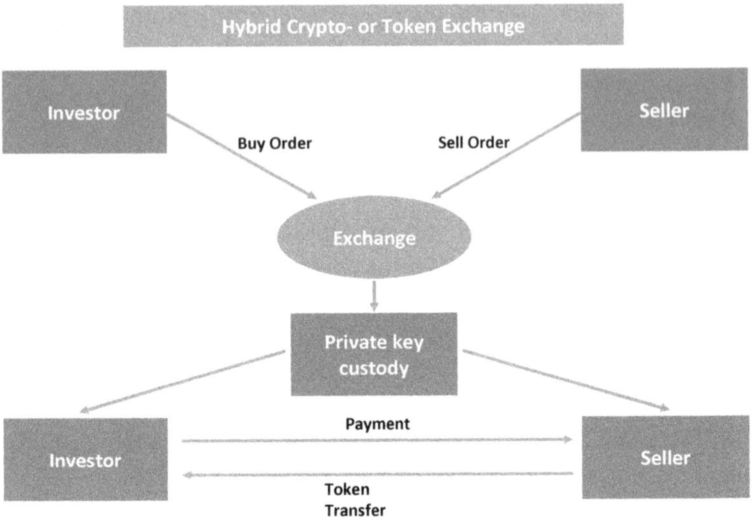

Figure 1: Hybrid Crypto- or Token Exchange.

The advantage of the concept of the private key custody is that the custodian could be changed easily by moving the access to the private keys to another custodian.

Currently, most crypto exchanges are set up as illustrated in Figure 1. The access to the assets is held and administered in a central wallet. This setup bears some risks for the security of assets as it was proven by several security failures (Fidelity Digital Assets, 2018) over the last years.

This centralized setup of the exchange does also not fit well into the decentralized approach of the fundamentals of distributed ledger technology.

A peer-to-peer trade creates a direct connection between the investor and the seller. These direct connections are called atomic swaps which are based on smart contracts allowing it to take place on-chain (on one blockchain) or off-chain (off a blockchain). The smart contracts contain specific security measures, i.e., hashlocks and timelocks (Herlihy, 2018).

The security of the delivery is important in a peer-to-peer trading setup. Both parties may not know each other, just their interests in selling

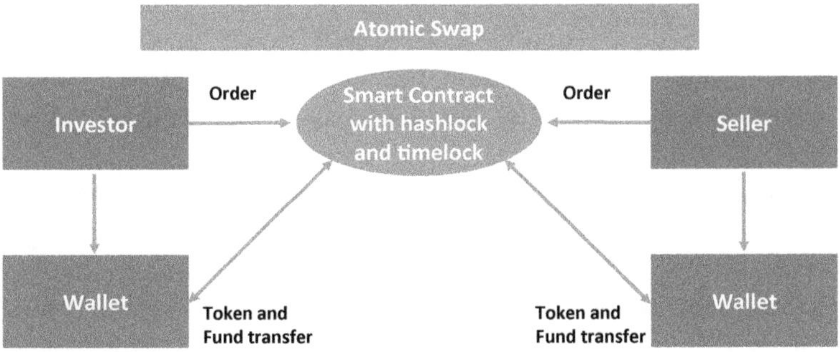

Figure 2: Atomic Swap.

and buying are documented. The security feature of hashlocks and timelocks is introduced in the trade as illustrated in Figure 2.

The first security feature is a hashlock consisting of two mechanisms, a challenge and a solution. The challenge is a condition in a contract (De Jong, 2018). The solution of the condition activates the contract, like a key for a lock.

The second security feature is a timelock that can be defined as a countdown. During the countdown, the solution for the challenge can be provided. When the amount of time encoded in the contract has elapsed, the solution cannot be entered anymore in the contract, i.e., no swap is executed (Herlihy, 2018).

The settlement of the atomic swap is direct between the parties, i.e., investor and seller. Both parties involved put their access to their assets (i.e., their digital assets, e.g., tokenized equity against a stablecoin) in escrow with the smart contract of the swap. If the solution of the hashlock is provided in time as set by the timelock, the swap is executed and the wallets receive the agreed access to the assets. If the solution is not supplied or the time has elapsed, the swap has failed, and the agreed access assets in escrow will be transferred back to the initial wallets.

In the case of atomic swaps, trading and settlement are done directly. Therefore, no intermediary is involved anymore. The investor and the seller hold their private keys for their assets, respectively.

The differentiation between the hybrid crypto- or token exchange and the atomic swap is the use of an exchange and with it the custody of the private keys. The private keys in the individual wallets are either with the exchange or with the individual parties.

1.7 *Custody of Tokens*

The investor may decide to hold the access to the tokens in a self-administered wallet, in a wallet at a custodian, or in a custody wallet at an exchange.

The wallet at a custodian is an administration service that takes care of the token, manages the fulfillment of rights from the token, and protects private keys (BaFin, 2020). These custodial services are ordered separately from the trading, either as hot storage, cold storage, or multi-signature service to provide safe and secure storage (Fidelity Digital Assets, 2018). For example, cold storage means that an offline address is created with an offline public and private key pair (Bitcoin.com n/a). The case of hot storage or multi-sig solution changes the public address as well, as the investor will send the tokens to a new address. The custodian will administer the new address, i.e., is managing the respective private keys of this new address.

The custody wallet at an exchange is administered by the exchange. The wallet holds all the tokens needed for trading, i.e., the ownership of the token is centralized.

The custodial services as well as the centralized solution at an exchange may add further risks to the decentralized system of distributed ledgers by centralizing the access to the tokens. In the case of exchanges, security failures were seen over the last years (Fidelity Digital Assets, 2018).

These kinds of custodial services are built on the basis of trust (KPMG, 2020), which indicates a fundamental difference to the trustless distributed ledger technology in a public permissionless blockchain.

If the investor uses a self-administered wallet, the individual tokens would directly belong to the investor, a fully transparent holding in the case of a public blockchain or a non-transparent holding in the case of a private blockchain. Even in the case of a private blockchain, the individual tokens could be mapped to the individual wallet.

The custody of the token will be based on individual preferences, i.e., personal administration, administration by a custodian, or even by an exchange. The atomic swap enables the direct mapping of individual tokens and their respective wallets.

1.8 *Implications of Custody*

The self-governance of assets, i.e., the administration of the wallet with its private key, may lead to direct communication between the token asset or the respective token issuer and the wallet and its owner. The transparency and/or identification opportunity of the wallet address enables this communication opportunity.

The communication can be initiated by each party, the holder of the token, the token issuer or the token asset itself. The token asset itself is an asset which communicates via smart contracts, for example, the communication can be started when specific conditions are met. The conditions are programmed inside the smart contracts, for example, elapsed time (as in the timelocks in atomic swaps) or external conditions observed by oracles.

The direct communication between wallet and token issuers or even between wallet and token assets enables the opportunity to have a direct corporate governance ability. The flow of information is unhindered, i.e., communication can be started or received without any intermediary.

An atomic swap enables direct communication, as the administrator and the owner are the same. The difference when compared to a centralized wallet is obvious because the communication would be directed to the exchange instead of the economic owner of the token. If custody solutions would create individual wallets for each economic owner, governance communication could be mapped directly to the investor, i.e., the economic owner.

The direct mapping would also be helpful for incoming distributions of tokens that will flow to the wallet as well. Distributions may be paid from the tokens directly or by staking the relevant token in a mechanism in which the token will be held in the investor's wallet. All income will be credited fully to the wallet of the investor.

1.9 *Tokens in Comparison to ETFs*

Tokenization may substantially improve the efficiency of the asset management industry but may create challenges of its own. The aim of this research is to find problematic areas of passive asset management, i.e., ETFs, and to compare these areas with the results of the application of tokenization on assets.

This research found the issues of the current passive asset management with ETFs and introduced tokenization, trading of tokens, custody of tokens, and the implications of custody.

As a next step, the identified issues of passive asset management with ETFs are listed in Table 1. The first column describes the area of the issue,

Table 1: A Comparison of ETFs and Tokens.

Issues	ETFs	Token
fees	trading commission	applicable on exchange and peer-to-peer platforms, none in direct peer-to-peer transactions
fees	operating expenses	none
fees	bid–ask spread	applicable on exchange, none on peer-to-peer platforms
fees	discounts and premium to NAV	none
fees	participation in securities lending fees	none
fees	transaction and rebalancing costs	applicable
indexation	partially inadequate quality of indices	applicable
predictability of index changes	exploited by professional investors	applicable
control function of capital markets	potentially impaired by index following	applicable
corporate governance function	intransparent decisions	individual direct participation

and the second column describes the issue itself using ETFs. The third column introduces the effects of the issue on a token solution. The issue may have no effect (i.e., none), may have the same effects as for ETFs (i.e., applicable), or has different effects on tokens and on digital asset management with tokens.

The same effects as for ETFs are valid on the quality of indexation and the predictability of index changes and its potential exploits by professional investors. The quality of the index and its set of rules are independent of the way the assets are managed. The indexation is an external input factor. Index changes are an external factor and will result in transaction and rebalancing costs that apply to ETFs and tokens in an equivalent way.

The control function of capital markets may be hurt by passive asset management, which would be the same for ETFs and tokens.

The weightings are given by external rules, while the investment amount is given by the investors being the same for investment in ETFs or tokens.

Trading commissions and bid–ask spreads would be applicable for ETFs and tokens if the tokens are traded on an exchange. None of these fees would be charged in a peer-to-peer only setup; however, most trades in a peer-to-peer setup are done on peer-to-peer exchanges. Here, fees as trading commissions are charged but no bid–ask spreads.

Tokens have further advantages over ETFs as no operating expenses must be paid for the ETF itself. In addition, the tokens are traded in fractions; hence, no discounts and premiums to NAV must be calculated in comparison to ETFs.

A substantial advantage is the difference in the returns of security lending and respectively token lending. ETF providers such as Blackrock charge a percentage of the overall fees as their cut, i.e., the ETF holder is getting less than 100% of the securities lending fees. Tokens are held directly by the investor, i.e., all possible returns of token lending could be credited fully to the wallet of the investor.

Another substantial advantage of the use of tokens is the ability to clearly identify the wallet in which the tokens are held. The transparency of a public blockchain and/or the possibility to map the holdings to an individual wallet creates the opportunity to communicate directly. The asset holder and the economic owner are the identical parties in the token application in differentiation to ETFs where the asset holder is the ETF and the economic owner is the investor. The described problems of the ETF providers would be prevented. Instead, the token owner could be directly contacted and vote in such corporate decisions as a proxy contest. This new direct way of communication may open up new opportunities in the overall functions of corporate governance of asset owners.

Tokenization may solve some substantial problems of ETFs, in particular, the corporate governance functions and the intransparent security lending returns of ETF providers. In addition, tokenization may be even more cost-efficient than ETFs.

However, tokenization could raise novel issues, especially as described in areas of external custody or additionally in the anonymity of trading parties. The anonymity of trading partners is certainly of relevance as knowledge about positions or about the trading strategy may create an economic advantage for others and an economic disadvantage for the holder. Newly developed blockchains such as Polymesh guarantee ownership privacy and confidentiality about restrictions while being able to report to the relevant regulators (Dossa *et al.*, 2020).

2. Conclusion

ETFs have a reputation for being an efficient asset management method. The reputation is based on the assumptions of easy handling processes, low resulting costs, and no added risk creation. This research has found inconsistencies in this assumed reputation.

Fiduciary asset management in the passive asset management industry is not fully transparent and contradictions in the ETF providers were described. Crypto-asset management with direct and decentralized communication may fulfill the corporate governance function better than centralized communication in the case of intransparent fiduciary asset management in the current passive asset management.

ETFs shall be a transparent product in the passive asset management industry. However, the providers of ETFs have implemented various stages of fees for ETFs in an intransparent way. Some of these fees are not considered to calculate the total expense ratio of a fund;, for example, the commissions of the traded baskets of underlyings are not included in the total expense ratio when "authorized" market participants create ETFs. In consequence, the published total expense ratio underrepresents the full costs of ETFs.

In contrast, crypto-asset management uses the fractionalization of tokenized assets to trade the relevant token directly, i.e., no intermediary as an "authorized" market participant is any longer required. Another benefit of the fractionalization of tokenized assets is the trading of all relevant tokens according to the weighting of the relevant index. Hence, there is no tracking error anymore in contrast to physically optimized ETFs.

Tokenization can also bring transparency to the asset lending area of the asset management industry. Currently, asset managers in the ETF industry charge a part of the security lending returns of an ETF without displaying these fees in the total expense ratio of an ETF. This is possible as the asset manager is holding the assets as an intermediary. In crypto-asset management, tokenized assets can be held without an intermediary; hence, the returns from token lending would flow fully to the owner of the token asset.

The reputation of ETFs being an efficient asset management method is not congruent with the research; however, ETFs may be more efficient as an asset management method than other asset management methods known so far.

Crypto-asset management and tokenization show the opportunity for being more efficient, more transparent, and solving existing corporate governance problems. Tokenization may disrupt asset management with ETFs in the future.

References

BaFin. 2020. "Guidance notice — Guidelines concerning the statutory definition of crypto custody business (Section 1 (1a) sentence 2 No. 6 of the German Banking Act (Kreditwesengesetz — KWG)." https://www.bafin.de/SharedDocs/Veroeffentlichungen/EN/Merkblatt/mb_200302_kryptoverwahrgeschaeft_en.html. Last accessed: 30.05.2020.

Bitcoin.com. n/a. "How to Setup Bitcoin Cold Storage." https://www.bitcoin.com/get-started/setting-up-your-own-cold-storage-bitcoin-wallet/. Last accessed: 27.05.2020.

Blocher, J., and R. E. Whaley. 2016. "Two-Sided Markets in Asset Management: Exchange-Traded Funds and Securities Lending." *Vanderbilt Owen Graduate School of Management Research* Paper No. 2474904. https://ssrn.com/abstract=2474904. Last accessed: 21.05.2020.

Chen, H., G. Noronha, and V. Singal. 2006. "Index changes and losses to index fund investors." *Financial Analysts Journal* 62:4, 31–47.

CoinGecko. 2020. "Tokenize." https://www.coingecko.com/en/exchanges/tokenize. Last accessed: 25.5.2020.

CoinMarketCap. 2020. "Top 100 Cryptocurrencies by Market Capitalization." https://coinmarketcap.com/. Last accessed: 25.5.2020.

De Jong, M. B. 2018. "Ledger Loops: Hashlocked IOUs make the world go round." Whitepaper. https://ledgerloops.com/doc/whitepaper.pdf. Last accessed: 21.04.2020.

Dossa, A., G. Moore, J. Lancaster, M. Buchanan, and P. Ruiz. 2020. "Polymesh Whitepaper." Online: https://polymath.network/polymesh-whitepaper. Last accessed: 31.05.2020.

ETF.com. n/a. "What Is the Creation/Redemption Mechanism." https://www.etf.com/etf-education-center/etf-basics/what-is-the-creationredemption-mechanism?nopaging=1. Last accessed: 22.05.2020.

ETFGI. 2020. "ETFGI reports assets in the global ETFs and ETPs industry which will turn 30 years old in March started the new decade with a record 6.35 trillion US dollars." https://etfgi.com/news/press-releases/2020/01/etfgi-reports-assets-global-etfs-and-etps-industry-which-will-turn-30. Last accessed: 22.05.2020.

Fidelity Digital Assets. 2018. "Custody in the Age of Digital Assets." https://www.fidelitydigitalassets.com/articles/custody-in-the-age-of-digital-assets. Last accessed: 30.05.2020.

Herlihy, M. 2018. "Atomic Cross-Chain Swaps." https://arxiv.org/pdf/1801.09515.pdf. Last accessed: 27.04.2020.

Hirsch, L. 2017. "P&G says shareholders reject Peltz's bid for board seat by slim margin, activist says vote a dead heat." https://www.cnbc.com/2017/10/10/procter-gamble-shareholders-vote-against-adding-nelson-peltz-to-board.html. Last accessed: 22.05.2020.

Ho, A. 2018. "How does tokenization work, anyway?" https://medium.freecodecamp.org/how-does-tokenization-work-anyway-afb5fed1ac47. Last accessed: 27.05.2020.

Houben, R., and A. Snyers. 2020. "Crypto-Assets." https://www.europarl.europa.eu/RegData/etudes/STUD/2020/648779/IPOL_STU(2020)648779_EN.pdf. Last accessed: 23.05.2020.

iShares. n/a. "How is an ETF created?" https://www.ishares.com/ch/individual/en/education/what-are-our-products/creation-and-redemption-process?switchLocale=y&siteEntryPassthrough=true. Last accessed: 22.05.2020.

Israeli, D., C. M. C. Lee, and S. A. Sridharan. 2017. "Is there a dark side to exchange traded funds?" *An Information Perspective. Review of Accounting Studies* 22, 1048–1083.

Kappou, K. 2017. "The Diminished Effect of Index Rebalances." http://dx.doi.org/10.2139/ssrn.2971211. Last accessed: 21.04.2020.

KPMG. 2020. "Cracking crypto custody." https://advisory.kpmg.us/content/dam/advisory/en/pdfs/2020/kpmg-cracking-crypto-currency.pdf. Last accessed: 30.05.2020.

Laurent, P., T. Chollet, M. Burke, and T. Seers. 2019. "The tokenization of assets is disrupting the financial industry. Are you ready?" *Inside Magazine* 19, Part 02 — From a core transformation technology perspective.

Lopez, C. 2017. "The asset management industry, systemic risk, and macroprudential policy." *Journal of Financial Transformation* 45, 121–128.

Nobel Media AB. 2020. "Press Release." https://www.nobelprize.org/prizes/economic-sciences/1990/press-release/. Last accessed: 22.05.2020.

Petajisto, A. 2017. "Inefficiencies in the pricing of exchange-traded funds." *Financial Analysts Journal* 73:1, 24–54.

PWC. 2017. "Asset & Wealth Management Revolution: Embracing Exponential Change." https://www.pwc.com/gx/en/asset-management/asset-management-insights/assets/awm-revolution-full-report-final.pdf. Last accessed: 25.05.2020.

Riedl, P. 2015. "Cost of ETFs: Total Expense Ratio (TER) vs. Total Cost of Ownership (TCO)." https://www.justetf.com/uk/news/etf/cost-of-etfs-total-expense-ratio-ter-vs-total-cost-of-ownership-tco.html. Last accessed: 15.05.2020.

SIX Swiss Exchange. 2018. "SIX Swiss Exchange Indices. Stand: 19.05.2020." https://www.six-swiss-exchange.com/downloads/indexinfo/online/share_indices/smi/smifamily_rules_de.pdf. Last accessed: 02.05.2020.

State Street Global Advisors. 2020. "SPDR® S&P 500® ETF Trust." https://us.spdrs.com/en/etf/spdr-sp-500-etf-SPY. Last accessed: 22.05.2020.

Stylianou, K., and N. Carter. 2019. "Calculating cryptoasset market shares." *Journal of Competition Law and Economics*, http://dx.doi.org/10.2139/ssrn.3346558, 2.

Tsalikis, G., and S. Papadopoulos. 2019. "ETFs — Performance, tracking errors and their determinants in Europe and the USA." *Risk Governance and Control: Financial Markets & Institutions* 9:4, 67–76.

https://doi.org/10.1142/9789811239670_0006

Chapter 6

Oversight and Regulation of Cryptocurrencies: BitLicense

Usman W. Chohan

Economics and National Affairs,
Centre for Aerospace and Security Studies Islamabad, Pakistan
uchohan2@gmail.com

Abstract

The question of regulation in the domain of cryptocurrencies has been tackled in various ways, exhibiting therein a desire to strike a balance between fostering innovation and promoting oversight. This chapter examines the case of BitLicense, issued by the New York Department of Financial Services (DFS), with the aim of contextualizing the relative merits of regulatory and oversight initiatives in the domain of cryptocurrencies. This includes an examination of the impact and critiques regarding BitLicense since its promulgation, along with the use of perspectives from public value theory (PVT) to contextualize the value creation efforts of the DFS using BitLicense as a regulatory instrument. The findings of the chapter suggest that contrasting views exist on the value creation of cryptocurrency regulations, and this is reflected both in a PVT approach as well as the evolving praxis of virtual currency regulatory and oversight efforts.

Keywords: cryptocurrency, regulation, BitLicense, Bitcoin, SEC, oversight

> *Regrettably, the abominable BitLicense has awakened. It is a creature so foul, so cruel that not even Kraken possesses the courage or strength to face its nasty, big, pointy teeth.*
>
> — *Krakenfx, Farewell, New York. Open Letter. 2015.*

1. Introduction

The emergence of cryptocurrencies has heralded a great promise for the development of innovative financial structures (Vigna and Casey, 2016; Rose, 2015). As Allaire remarks, "the underlying promises of Bitcoin — security, privacy, efficiency, global interoperability — are innovations that policy makers are eager to see pursued" (Allaire, 2014). At the same time, the growth of the field has also been mired with various setbacks, including thefts, shutdowns, and abuse by criminals for nefarious activities (Foley *et al.*, 2019; Chohan, 2018). This shadowy aspect, coupled with the investor distress at great downswings in price since the Great Crypto Crash of 2018, has led to increased public calls for the existing structures of government to engage in *some* degree of regulatory oversight (Chohan, 2019b, 2019c). The legal issues surrounding cryptocurrencies are in fact a domain of growing academic and practitioner interest (Girasa, 2018; Bheemaiah, 2017). In some ways, perhaps, the regulation of blockchain may draw upon the industries of yore (Bostoen, 2019), but in many other ways, it is a novel field that requires unique attention (Bheemaiah, 2017). Yet, cryptocurrencies are not automatically inclined towards regulatory oversight, if anything due to their ideological rooting in cryptoanarchism (May, 1992; Ludlow, 2001; Chohan, 2017b), which aspires towards greater digital autonomy for the individual while protecting her rights to data access and privacy (May, 1994; Chohan, 2017b).

Nevertheless, different jurisdictions have meted out different regulatory treatments to cryptocurrencies (Inshyn *et al.*, 2018; Chohan, 2017c), ranging from outright banning to a comparatively lax position on their evolving praxis. Leading the charge, in this regard, have been American regulatory agencies, particularly the joint work by the Securities and Exchange Commission (SEC) and the Commodities and Futures Trading Commission (CFTC) at the federal level (Clayton, 2017; Clayton and Giancarlo, 2018), and the Department of Financial Services (DFS) at the subnational level (the State of New York). All have announced their keen interest in the space, along with a desire for proactive regulatory function that strikes a balance between innovation and accountability (DFS, 2015; Clayton, 2017; Giancarlo and Clayton, 2018). Yet, given that accountability and oversight are complex, cyclical, and multi-stakeholder processes (Chohan, 2017a, 2019a), the ability to strike a balance between innovation and accountability might, at times, appear elusive. Too much regulation risks stifling innovation (Amable *et al.*, 2016), but insufficient regulation leaves the public at risk to various forms of predation (see cryptocurrency examples in Chen *et al.*, 2019; Gandal *et al.*, 2018; Chohan, 2019b, 2018).

Given the comparatively novel nature of cryptocurrencies (Chohan, 2017d), it is particularly timely for academics and practitioners to consider how well new regulatory and oversight initiatives might be structured to contend with the gap that is left by a field that is developing ever so rapidly. Towards that end, this chapter presents a study of BitLicense, a form of regulatory license granted by the New York DFS for certain types of virtual currency business activities. Its greatest significance, as Allaire observed, has been that BitLicense was "the first material attempt at government rule-making around digital currency" (Allaire, 2014). Although described by some as "controversial" (del Castillo, 2015; Baker, 2017), BitLicense offers an example of proactive regulatory measures taken at an early juncture (pre-2015) to shape an amorphous commercial and transactional space, thus setting an example for other regulatory agencies around the world that wish to localize the functions of cryptocurrencies in their jurisdiction. Indeed, "given the significant role that New York plays in defining rules for the financial industry, this is a historic and crucial milestone for the development of the Bitcoin industry globally" (Allaire, 2014).

The structure of the remainder of this chapter is as follows. First, it provides an overview of BitLicense's dimensions, including what it does and doesn't cover in its remit. This helps to elucidate the underlying reasoning behind pursuing a limited but powerful exercise of control over the ability of agents to commercially engage in the cryptocurrency space. The next section considers its implications for cryptocurrency players, along with various practitioner critiques that have evolved since BitLicense was launched. The following section draws upon public value theory to briefly discuss certain implications of BitLicense as a value-creating proposal driven by public managers (the DFS). A concluding section discusses how the need for adaptation to a rapidly changing field requires continued oversight and regulation enforcement that still strikes the balance between the innovative impulses of cryptocurrency developers and the requisite accountability architecture that provides protections for the public.

2. BitLicense: An Overview

The State of New York has long been an avant-garde jurisdiction with respect to financial regulation (Allaire, 2014), and this was no less true of its early engagement with virtual currencies. In 2011, the state legislature established the DFS to regulate certain types of "issuance, banking and financial services," with a particular focus on new forms of financial instruments to maintain the soundness of prudence of the New York banking system (Baker, 2017). In August 2013, the DFS announced that it had initiated an inquiry into regulatory guidelines for virtual currencies (Lawsky, 2013). By any measure, and given the comparative recency of cryptocurrencies as a phenomenon (see Chohan, 2017d), the DFS was acting precociously to develop a scope for presenting an effective regulatory framework. It had determined, at the time, that "virtual currency exchangers may be engaging in money transmission as defined in New York law, which is an activity that is licensed and regulated by DFS" (Lawsky, 2013), arriving also at the conclusion that the existing framework for regulating money transmission businesses wasn't adequately covering the cryptocurrency space, hence the need for BitLicense.

BitLicense is thus a manifestation of the DFS's regulatory coverage of "virtual currency business activity" (DFS, 2015), and is part of the mandate of the office of the Superintendent of Financial Services (SFS; code: 23 CRR-NY 200). BitLicense has three central aims: "to establish regulations that prevent money laundering, protect consumers, and lay out rules related to cyber security" (see Klein, 2019). It has a "30-page application [which] includes a $5,000 fee to the [DFS], and an additional 20 pages of rules to follow" (del Castillo, 2015). The cost associated with an application for a BitLicense has, in one reported instance (Coinsetter), amounted to roughly $50,000 (del Castillo, 2015). Although the terms "cryptocurrencies" and "virtual currencies" are used interchangeably in this chapter, BitLicense offers an explicit definition of virtual currencies as "any type of digital unit that is used as a medium of exchange or form of digitally stored value or that is incorporated into payment system technology" (DFS, 2015), which casts a wide net over a space (see also Chohan, 2017c). The essence of BitLicense's stipulations are that entities engaging in virtual currency business activity within the state must be licensed, maintain requisite capital requirements, engage in proper book- and record-keeping, file regularized financial reports, and subject themselves to examination by the DFS (see also Hughes and Middlebrook, 2015). It is confined to New York State, activities involving the State of New York, or a New York resident; here the term "resident" is defined as residing in, located in, having a place of business in, or conducting business in the state. It follows from the stipulation of 23 NYCRR 200.3(a) that "No Person shall, without a license obtained from the superintendent, engage in any Virtual Currency Business Activity."

BitLicense require*s* licensees to maintain customer protection in three ways: "(1) maintenance of basic capital in the form of permissible investments, (2) maintenance of 'a bond or trust account in United States for the benefit of its customers', virtual currency of the 'same type and amount as that which is owed or obligated to' a third person, and (3) observance of the prohibition on 'selling, transferring, lending, hypothecating, pledging, or otherwise using or encumbering assets ... held, stored, or maintained by, or under the custody or control of, [the] Licensee on behalf of another Person" (Hughes and Middlebrook, 2015, p. 495). For the purposes of BitLicense, the scope of "virtual currency business activity" is relegated to the following five activities (DFS, 2015):

1. receiving Virtual Currency for Transmission or Transmitting Virtual Currency, except where the transaction is undertaken for non-financial purposes and does not involve the transfer of more than a nominal amount of Virtual Currency;
2. storing, holding, or maintaining custody or control of Virtual Currency on behalf of others;
3. buying and selling Virtual Currency as a customer business;
4. performing Exchange Services as a customer business;
5. controlling, administering or issuing a Virtual Currency.

Although ostensibly wide-ranging, the definition of business activity intentionally excludes certain forms of activity and agents. For example, an ordinary consumer does not need a BitLicense to purchase goods or services using cryptocurrencies. Nor does a merchant require a BitLicense in order to accept cryptocurrency as payment for goods or services that it provides. Nor too is a BitLicense required for nominal payments of virtual currency for non-financial purposes, such as for sole use in online gaming or code-writing (see Baker, 2017, p. 10; Lawsky, 2013). In addition, the development of cryptocurrencies and virtual instruments in and of itself does not require a BitLicense, and licensees do not need DFS approval for minor software and app updates (DFS, 2015). For jurisdictional purposes, any entity that is chartered under New York Banking Law does not require a BitLicense, but it must receive prior approval from the DFS to engage in virtual currency activity. Meanwhile, out-of-state businesses are required to obtain a BitLicense if they are to engage in virtual currency business activities within the State of New York. The issuance of BitLicenses has been subject to rigorous reviews by the DFS. At its discretion, however, the DFS has stated that it can offer conditional two-year BitLicenses subject to a more stringent review later on (DFS, 2019). BitLicenses may need to be paired with money transmitter licenses in the case of certain businesses, and then cross-satisfaction of requirements is acceptable to the DFS. To maintain the requirements of anti-money laundering and countering the financing of terrorists (AML/CFT), the BitLicense rules stipulate that when a licensee is involved in a cryptocurrency-to-cryptocurrency transaction in an aggregate amount above $10,000 per day by a single person, the licensee must notify the DFS. This coheres with international AML/CFT practices as stipulated by international bodies such as the FATF (see Blazejewski, 2008; Chohan, 2019d).

3. Impact and Critique

Given that the BitLicense system was the first major regulatory attempt to present an oversight and accountability architecture for virtual currencies, it was carefully studied by practitioners for its implications. Allaire pointed out that its scope was very broad and that it might compel many entities to withdraw from New York State for their cryptocurrency business activity (Allaire, 2014). Baker remarked that "I can think of no potential avenue for the issuer of an ICO [initial coin offering] to escape regulation under the BitLicense based on the category of activity that is subject to regulation in this provision" (Baker, 2017, p.12; see also ICOs in Chohan, 2019b, 2019c). One critique of BitLicense emerged from the ambiguities of language as stipulated in the law regarding the activities that it covers (Baker, 2017). However, the use of ambiguous language is also a reflection of an ever-rapidly transforming field, with new cryptocurrency technologies emerging by the day (Chohan, 2017c). Leaving room for greater interpretation would make BitLicense a more adaptive legal instrument with coverage of growing technologies. In terms of the aforementioned trade-off between fostering innovation and promoting accountability, some critics have asserted that BitLicense veers too far down the line of suppressing innovation, and so, "many feel that it simply stifles development and essentially prohibits the use of value-based blockchain technology in the state [of New York]" (Baker, 2017). As Allaire had forecast prior to its launch, "BitLicense is likely to have the opposite impact — radically limiting those who can participate in this industry, pushing firms offshore and into sometimes shadier jurisdictions" (Allaire, 2014).

This was manifest in an important event relating to BitLicense that came to be known in popular culture as the *Great Bitcoin Exodus* (GBE), referring to the departure of numerous cryptocurrency players from New York under compulsion from the regulatory pinch they anticipated under BitLicense. As del Castillo remarks, "the burden, it turns out, concerning both capital required and time invested, wasn't worth the potential benefits" (del Castillo, 2015). As mentioned earlier, given that the costs associated with an application for a BitLicense have, in one reported instance (Coinsetter), amounted to roughly $50,000 (del Castillo, 2015), the license can be considered discriminatory towards new entrants ("start-ups") in that it creates too high a legally compliant financial barrier to entry. As the founders of Kraken, a bitcoin exchange with $6.5 million in venture capital that joined in the exodus, wrote in an open letter: "while we're sure that the protection from New York law enforcement is valuable, it comes at a price that exceeds the market opportunity of servicing New York residents. Therefore, we have no option but to withdraw our service from the state" (Krakenfx, 2015). In fact, Kraken stipulated that BitLicense was prohibitive to a new cryptocurrency business for a host of reasons, including the following: no guarantee of support from New York banks; no guarantee of enforcement against unlicensed competitors; a reduced degree of consumer protection; an "unjustifiable burden" and restrictions on global operations; a similarly "unjustifiable bifurcation" of the service for New York alone; an "unjustifiable expense" for the opportunity to compete for the small market (of New York); "no exemption from traditional money transmission licensing" (although DFS did amend this); "no onramp" for small businesses; and in Kraken's view, "dubious value to the consumer" (Krakenfx, 2015).

During the GBE, many large and small cryptocurrency-related ventures chose to exit the market, but the most well-known among the pack at the time was ShapeShift. IO, due to the popular reputational element behind the founder Erik Voorhees, whose earlier company Satoshi Dice had made the first multi-million dollar exit for a bitcoin company. Lambasting BitLicense's "curbs" on virtual currency trading, Voorhees tweeted the following: "BitLicense is officially law in NY today. Shed a tear for freedom, capitalism, and innovation. Then, comply citizen. #bitcoin #USSA" (see Klein, 2019). In addition, other international names operating in New York also chose to leave the market, including the Hong Kong-based giant Bitfinex, the Montana-based Poloniex, and the Finnish LocalBitcoins.com. Their rationale was not simply that the DFS requires companies to share in-depth information about their own operation in a regularized manner, but also that there would be ongoing Know Your Customer (KYC) requirements designed to combat AML/CFT issues (see also Financial Action Task Force practices on laundering in Blazejewski, 2008; Chohan, 2019d). As mentioned earlier, the cryptoanarchist ideological leanings (May, 1994; Ludlow, 2001) of cryptocurrencies made them recalcitrant towards excessive oversight and regulatory intrusion (Chohan, 2017b). For BitLicense, this meant that "bitcoin's early adopters saw it as a watering down of the anonymity they like about bitcoin in the first place" (del Castillo, 2015). Indeed, the GBE was not just a movement by some virtual currency entities to find a safer harbor from regulations, but also a response from many private customers to divert their cryptocurrency holdings. As del Castillo reported, many customers also closed accounts in entities that operated in New York pending the enactment of BitLicense (del Castillo, 2015).

Another salient critique of BitLicense resided in the fact that not too many licenses were eventually issued (Baker, 2017). As of this writing, a total of 18 BitLicenses have been issued since 2014 (see also Klein, 2019). Given the proliferation of cryptocurrency-based technologies, virtual currencies, and initial coin offerings (Chohan, 2019b, 2019c), a figure of 18 is indeed a paltry sum. Many of the players that have received BitLicenses are either larger-scale developers or institutional players with heavy backing, such as the recent recipient Tagomi Trading LLC, which trades cryptocurrencies on behalf of hedge funds and wealthy individuals, and includes a co-founder who was previously head of Goldman Sach's digital trading desk (Klein, 2019). For the purposes of reference, some other large licensees include (in chronological order) Gemini, Ripple, Coinbase, Square, BitPay, Coinsource, and Robinhood. Gemini was founded by the Winklevoss twins of Facebook fame (Popper and Latman, 2013) and is one of the largest cryptocurrency exchanges in the world.

Coinbase is a similarly large cryptocurrency exchange with revenues of more than $1 billion (Gjermundrod *et al.*, 2016), while Bitpay and Square are international bitcoin payment service providers. Meanwhile, Ripple is a real-time gross settlement system, and currency exchange and remittance network (see Dierksmeier, 2018). As such, these cryptocurrency juggernauts are well-positioned to receive licenses and to comply with BitLicense stipulations, while they also gain from the legitimization that this license provides to their scale and to their function. For smaller players with new cryptocurrency approaches or ideas, however, the critique of barriers to entry stifling innovation perhaps rests against BitLicense.

With this in mind, the DFS proposed two new measures in December 2019 "to enhance efficiency and enable DFS-regulated virtual currency businesses to offer and use new coins in a timely fashion" (DFS, 2019). The first was to provide a public (open-access) list of coins that are permitted for the Virtual Currency Business Activities of DFS-regulated virtual currency businesses without DFS's prior approval. The second was the proposed model framework for the self-certification (without prior DFS approval) of virtual currency businesses in company-specific listing or adoption policies for coins. The question whether such incremental measures lead to a wider adoption, compliance, and application by cryptocurrency companies is still an open question. Given all of the aforementioned critiques, it is worth asking whether BitLicense is indeed fostering sufficient levels of better oversight, regulation, and accountability within the domain of cryptocurrencies. To address this question, one might rely on public value theory (PVT), and its emphasis on creating value for the wider public, to frame the impact of BitLicense. This discussion constitutes the following section.

4. A Public Value Perspective on BitLicense

Public value theory (PVT, see Moore, 1994; Chohan and Jacobs, 2017, 2018; Chohan, 2019a) is a discourse in the public administration literature which seeks to identify the role of "public managers" (bureaucrats, such as the DFS) in the value creation processes of society. The most commonly used tool and "central symbol" of public value is the *strategic triangle* (Alford and O'Flynn, 2009; Moore, 1995). It rests on three nodes: legitimacy, recognition of value, and operational resources. Legitimacy refers to the degree to which a project is being conferred legitimacy by members of the public, as well as to the legitimization that an institution might confer on projects undertaken by the public (Gains and Stoker, 2009). A recognition of public value refers to the degree to which a project or initiative is accorded the requisite recognition and acceptance by public stakeholders (Alford and O'Flynn, 2009). Operational resources refer to the methods, capabilities, institutional means, and assets that an organization of public managers has at its disposal to execute value-creating projects (Moore, 1995). When all three nodes are adequately met, there is an opportunity for public managers to engage in meaningful public value creation (Chohan and Jacobs, 2017, 2018). BitLicense is an instrument created by public managers (the DFS) to put greater regulation over the emergent domain of cryptocurrencies, which is of keen interest to a growing segment of the public. It is thus possible to transpose the BitLicense project onto the strategic triangle to examine whether public value creation is being made possible through the DFS's efforts. This is presented in Table 1 using contrasting perspectives (pros/cons) regarding each node.

Table 1: The Strategic Triangle on Bitlicense.

Node	Pros	Cons
Legitimacy	BitLicense acts as a legitimizing force in the cryptocurrency domain, allowing compliant companies to assure the public of responsible virtual currency business activity.	Cryptocurrencies veer ideologically towards cryptoanarchism, which seeks refuge from the exertion of government power and government "legitimization." Many cryptocurrencies thus shun government intrusion.
Recognition of Value	There is an increasing recognition by governments and civil society that some degree of regulation is necessary to protect the public from dangers of unregulated crypto-proliferation.	Many private agents do not see sufficient value in adhering to the costly, tiresome, exhaustive, and exacting requirements of a BitLicense. The cost-prohibitive nature of the licensing process also disfavors new entrants/small players.
Operational Resources	The DFS has strong regulatory know-how, a large budget, well-trained staff and prudent leadership.	The long application and compliance processes suggest that the DFS's resources face a degree of constraint in processing license applications in a timely manner.

Legitimacy: Even though only 18 licenses have been issued since BitLicense's inception, those that have received the DFS's imprimatur can operate under an umbrella of legitimacy, based on their rigorous compliance with regularized requirements. BitLicense creates value in this regard because it serves as a "legitimating device" (see Chohan, 2019a) for entities wishing to transact in virtual currency business activity. The public, in turn, rests more assured that these 18 entities adhere to a strict compliance regime that involves an office of public managers. Although this can never entirely dispel the risks of cryptocurrency malpractices (see Gandal *et al.*, 2018; Chen *et al.*, 2019; Chohan, 2018), it does provide some degree of assurance that public managers are engaging in oversight and holding virtual currency agents accountable. As del Castillo comments, "for [those] who decided to tough out this new era of BitLicenses and agree to share not only information about themselves — but their customers — could find themselves at the head of a very thinned out herd" (del Castillo, 2015). Meanwhile, the contrasting aspect of legitimization is rooted in the cryptoanarchist ideological leanings of many cryptocurrency developers, transactors, and investors (May, 1994; Ludlow, 2001). They do not therefore see the "need" for seeking out government legitimization as this is the specific force from which they yearn to escape (Chohan, 2017b). To such cryptoanarchists, the term "cryptocurrency regulation" is itself an oxymoron and deserves short shrift. The tussle between these two contrasting views on legitimization persists.

Recognition of value: The emergence of cryptocurrencies in the popular conscience has also been mired with various setbacks, including thefts, shutdowns, and abuse by criminals for nefarious activities (Foley *et al.*, 2019; Chohan, 2018). This shadowy aspect, coupled with the investor distress at great downswings in price since the Great Crypto Crash of 2018, has led to increased public calls for the existing structures of government to engage in some degree of regulatory oversight (Chohan, 2019b, 2019c). There is thus a heightened recognition of the value that greater regulation through instruments such as BitLicense provides. At the same time, the aforementioned critiques of BitLicense demonstrate that many private agents do not see sufficient value in adhering to the costly, tiresome, exhaustive, and exacting requirements of a BitLicense. The cost-prohibitive nature of the licensing process also disfavors new entrants/small players. As Kraken's open-letter lamented, there is: no guarantee of support from New York banks; no guarantee of enforcement against unlicensed competitors; a reduced degree of consumer protection; an "unjustifiable burden" and restrictions on global operations; a similarly "unjustifiable bifurcation" of the service for New York alone; an "unjustifiable expense" for the opportunity to compete for the small market; "no exemption from traditional money transmission licensing"; "no onramp" for small businesses; and "dubious value to the consumer" (Krakenfx, 2015). Therefore, there are equally contrasting views on the level of recognition that is accorded to the value of BitLicense more specifically and cryptocurrency regulation more broadly.

Operational resources: According to the Division of the Budget (DOB) of New York State, the DFS has an annual budget in excess of $400 million, with more than 1500 employees and countless financial services experts (DOB, 2019). Together, they oversee a financial sector including both bank and non-bank entities with cumulative assets exceeding $6.2 trillion (DFS, 2019), under prudent leadership and highly specialized cadres of financial-expert public managers. It may be gleaned from this that the DFS enjoys the requisite operational resources to pursue active financial regulatory oversight. At the same time, the long waiting times for the issuance of BitLicenses (Klein, 2019; del Castillo, 2015) suggest that the DFS's operational resources, efficiently as they may be deployed by its public managers, face constraints nonetheless; this is particularly so given the vast array of financial institutions and instruments for which they provide a regulatory and oversight role.

5. Conclusion

The foregoing discussion on the strategic triangle indicates that there are diametrically opposed views regarding each of the nodes of the strategic triangle. On the one hand, the effort to legitimize virtual currency business activities is being well-received, with many large agents and exchanges adhering to the rigorous compliance requirements in a manner that can bring greater legitimacy and assurance to the public about their activities. This is a strong indication of public value creation. On the other hand, the Great Bitcoin Exodus demonstrated the strong cryptoanarchist inclinations of many cryptocurrency players, for whom BitLicense was more of a regulatory threat than opportunity. As del Castillo observed, "bitcoin's early adopters saw it as a watering down of the anonymity they like about bitcoin in the first place" (del Castillo, 2015). Similarly, on the one hand, there is a growing recognition of the values created by stronger regulatory oversight of the virtual currency domain, both from governments around the world as well as civil society and private investors. The DFS addresses these values in providing a rigorous framework and compliance requirement through BitLicense. At the same time, various aspects of the compliance (cost, time, recourse, etc.) make it prohibitive for many virtual currency businesses, particularly for newer and smaller players.

What might be gleaned from the public value approach is that there is a mixed verdict for BitLicense, which is a reflection of the contrasting and conflicting values of segments within the public (see also Chohan and Jacobs, 2018). For scholars of PVT, the cryptocurrency analysis through the strategic triangle brings out a scholarly nuance: the strategic triangle itself can be applied using a pros/cons approach to highlight conflicts within the values held by the public, which is an advance in the PVT discourse (see also Alford and O'Flynn, 2009; Chohan, 2019a). What the strategic triangle evinces does reflect the wider debate about regulation in cryptocurrencies itself, for on the one hand, there is a pressing need for governments to contend with the meteoric rise of cryptocurrencies (see Chohan, 2017c), and yet there are complexities in developing a praxis for regulating something as amorphous as the field of virtual currencies. This challenge is echoed in the experience of other proactive regulators such as the SEC and CFTC (Clayton, 2017; Clayton and Giancarlo, 2018). Indeed, the question whether value is being created is likely to receive heated and continuous debate insofar as diametrically opposed views on regulation for cryptocurrencies persist. What was mentioned at the very outset in this chapter was that a balance is desired in regulation between fostering accountability and promoting innovation. This is an elusive goal, and the case study of BitLicense helps to illustrate that dilemma in a telling fashion. Further regulatory efforts, shifting public attitudes, and technological breakthroughs are all likely to steer this debate in the years to come.

References

Alford, J., and J. O'Flynn. 2009. "Making sense of public value: Concepts, critiques and emergent meanings." *International Journal of Public Administration* 32:3–4, 171–191.

Allaire, J. 2014. "Thoughts on the New York BitLicense Proposal." *Circle.* August 13.

Amable, B., Ledezma, I., and Robin, S. 2016. "Product market regulation, innovation, and productivity."*Research Policy* 45:10, 2087–2104.

Baker, B. 2017. "Application of the New York BitLicense to Initial Coin Offerings." Available at SSRN 3319540.

Bheemaiah, K. 2017. "Innovating Capitalism." In *The Blockchain Alternative*, 83–154. Berkeley, CA: Apress.

Blazejewski, K. S. 2008. "The FATF and its institutional partners: Improving the effectiveness and accountability of transgovernmental networks." *Temple International and Comparative Law Journal* 22, 1–17.

Bostoen, F. 2019. "Regulating online platforms: Lessons from 100 years of telecommunications regulation." *Technology Review* 335:2, 335–40.

Chen, W., W. Jun, Z. Zheng, C. Chen, and Y. Zhou. 2019. "Market manipulation of bitcoin: Evidence from mining the Mt. Gox transaction network." *IEEE INFOCOM 2019 — IEEE Conference on Computer Communications*, 964–972. IEEE.

Chohan, U. W. 2017a. "Budget Reform and Political Reform." In Ali Farazmand (ed.), *Global Encyclopedia of Public Administration, Public Policy, and Governance.* New York: Springer.

Chohan, U. W. 2017b. "Cryptoanarchism and cryptocurrencies." *Philosophy & Methodology of Economics eJournal*. SSRN.

Chohan, U. W. 2017c. "Assessing the differences in bitcoin & other cryptocurrency legality across national jurisdictions." *International Political Economy: Monetary Relations eJournal.*SSRN.

Chohan, U. W. 2017d. "A History of Bitcoin." *Monetary Economics: Financial System & Institutions eJournal.* SSRN.

Chohan, U. W. 2018. "The problems of cryptocurrency thefts and exchange shutdowns." *Information Systems & Economics eJournal*. SSRN.

Chohan, U. W. 2019a. *Public Value and Budgeting: International Perspectives*. London: Routledge.

Chohan, U. W. 2019b. "Are Cryptocurrencies Truly Trustless?" In Gouette *et al.* (eds.), *Cryptofinance and Mechanisms of Exchange: The Making of Virtual Currency*, 77–89. Cham: Springer.

Chohan, U. W. 2019c. "Initial coin offerings (ICOs): Risks, regulation, and accountability." In Gouette *et al.* (eds.), *Cryptofinance and Mechanisms of Exchange: The Making of Virtual Currency*, 165–177. Cham: Springer.

Chohan, U. W. 2019d. "The FATF in the global financial architecture: Challenges and implications." *CASS Working Papers on Economics and National Affairs.* EC001UC.

Chohan, U. W., and K. Jacobs. 2017. "Public value in politics: A legislative budget office approach." *International Journal of Public Administration* 40:12, 1063–1073.

Chohan, U. W., and K. Jacobs. 2018. "Public value as rhetoric: A budgeting approach." *International Journal of Public Administration* 41:15, 1217–1227.

Clayton, J. 2017. Statement on Cryptocurrencies and Initial Coin Offerings. Securities and Exchange Commission [SEC], Washington, DC.

Clayton, J., and J. C. Giancarlo. 2018. Statement by SEC Chairman Jay Clayton and CFTC Chairman J. C. Giancarlo: Regulators are Looking at Cryptocurrency [Press release].

del Castillo, M. 2015. "The 'Great Bitcoin Exodus' has totally changed New York's bitcoin ecosystem." *New York Business Journal.* August 12.

Department of Financial Services (DFS). 2015. *Virtual Currency Business Activity*. Licenses Memorandum. New York: DFS.

DFS. 2019. *Guidance: Virtual Currency Business Activity*. New York: DFS.

Dierksmeier, C. (2018). "Just HODL? On the moral claims of bitcoin and ripple users." *Humanistic Management Journal* 3:1, 127–131.

Foley, S., J. R. Karlsen, and T. J. Putniņš. 2019. "Sex, drugs, and bitcoin: How much illegal activity is financed through cryptocurrencies?" *The Review of Financial Studies* 32:5, 1798–1853.

Gains, F., and G. Stoker. 2009. "Delivering 'public value': Implications for accountability and legitimacy." *Parliamentary Affairs* 62:3, 438–455.

Gandal, N., J. T. Hamrick, T. Moore, and T. Oberman 2018. "Price manipulation in the Bitcoin ecosystem." *Journal of Monetary Economics* 95, 86–96.

Gjermundrød, H., K. Chalkias, and I. Dionysiou. 2016. "Going beyond the Coinbase transaction fee: Alternative reward schemes for miners in blockchain systems." In *Proceedings of the 20th Pan-Hellenic Conference on Informatics*, 1–4.

Girasa, R. 2018. "Legal issues of digital technology." In *Regulation of Cryptocurrencies and Blockchain Technologies*, 57–69. Cham: Palgrave Macmillan.

Hughes, S. J., and S. T. Middlebrook. 2015. "Advancing the framework for regulating cryptocurrency payments intermediaries." *Yale Journal of Regulation* 32:4, 495.

Inshyn, M., L. Mohilevskyi, and O. Drozd. 2018. "The issue of cryptocurrency legal regulation in Ukraine and all over the world: A comparative analysis." *Baltic Journal of Economic Studies* 4:1, 169–174.

Klein, J. 2019. "New York just granted its 18th BitLicense." *Breakermag.* March 28.

Krakenfx. 2015. "Farewell, New York." Krakenfx. August 9.

Lawsky, B. M. 2013. "Notice of Inquiry on Virtual Currencies." New York State Department of Financial Services. August 12.

Ludlow, P. 2001. *Crypto Anarchy, Cyberstates, and Pirate Utopias*. Boston: MIT Press.

May, T. C. 1992. "The cryptoanarchist manifesto." *High Noon on the Electronic Frontier: Conceptual Issues in Cyberspace.*

May, T. C. 1994. *Crypto Anarchy and Virtual Communities.* T. C. May.

Moore, M. H. 1994. "Public value as the focus of strategy." *Australian Journal of Public Administration* 53:3, 296–303.

Moore, M. H. 1995. *Creating Public Value: Strategic Management in Government.* Cambridge, MA: Harvard University Press.

Popper, N., and P. Lattman. 2013. "Never mind Facebook; Winklevoss twins rule in digital money." *New York Times.*

Rose, C. 2015. "The evolution of digital currencies: Bitcoin, a cryptocurrency causing a monetary revolution." *International Business & Economics Research Journal (IBER)* 14:4, 617–622.

Vigna, P., and M. J. Casey. 2016. *The Age of Cryptocurrency: How Bitcoin and the Blockchain Are Challenging the Global Economic Order*. New York: Macmillan.

https://doi.org/10.1142/9789811239670_0007

Chapter 7

Cryptocurrencies: Key Risks and Challenges

Sonia Arsi[*,†], **Soumaya Ben Khelifa**[*,‡], **Yosra Ghabri**[*,§], **and Hela Mzoughi**[*,¶]

[*]*University Tunis Carthage — Carthage Business School, Tunis, Tunisia*

[†]*sonia.arsi@utctunisie.com*

[‡]*soumaya.benkhelifa@utctunisie.com*

[§]*yosra.ghabri@utctunisie.com*

[¶]*hela.mzoughi@utctunisie.com*

Abstract

Cryptocurrencies are witnessing a growing interest from investors and the media. They are increasingly perceived as a new class of assets through added benefits, such as hedging capabilities and diversification. However, this does not preclude the fact that cryptocurrencies can be risky assets. Within such a context, diverse studies were carried out at various risk levels. Our chapter bridges this gap and tries to reconcile varying positions on risk across cryptocurrencies. Particularly, we provide a detailed overview on the main risks to be considered by crypto-traders, namely, technology, fraud, legal, market, liquidity, and COVID-19 pandemic risks. The main findings show that the occurrence of any technological failure tends to raise insecurity and distrust in the cryptocurrency technology. This fact can be even further spoiled through fraud schemes and fake trading volumes. Additionally, the legal framework of the cryptocurrencies is still inconclusive. In terms of market risk, these crypto-assets are riskier than fiat currencies and there is a significant risk contagion across large-cap cryptocurrencies. Then, a significant relationship exists between liquidity and efficiency in the cryptocurrency market, since price dynamics can influence the market liquidity. Finally, it sorts out that the COVID-19 pandemic heavily affected the cryptocurrency markets. This chapter underlines current challenges for investors, regulators, and policymakers.

Keywords: cryptocurrency Market, Bitcoin, risk, technology, fraud, regulation, liquidity and COVID-19 pandemic

1. Introduction

In today's global financial markets, cryptocurrencies represent a remarkable innovation that has attracted noteworthy attention from theorists, analysts, and traders. Using a fully decentralized system, this new form of currency introduces advancements in money transfers and electronic payments, lowering the transaction costs and increasing users' privacy. In addition to the potential benefits that digital currencies offer, they also pose different risks to investors and traditional financial companies. Hence, understanding the risks associated with this new asset class and their underlying technology, blockchain, is a major concern for investors, policymakers, and regulators in order to avoid asset bubbles, manage liquidity, and optimally diversify portfolios.

Cryptocurrencies have recently proliferated through Initial Coin Offerings (ICOs), blockchain forks, and token sales. The relevance and the popularity of their underlying technologies will explicitly affect their market value. Accordingly, when it comes to the cryptocurrency market, financial risks cannot be examined without taking into account technology risks. For instance, financial risks are associated with volatility spillovers (e.g., Canh *et al.* (2019)), extreme values and bubbles (e.g., Baek and Elbeck (2015)), contagion risk (e.g., Tiwari *et al.* (2020)), systematic and idiosyncratic risks (e.g., Borri (2019)), and liquidity risk (e.g., Koutmos (2018)). However, to sustain cyber security and protect private keys, the cryptocurrency market requires managing the risks of "outages" in the infrastructure components (e.g., Bosu *et al.* (2019)), the crypto-scalability (e.g., Judmayer *et al.* (2017)), and the cyber security or hacking risk (e.g., Taylor *et al.* (2019)). Equally, the fraud/theft risk emerges as cryptocurrency exchanges manipulate investors and release fake data (e.g., Transparency Institute Blockchain (2019a, 2019b)). Another key risk related to the cryptocurrency market is the legal uncertainty and the lack of clarity and coordination on regulatory treatment between different jurisdictions across the world (e.g., Stratfor (2016)). Nevertheless, one cannot ignore the COVID-19 pandemic risk and how it reshaped the picture of cryptocurrencies. Thus, exploring how these different risks interplay with the cryptocurrency market is crucial to help protect investors from illegal activities and market manipulation. Furthermore, it supports regulators to control cryptocurrency exchanges and prevent market misconduct and financial crimes. The ultimate goal is to increase the legitimacy of crypto activities.

In this context, the aim of this chapter is to review and assess the key risks to which cryptocurrency investors are exposed. More precisely, we explore the technology, fraud/theft, legal, market, liquidity and pandemic risks related to cryptocurrency activities to draw and provide important policy and managerial implications for regulators and practitioners. The rest of the chapter is structured as follows. Section 1 analyzes the technology risk of cryptocurrencies. Section 2 underlines the fraud/theft risk. Section 3 spotlights the regulation risk. Section 4 focuses on the market risks. Section 5 deals with liquidity risk. Section 6 emphasizes on the COVID-19 pandemic risk. Section 7 concludes and discusses potential implications.

2. Technology Risk

The technology risk, or "Information Technology (IT)" risk, refers in general to the occurrence probability of technology deficiencies that may hamper the smooth running of a considered business, such as cyber security incidents, services interruptions, etc. (e.g., Subriadi and Najwa (2020)). Within the cryptocurrency context, the literature highlighted diverse aspects of technological incidences, emphasized on hereafter. The main feature of cryptocurrencies lies in their use of a specified mechanism called the "blockchain technology," also known as "Distributed Ledger Technology (DLT)." It is defined as a ledger that records and stores data in the form of "blocks." Each transaction is verified and secured (e.g., Houben and Snyers (2018) and Taylor *et al.* (2019)). Nevertheless, since crypto-technologies are praised for their privacy and security features, to what extent can they be unfailing?

A first risk can be referred to as "outages" in the infrastructure components. Palladino (2017) mentioned that the emergence of bugs, due to encoding problems, contributed to a theft of 150,000 ETH (approximately $30 million). Bosu *et al.* (2019) pointed out that such technical failures, while they seem to be "innocent-looking," can lead to devastating consequences. Also, Krause and Tolaymat (2018) cited that power and computing resource requirements for cryptocurrency mining play an important role in shaping the speed and trust around cryptocurrencies. The authors reported that Bitcoin is consuming energy "as much as Angola or Panama."

Another potential risk is the crypto-scalability, defined as the number of transactions handled by the network; it represents a limitation to cryptocurrency technologies (e.g., Herrera-Joancomartí and Pérez-Solà (2016)). For example, considering the Bitcoin network, Judmayer *et al.* (2017, p. 87) highlighted that it has a restricted processing time, which is seven transactions per second, compared to PayPal and VISA (in terms of hundreds and thousands of transactions per second). The authors pointed out that such a shortage can weaken the cryptocurrency technologies' performance and endanger their security features.

This sorts out an additional IT risk of cryptocurrencies, which is the "cyber security risk" or "hacking risk" (e.g., Soehartono and Pati (2019, p. 210)). Indeed, Taylor *et al.* (2019) underlined that the blockchain technology is a magnet to "cyber attacks." The literature stated different aspects. Judmayer *et al.* (2017, p. 53) stressed that the loss of private keys or even an "unintentional key sharing" can contribute to unsecure crypto-transactions with covering the real owners of private keys (e.g., Wang *et al.* (2018)). An example is the hack of Mt. Gox, one of the largest cryptocurrency exchanges, in 2014 due to a theft of private keys (e.g., Kim and Lee (2018)). Further, Konoth *et al.* (2019) showed how infectious codes, better known as "Trojan malwares" that "encrypts the entire drivers to file to infect computers," stole cryptocurrencies and damaged the market in turn.

Within this framework, Soehartono and Pati (2019) underlined that hacking entails expensive costs as it needs powerful computers to fathom the block. Interestingly, this additional privacy can be a double-edge sword. It can be not only a source of problems as law enforcement officers will have a hard task to control it (e.g., Hackett (2017) and Min (2019)), but also an incentive to manipulation and fraud (e.g., Twomey and Mann (2020)).

3. Fraud/Theft Risk

Subsequently to IT deficiencies, cryptocurrencies are particularly prone to identity theft and fraud. Here, a nuance is provided; identity theft consists of stealing the identity of crypto-traders including their personal details, and banking information, among others, while identity fraud refers to the use of stolen information to commit illegal or unethical practices. Koops and Leenes (2006) stated that identity fraud is a broader term that encompasses "identity theft"; it's all about "identity-related crime." Within the cryptocurrency context, the *fakeness* of trading volume is considered to be among the main scandals of identity fraud.

According to its report presented to the Securities and Exchange Commission (SEC), Bitwise Asset Management (2019) emphasized that around 95% of Bitcoin trading volume reported by CoinMarketCap is fake. Though the daily Bitcoin trading volume specified by CoinMarketCap is about $6 billion, the truth uncovers only $273 million. Then, following this scandal, further investigations came up. Through the launch of the "BTI Verified program," Transparency Institute Blockchain (2019a) aimed to detect "wash trading" activity, i.e., fake transactions. It stated that 17 among the top 25 CoinMarketCap exchanges decipher over 99% as fictitious volumes. In a later report, Transparency Institute Blockchain (2019b) released that around 25% of the aforementioned exchanges reveal accurate data on their volume patterns. Figure 1 displays the names of exchanges with the highest rates of wash trades.

They stated that such scams create fictitious liquidity and overblow cryptocurrency markets, which mislead inescapably the traders. Besides, this *inflation* contributes to the apparently endless proliferation of new

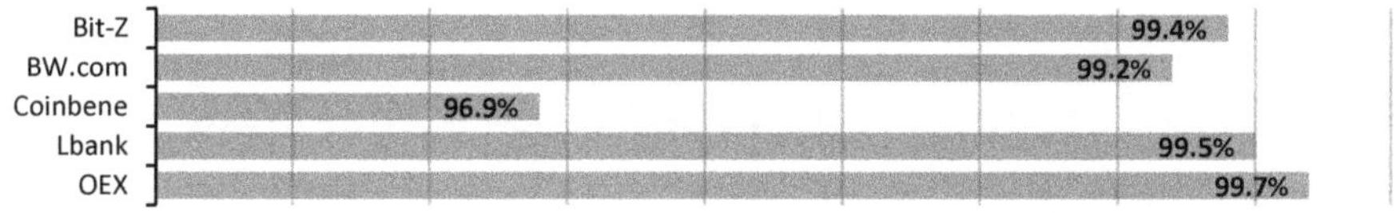

Figure 1: Highest Fake Volume Rate per Cryptocurrency Exchange.

Source: Data extracted from September's report established by Transparency Institute Blockchain (2019b).

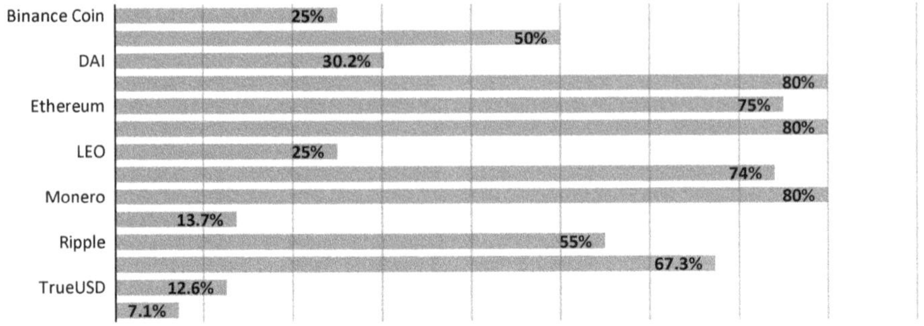

Figure 2: Fake Volume Rate per Cryptocurrency.

Source: Data extracted from September's report established by Transparency Institute Blockchain (2019b).

exchanges (e.g., Bovaird (2019) and Kauflin (2019)). For further highlights, Transparency Institute Blockchain (2019b) draws a distinction between cryptocurrencies according to their fake and true volume trades as displayed in Figure 2. This portrait alters the truthiness of cryptocurrency markets and presents a considerable risk for investors.

Recently, the National Internet Finance Association of China (2020) underlined that crypto exchanges tamper volume trades, especially during low prices (a fact equally confirmed by Griffin and Shams (2019) for Bitcoin and Tether). Lo and behold, traders will take the bait and another set of "manipulation" is implemented to take over their investment. The study reported examples of fraudulent trading programs and strategies, and provoked IT shortages.

While these secrecies on trading volume tend to grab the traders' attention, it leads inevitably to a tarnished reputation of the cryptocurrency markets. This picture stems from one main reason: the lack of an efficient "regulatory crackdown" (e.g., National Internet Finance Association of China (2020), Twomey and Mann (2020), and Joshi (2020)).

4. Cryptocurrency Regulations and Legal Risk

The debate about the legal aspects of crypto-assets and in particular how to regulate decentralized cryptocurrencies is still inconclusive. The rapid growth of cryptocurrencies and their "DLT" has forced central banks, financial institutions, and regulators to recognize a growing gap between the technology, policymakers, and legislators.

According to the Financial Action Task Force (FATF), Bitcoin is a digital representation of value that does not have legal tender status in any jurisdiction. As opposed to centralized fiat currencies, cryptos are not regulated by any government and can be owned by any individual without the control of central banks and financial institutions (e.g., Yeoh (2017)). Cryptocurrencies are administered through blockchain, a decentralized network based on cryptographic protocols to track purchases and secure financial transactions (e.g., Arslanian and Fischer (2019)). Anonymity is a key feature in the cryptocurrency market, making it difficult to determine the identity of cryptocurrency users within the system. Their decentralized and global nature creates an attractive environment for hacking, frauds, and criminal activities (e.g., Levine (2018)). There is no central authority or administrator that could be subject to regulation. Miners and developers substitute the central authority and control the system operations.

Cryptocurrencies cannot be classified as a single type of asset. They combine the characteristics of currencies, commodities, payment systems and securities. Furthermore, cryptocurrencies have different types (coins, tokens, stablecoins, etc.) which gave them different legal statuses. This leads to ambiguity regarding which regulatory framework to apply. The absence of geographic limitations and regulated institutions facilitates tax avoidance (e.g., Foley *et al.* (2019)). A key threat to cryptocurrencies is their association with fraud, cybercrime, high volatility, hacking, Ponzischemes, and market manipulation (e.g., Ahlstrom *et al.* (2018)). Cryptocurrency users remain unprotected against these risks and illicit activities. Wallets could be hacked, users could be duped by fraudsters, and the unscrupulous could make illegal purchases and evade taxes (European Banking Authority (2014)).

Regarding these challenges, governments around the world are taking different regulations and legal approaches to cryptocurrencies. Some jurisdictions have adopted specific regulations to manage cryptocurrency activities; some have no formal regulatory policy, while others have banned their use.

The United States was one of the few countries that have adopted a regulatory policy to manage cryptocurrency exchanges and control fraud risk. In March 2013, guidance was issued by the Financial Crimes

Enforcement Network (FinCEN) that considers cryptocurrency activities as money transmitters. Under this regulation, the administrators are required to maintain certain transaction records in relation to suspicious or large cash transactions and file reports with FinCEN, to implement counter-terrorist financing and anti-money laundering programs. In order to monitor cryptocurrency activities, other jurisdictions impose rules to put in place "know your customer" (KYC) regimes to prevent financial crimes. In 2017, the U.S. Uniform Law Commission prepared the "Uniform Regulation of Virtual Currency Businesses Act" to determine which businesses and activities require licensing regimes in order to operate in the U.S. market. As cryptocurrencies are not a homogeneous asset class (currency units, securities or commodities), the SEC issued guidelines to identify cryptocurrencies that would be regulated as securities. The users providing trading services dealing with this asset class should comply with securities regulation. However, enforcement actions have been issued by the SEC against the ICO activities to not violate securities regulation. In fact, ICOs should comply with specific disclosure requirements similar to securities to allow the access of investors to sufficient information and help them in their investment decisions (e.g., Zetzsche *et al.* (2019)).

Despite facing challenges, U.S. securities regulators and government agencies are still developing procedures to implement regulations dealing with market misconduct, cryptocurrency fraud, and other illicit activities.

Considered as the global leader in the development of cryptocurrencies, Japan promulgated specific laws and legislative provisions that support the technological development of cryptos and encourage their usage. The Bank of Japan announced, in April 2017, that Japan will take the required procedures in order to advance the payment infrastructures and provide the optimum functions of cryptocurrency exchanges (e.g., Nakaso (2017)). On the same date, the Japanese "Virtual Currency Law" was developed to address the nature of cryptocurrencies, the operation of cryptocurrency exchanges, and how to prevent financial crimes. These legislative provisions include revised sections of the Payment Services Act, the Amendment Act for the Prevention of Transfer of Criminal Proceeds, and Guidelines issued by the Financial Services Agency of Japan. The amended Payments Services Act declares cryptocurrencies as a legal method of payment in Japan.

Australia is another leading jurisdiction in innovation and cryptocurrency research. The Australian Securities and Investments Commission

(ASIC) launched, in 2017, the regulatory sandbox scheme which provides regulatory exemptions to test certain financial products for some companies in order to sustain public confidence in the long run (e.g., Price (2018)). Similar programs and regulations were also created by other jurisdictions in South Africa and the United Kingdom to provide stable regulatory policies for virtual currencies. Furthermore, Venezuela and Zimbabwe have accepted cryptocurrencies, and started to explicitly trade with Bitcoin. To create "Crypto Valley," a cryptocurrency industry associated with the technology companies in Silicon Valley, Switzerland adopted guidelines and low tax rates in order to provide regulatory certainty and attract exchanges and cryptocurrency companies. Similarly, Malta developed a blockchain taskforce strategy and "crypto-friendly" frameworks aiming to advise the government and attract cryptocurrency exchanges. Singapore also explored ways to adopt transparent and well-informed regulations to become a major location for ICOs.

Many European Union (EU) countries don't have any view on Bitcoin and have not banned it. In 2016, the European Parliament proposed to set up a taskforce by the European Commission to monitor cryptocurrency activities and stop fraud risks and tax evasion practices. In 2017, the proposal involved cryptocurrency wallets to control doubtful movements and terrorist fundraising (e.g., Coleman (2017)). In 2018, the European Banking Authority proposed to prevent banks and financial institutions from trading virtual currencies rather than putting many restrictions on financial innovations and crypto exchanges (e.g., Binham (2018)). Finally, in 2019, some EU countries such as France adopted specific licensing regulations imposed on cyber-security requirements, cryptocurrency service providers prudential, and "know your customer" requirements.

Other jurisdictions such as India, Nepal, Hong Kong, and Indonesia announced Bitcoin as illegal currency and mode of exchange and imposed outright bans on cryptocurrency trading (e.g., Bloomberg (2018)). They issued warnings to users about the potential risks associated with investing in cryptocurrencies. In April 2017, an official statement was issued by the Central Bank of Bolivia to restrict cryptocurrency exchanges that are not regulated or issued by central banks or states. Similarly, in 2017, a series of official announcements, notices, and circulars were issued by the National Internet Finance Association (NIFA) to deter investors and organizations from engaging in ICO activities. Consequently, China and South Korea have banned ICOs and severely restricted cryptocurrency trading (e.g., Borri and Shakhnov (2019)). Pakistan, Vietnam, Morocco, and Algeria banned all cryptocurrency activities. Taiwan, Colombia, Bangladesh, Thailand, Iran, Lesotho, and Lithuania have prohibited banks and financial institutions from accepting transactions involved with cryptocurrencies.

Countries around the world are taking different guidelines and regulations to manage and control cryptocurrency activities, applying different approaches and legal rules. The restrictive and uncertain regulatory policies need to be harmonized across governments. The lack of clear regulatory policies and common standards regarding cryptocurrencies will make their future value usually volatile and create instability and further financial risks may arise in turn.

5. Market Risk

The market risk can be defined as a decrease in the investment value due to factors that may have an impact on the overall financial market performance and cannot be reduced through diversification. The performance of the cryptocurrency market, like the traditional financial markets, may be influenced by potential losses due to the excess volatility-stylized fact of these digital assets.

The volatility risk of the cryptocurrencies gained intensive attention due to its vital implications for asset-pricing analysis, portfolio selection, market efficiency, capital budgeting decisions, and risk management practices. Many studies (e.g., Vejačka (2014), Dyhrberg (2016), Bouoiyour and Selmi (2016), and İçellioğlu and Öner (2019)) dealt with the volatility risk of cryptocurrency. Unquestionably, the low-volatility anomaly runs counter to the primary intuition that high-volatility assets must deliver commensurately high returns. According to Siswantoro *et al.* (2020), this character is qualified by huge volatility when evaluating the suitability of cryptocurrency as money from the Islamic perspective. The results affirm that cryptocurrency is prohibited in Islam as it is used for speculation.

High volatility in the cryptocurrency market can cause a risk such as bubbles and important downturns, which may attract speculative investors (e.g., Baek and Elbeck (2015)). On the other hand, Fry (2018) presents robust evidence on bubbles in Bitcoin and Ethereum by using rational bubble models and considering both heavy tails and the probability of a complete decline in asset prices.

Katsiampa (2019) notes that a lot of research has been conducted on cryptocurrencies' price volatility; nevertheless, univariate models are not appropriate for studying their co-movements. In addition, the extreme value behavior of cryptocurrencies has been studied by Osterrieder and Lorenz (2017), Osterrieder *et al.* (2017), and Gkillas and Katsiampa (2018). The latter showed that cryptocurrencies exhibit heavier tail behavior and are thus riskier than fiat currencies. The existence of cryptocurrencies' conditional volatility and asymmetric effects between good and bad news are confirmed following their results. The risk of extreme volatility is directly related to the dynamic interdependencies between log-returns of cryptocurrencies and the transmission of demand shocks within clusters.

Therefore, examining the interconnectedness between different types of cryptocurrencies can be meaningful for both investment and risk prevention. In this context, the research of Zięba *et al.* (2019) and Antonakakis *et al.* (2019) investigates the transmission mechanism in the cryptocurrency market and find that periods of high (low) market uncertainty correspond to strong (weak) connectedness.

The study of Canh *et al.* (2019) provides a formal analysis of the structural breaks and volatility spillovers with strong positive correlations in the cryptocurrency market. The detection of systematic structural breaks indicates market integration, which in turn limits the diversification benefit. These findings highlight the important degree of non-diversifiable risk within this emerging financial asset class. In this context, Borri and Shakhnov (2019) focus on the conditional tail-risk in the cryptocurrency market and show that these cryptocurrencies are highly correlated and exposed to tail-risk. They affirm that idiosyncratic risk can be significantly reduced and cryptocurrencies' portfolios offer better risk-adjusted and conditional returns than individual cryptocurrencies. In opposition, Borri (2019) affirm that these cryptocurrencies are not exposed to tail-risk in relation to other global assets (equity market or gold). The returns on these cryptocurrencies are not only highly correlated but also exhibit idiosyncratic risk.

High degrees of contagion risk are examined in the research of Yi *et al.* (2018), Koutmos (2018), and Tiwari *et al.* (2020), among others. Indeed, the results reveal a steady rise in return and volatility spillovers over time and show heavy tail dependence between each pair of cryptocurrencies. The results provide evidence of a significant risk contagion among price returns of major cryptocurrencies in bull and bear markets, while small cap cryptocurrencies are more likely to receive volatility shocks than others.

An examination of contagious cryptocurrencies will help market participants and policymakers to anticipate the presence of a systematic risk, and thus will help them better manage the cryptocurrency risks. The article by Handika *et al.* (2019) deals with systematic risk in the Asian financial markets. Their outcomes are somewhat consistent with others and document a systematic risk in some financial market regions (e.g., Forbes and Rigobon (2002), Dungey *et al.* (2005), Białkowski and Serwa (2005), Boschi (2005), and Martínez-Jaramillo *et al.* (2010)).

A popular behavioral explanation for the excess of volatility is herding behavior. The analysis of herding existence in the cryptocurrency market is of paramount importance, since the presence of this phenomenon would give rise to an inefficient market, in which asset pricing models, based on rational economic behavior, cannot be properly applied. Indeed, da Gama Silva *et al.* (2019) identify and analyze the herding and contagion behavior in cryptocurrency markets. The herding behavior of cryptocurrency is also analyzed by Bouri *et al.* (2019), who highlight the existence of herding in a market with 14 cryptocurrencies. In addition, Vidal-Tomás *et al.* (2019) analyze the existence of herding in the cryptocurrency market through the cross-sectional standard (absolute) deviation of returns. The results show that extreme dispersion of returns is explained by rational asset pricing models although it is possible to observe herding during down markets, which highlights the inefficiency and risk of cryptocurrencies. They also observe that the smallest digital currencies are herding with the largest ones. As a consequence, assets will not be priced appropriately given that traders are not including all the information available in the market properly due to their irrational behavior.

To manage the risk of investment in crypto-assets, Białkowski (2019) examines rules that are actually used by banks and hedge funds. These are integral parts of risk management practice in the professional trading community and serve to reduce a portfolio's exposure after its cumulative losses reach some predetermined level. The results also highlight the importance of the development of crypto-asset specific stop-loss rules to deal with the low survival rate.

6. Liquidity Risk

The top ten cryptocurrencies, such as Bitcoin, Ethereum, and Litecoin, have achieved market capitalization higher than 2 billion USD. Particularly, the Bitcoin reached a value close to 190 billion USD in

February 2020 (e.g., www.coinmarketcap.com). Recently, cryptocurrencies intensively attracted many investors and market-makers. They brought to the attention of researchers very good issues. However, concerns have been expressed about increased speculation and price manipulation in cryptocurrency markets. This brings us to a further issue about the liquidity risk of cryptocurrencies. The current literature on the cryptocurrency market focuses mainly on the relationship between liquidity and the following aspects: trading, market volatility and price dynamics, and market efficiency.

Recently, some studies examined the trading dynamics and market microstructure of cryptocurrencies. While cryptocurrencies such as Bitcoin represent a digital medium of exchange, it is also an investment asset which is traded seven days a week (Dyhrberg *et al.* (2018)). However, little attention had been addressed to its determinants and the development of its liquidity (e.g., Scharnowski (2020)). Koutmos (2018) and Dyhrberg *et al.* (2018) investigate the trading and market microstructure of Bitcoin using the spread as a measure of liquidity. Particularly, Dyhrberg *et al.* (2018) focus on the Bitcoin/US dollar exchange rate market. They collect intraday and quote data of individual trades from three marketplaces (Kraken, GDAX and Gemini) and they measure the trading costs using the average quoted spread and the average effective spread. Their results suggest that these two spreads are lower than those on equity exchanges, indicating that Bitcoin is highly investible. It is also important that the liquidity of Bitcoin has improved considerably in the last years (e.g., Scharnowski (2020)). Koutmos (2018) developed a new model based on the bid-ask spread data to assess the liquidity uncertainty of Bitcoin. To explain this variable, he incorporates microstructure variables such as price, trading volume, size, transaction fees, etc. The findings show that, for the low liquidity uncertainty regime, the "liquidity uncertainty" is positively related to Bitcoin returns and range volatility and it is negatively associated with other microstructure characteristics, namely, market capitalization, trade volume and transactions fees. However, for "the high liquidity uncertainty regime," microstructure characteristics have no impact on liquidity uncertainty. Hence, such regimes should be taken into account to conduct further tests on Bitcoin.

Makarov and Schoar (2020) examine the arbitrage and price deviations in the cryptocurrency market. They show that deviations in the prices are greater across than within countries and are lower between cryptocurrencies. By dividing the signed volume into two components (common and idiosyncratic), they find that the idiosyncratic component is a determinant of arbitrage spreads between exchanges. Al Janabi *et al.* (2019) propose a new approach to evaluate liquidity-adjusted Value-at-Risk optimization of portfolios and apply it to Bitcoin and other assets. They find that Bitcoin is more performant under a scenario of only long positions. Naeem *et al.* (2019) investigate the relationship between trading volumes and returns of cryptocurrencies. He chooses the largest crypto-assets: Ethereum, Bitcoin and Litecoin. Using GARCH-copula models, the results suggest that the dependence is asymmetric and extreme returns are related to extreme trading volume.

The nascent research studies on cryptocurrencies seem to find evidence that there is a significant relationship between cryptocurrencies' liquidity and efficiency. For example, Wei (2018) finds that market efficiency is high when market liquidity is high and there is anti-persistence in the form of a low Hurst exponent in illiquid markets. Köchling *et al.* (2019) examine the market efficiency of 75 cryptocurrencies and they show that the price delay is strongly correlated with liquidity. Brauneis and Mestel (2018) also examine the drivers of efficiency towards the relationship between cryptocurrencies' liquidity and predictability. They evaluate the liquidity of 73 cryptocurrencies using the time series mean of different measures: the log-dollar volume, the turnover ratio, Amihud (2002)'s illiquidity ratio and the bid-ask estimated by Corwin and Schultz (2012). Multivariate regressions were run to investigate the impact of these four variables on efficiency. The findings show that this latter has a positive relationship with the turnover ratio. However, it is negatively related to the bid-ask (e.g., Corwin and Schultz (2012)).

The investors, market participants, and managers have been attracted by the huge volatility of the cryptocurrency market since its creation. Hence, it is worthwhile to investigate whether bubbles and price dynamics could affect the liquidity of such a market. The relationship between the liquidity and volatility of cryptocurrencies is the subject of some recent academic interest. Fry (2018) proposes a rational bubble model that considers heavy-tails and the possibility of total collapse in cryptocurrency prices. He finds that liquidity risk can lead to heavy-tails in these crypto-assets and that bubbles can occur, particularly, for Bitcoin and Ethereum. Wei (2018) assesses the illiquidity of 456 cryptocurrencies using Amihud's illiquidity ratio. He classifies them into five groups in accordance with their liquidity. He finds that liquidity is strongly related to volatility for this type of asset. Furthermore, crypto-investors do not require a return premium for illiquid cryptocurrencies. Ghysels and Nguyen (2019) study the liquidity provision of Bitcoin. Their results show that aggressive orders are more informative when market volatility is high and become more attractive to informed agents. In such an environment, the liquidity deteriorates. However, in low market volatility, market orders and best limit orders are less informative, which explains the improvement in global liquidity.

7. Cryptocurrency Market at the Time of the COVID-19 Pandemic

Previous studies revealed that Bitcoin has similar properties to gold and acts as a hedge and a safe haven against global economic uncertainty. The weak correlation of cryptocurrencies, in particular, Bitcoin, with traditional asset classes during the European debt crisis of 2010–2013 and the Cypriot banking crisis of 2012–2013, makes it a valuable diversification and hedging tool against equity and commodity indices (e.g., Baur *et al.* (2018), Bouri *et al.* (2017), Bouri, Molnár, *et al.* (2017), Ji *et al.* (2018), Kristoufek (2015), Luther and Salter (2017) and Urquhart and Zhang (2019)). As financial markets move to a bearish state during such stress periods, Bitcoin reacts positively to adverse market conditions and spikes in value.

Although the previous literature argues that Bitcoin is somewhat comparable to gold, its hedging and safe-haven features are affected by the recent coronavirus crisis. Figure 3 exhibits the dynamics of the MSCI World Index and Bitcoin prices during the pandemic. It is shown that the global corona pandemic has a negative impact on Bitcoin prices and consequently on returns. The figure shows that Bitcoin moves in tandem with the MSCI World Index; thus Bitcoin has lost its safe-haven benefits against stock market turmoil during the global pandemic. Specifically, at the end of February 2020, the global markets were in freefall following the rhythm of the coronavirus, much faster than prior epidemics (SARS and swine flu). According to CNBC, cryptocurrency markets have plunged after the historic drop in oil prices and the continued sales of stocks. Particularly, this violent sale in the cryptocurrency market comes after the Brent Crude oil, considered as an international oil benchmark, fell down to 30%, reaching a price of $31.02 per barrel, its lowest level since 2016. On March 8, more than $26 billion wiped out cryptocurrency

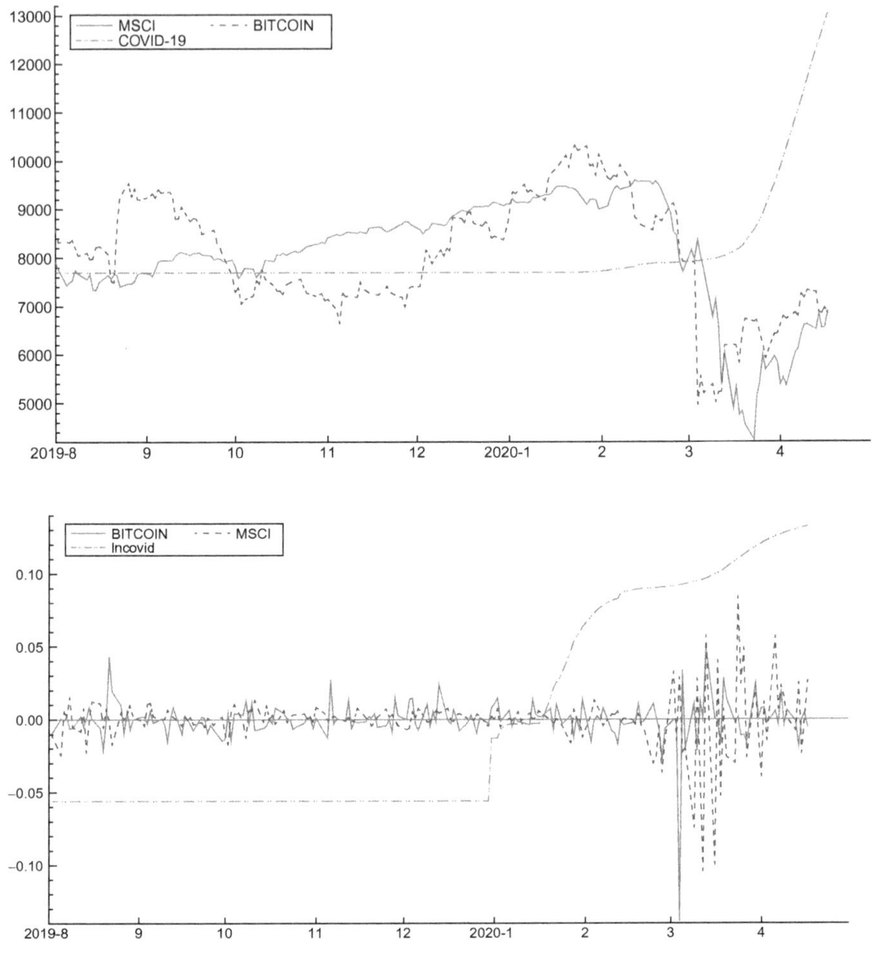

Figure 3: Dynamics of Prices and Returns for MSCI World Index and Bitcoin during the COVID-19 Pandemic.

Notes: COVID-19 refers to the number of global confirmed cases since December 31, 2019. MSCI World Index data are sourced from Bloomberg, and Bitcoin data are collected from the Coinmarketcap.com website. The sample period is from August 2, 2019 to April 30, 2020.

market capitalization in 24 hours according to the data sourced from Coinmarketcap.com. Bitcoin, the largest cryptocurrency in value, fell over 10% in 24 hours around the same time. The other large digital coins, Ethereum, Ripple, and Bitcoin Cash, displayed double-digit percentage point losses.

The huge price movements of cryptocurrencies are not unusual and these digital coins are known for their volatility. Market players have said, however, that this could be an opportunity to buy Bitcoin. The hedging effectiveness of cryptocurrencies for traditional assets decreases significantly when considering the recent COVID-19 crisis. The noteworthy effect of the coronavirus highlights the fragile role of Bitcoin and shows that the latter is not resilient to crisis periods and could lose its safe-haven feature during pandemics.

8. Conclusion

This chapter presented an overview of the diverse risks associated with the cryptocurrency industry. We mainly handled five risks, namely, technological, fraud/theft, legal, market, liquidity, and COVID-19 pandemic risks. Considering the technology risk, the occurrence of any technological failure, like networks bugs or loss of private keys, among others, tends to raise insecurity and distrust in the cryptocurrency technology. Incidents in the form of hacks and exchange breakdowns are most likely inclined to take place. For the fraud/theft risk, crypto-exchanges tend to release wash trading volumes and manipulate crypto-traders in order to take control of their wealth. The literature partly indicated the regulation set in the cryptocurrency market. In fact, the legal framework is still inconclusive, which indicates a lack of transparency in such a market. All of these factors can enhance market risk across cryptocurrencies. We provided evidence of their riskiness compared to fiat currencies and the presence of a significant risk contagion across large-cap cryptocurrencies. Furthermore, we stress that scarce investigations have dealt with the liquidity issue in the cryptocurrency market. It sorts out that such assets are highly investible. Nonetheless, a substantial connectedness exists between liquidity and efficiency in the cryptocurrency market, since price dynamics can influence the market liquidity. Finally, in the aftermath of the ongoing COVID-19 pandemic spread, major cryptocurrencies were heavily affected and lost their hedge and safe-haven capabilities.

8.1 *But What Comes Afterwards?*

Understanding the concepts of risk across cryptocurrencies can help give effective implications for market makers, investors, and regulators.

Hussain Shahzad *et al.* (2019) underlined that technology features of cryptocurrencies are prone to hinder the entry of new traders and can potentially increase the liquidity risk in the cryptocurrency market. Following the research of Liu (2019), the cryptocurrencies' mechanisms and their "complexity" features should be explained to the grand public. Otherwise, it would impede the effective estimation of risk for optimal and diversified portfolios.

Considering the diversification matter, crypto-traders can explore "low-risk opportunities" (e.g., Brauneis and Mestel (2019)). Alternatively, liquidity can play an important role in diversification. Hussain Shahzad *et al.* (2019) pointed out that investors should carry out the liquidity risk assessment, as these periods are witnessing an expanded number of new cryptocurrencies and volatile trading volumes. However, Al-Yahyaee *et al.* (2020) emphasized that high liquidity degrees can give information on the return predictability of the cryptocurrency.

Within this framework, the role of regulators has to be recognized. In fact, regulation should focus on reducing the liquidity risk in the cryptocurrency market. Particularly, it should mutinously search for its main drivers and its relationship with market efficiency and volatility. Likewise, market makers may implement specific regulations in order to decrease volatility across cryptocurrencies and ensure additional security for investors. Even with the lack of an authority regulator, Kajtazi and Moro (2019, p. 7) reported that "regulators have the power to set up rules that limit the possibility for any regulated investment tool (e.g., trust funds, insurance policies, pension funds, etc.) to invest" in cryptocurrencies.

References

Ahlstrom, D., D. J. Cumming, and S. Vismara. 2018. "New methods of entrepreneurial firm financing: Fintech, crowdfunding and corporate governance implications." *Corporate Governance: An International Review* 26, 310–313. https://doi.org/10.1111/corg.12258.

Al-Yahyaee, K. H., W. Mensi, H.-U. Ko, S.-M. Yoon, and S.-H. Kang. 2020. "Why cryptocurrency markets are inefficient: The impact of liquidity and volatility." *The North American Journal of Economics and Finance* 52. https://doi.org/https://doi.org/10.1016/j.najef.2020.101168.

Al Janabi, M. A. M., R. Ferrer, and S. J. H. Shahzad. 2019. "Liquidity-adjusted value-at-risk optimization of a multi-asset portfolio using a vine copula approach." *Physica A: Statistical Mechanics and Its Applications*, 536(December). https://doi.org/10.1016/j.physa.2019.122579.

Amihud, Y. 2002. "Illiquidity and stock returns: Cross-section and time-series effects." *Journal of Financial Markets* 5, 31–56. https://doi.org/10.1016/S1386-4181(01)00024-6.

Antonakakis, N., I. Chatziantoniou, and D. Gabauer. 2019. "Cryptocurrency market contagion: Market uncertainty, market complexity, and dynamic portfolios." *Journal of International Financial Markets, Institutions and Money* 61, 37–51. https://doi.org/10.1016/j.intfin.2019.02.003.

Arslanian, H., and F. Fischer. 2019. "The Rise of Bitcoin." *The Future of Finance*, Cham: Palgrave Macmillan, 95–111. https://doi.org/10.1007/978-3-030-14533-0_9.

Baek, C., and M. Elbeck. 2015. "Bitcoins as an investment or speculative vehicle? A first look." *Applied Economics Letters* 22:1, 30–34. https://doi.org/10.1080/13504851.2014.916379.

Baur, D. G., K. H. Hong, and A. D. Lee. 2018. "Bitcoin: Medium of exchange or speculative assets?" *Journal of International Financial Markets, Institutions and Money* 54, 177–189. https://doi.org/10.1016/j.intfin.2017.12.004.

Białkowski, J. 2019. "Cryptocurrencies in institutional investors' portfolios: Evidence from industry stop-loss rules." *Economics Letters*, November. https://doi.org/10.1016/j.econlet.2019.108834.

Białkowski, J., and D. Serwa. 2005. "Financial contagion, spillovers and causality in the Markov switching framework." *Quantitative Finance* 5:1, 123–131. https://doi.org/10.1080/14697680500117716.

Binham, C. 2018. "EU body strikes back at cryptocurrency regulation." *Financial Times*. https://www.ft.com/content/bc48eafc-2301-11e8-ae48-60d3531b7d11.

Bitwise Asset Management. 2019. "*Presentation to the U.S. Securities and Exchange Commission.*" https://www.sec.gov/comments/sr-nysearca-2019-01/srnysearca201901-5164833-183434.pdf.

Bloomberg. 2018. "Making sense to the world's cryptocurrency rules." *Bloomberg News*. https://www.bloomberg.com/news/articles/2018-03-19/is-this-legal-making-sense-of-the-world-s-cryptocurrency-rules.

Borri, N. 2019. "Conditional tail-risk in cryptocurrency markets." *Journal of Empirical Finance* 50, 1–19. https://doi.org/10.1016/j.jempfin.2018.11.002.

Borri, N., and K. Shakhnov. 2019. "Regulation spillovers across cryptocurrency markets." *Finance Research Letters*, https://doi.org/10.1016/j.frl.2019.101333.

Boschi, M. 2005. "International financial contagion: Evidence from the Argentine crisis of 2001–2002." *Applied Financial Economics* 15:3, 153–163. https://doi.org/10.1080/0960310042000306943.

Bosu, A., A. Iqbal, R. Shahriyar, and P. Chakraborty. 2019. "Understanding the motivations, challenges and needs of blockchain software developers: A survey." *Empirical Software Engineering* 24, 2636–2673. https://doi.org/10.1007/s10664-019-09708-7.

Bouoiyour, J., and R. Selmi. 2016. "Bitcoin: A beginning of a new phase?" *Economics Bulletin* 36:3, 1430–1440.

Bouri, E., R. Gupta, and D. Roubaud. 2019. "Herding behaviour in cryptocurrencies." *Finance Research Letters* 29, 216–221.

Bouri, E., N. Jalkh, P. Molnár, and D. Roubaud. 2017. "Bitcoin for energy commodities before and after the December 2013 crash: Diversifier, hedge or safe haven?" *Applied Economics* 49:50, 5063–5073. https://doi.org/10.1080/00036846.2017.1299102.

Bouri, E., P. Molnár, G. Azzi, D. Roubaud, and L. I. Hagfors. 2017. "On the hedge and safe haven properties of bitcoin: Is it Really more than a Diversifier?" *Finance Research Letters* 20, 192–198. https://doi.org/10.1016/j.frl.2016.09.025.

Bovaird, C. 2019. "95% of reported bitcoin trading volume is fake, says bitwise." *Forbes*. https://www.forbes.com/sites/cbovaird/2019/03/22/95-of-reported-bitcoin-trading-volume-is-fake-says-bitwise/#57e3ef156717.

Brauneis, A., and R. Mestel. 2018. "Price discovery of cryptocurrencies: Bitcoin and beyond." *Economics Letters* 165, 58–61. https://doi.org/10.1016/j.econlet.2018.02.001.

Brauneis, A., and R. Mestel. 2019. "Cryptocurrency-Portfolios in a mean-variance framework." *Finance Research Letters* 28, 259–264. https://doi.org/10.1016/j.frl.2018.05.008.

Canh, N. P., U. Wongchoti, S. D. Thanh, and N. T. Thong,. 2019. "Systematic risk in cryptocurrency market: Evidence from DCC-MGARCH model." *Finance Research Letters* 29, 90–100. https://doi.org/10.1016/j.frl.2019.03.011.

Coleman, L. 2017. "The european union wants to identify bitcoin users." *Cryptocoins News*. https://www.cryptocoinsnews.com/the-european-union-wants-to-identify-bitcoin-users/.

Corwin, S. A., and P. Schultz. 2012. "A simple way to estimate bid-ask spreads from daily high and low prices." *Journal of Finance* 67, 719–760. https://doi.org/10.1111/j.1540-6261.2012.01729.x.

da Gama Silva, P. V. J., M. C. Klotzle, A. C. F. Pinto, and L. L. Gomes. 2019. "Herding behavior and contagion in the cryptocurrency market." *Journal of Behavioral and Experimental Finance* 22, 41–50. https://doi.org/10.1016/j.jbef.2019.01.006.

Dungey, M., R. Fry, B. González-Hermosillo, and V. L. Martin. 2005. "Empirical modelling of contagion: A review of methodologies." *Quantitative Finance* 5:1, 9–24. https://doi.org/10.1080/14697680500142045.

Dyhrberg, A. H. 2016. "Hedging capabilities of bitcoin. Is it the virtual gold?" *Finance Research Letters* 16, 139–144. https://doi.org/10.1016/j.frl.2015.10.025.

Dyhrberg, A. H., S. Foley, and J. Svec. 2018. "How investible is bitcoin? Analyzing the liquidity and transaction costs of bitcoin markets."

Economics Letters 171, 140–143. https://doi.org/10.1016/j.econlet.2018.07.032.

European Banking Authority. 2014. "EBA opinion on virtual currencies." *European Banking Authority*. https://eba.europa.eu/sites/default/documents/files/documents/10180/657547/81409b94-4222-45d7-ba3b-7deb5863ab57/EBA-Op-2014-08 Opinion on Virtual Curr.

Foley, S., J. R. Karlsen, and T. J. Putnins, 2019. "Sex, drugs, and bitcoin: How much illegal activity is financed through cryptocurrencies?" *Review of Financial Studies* 32, 1798–1853. https://doi.org/10.1093/rfs/hhz015.

Forbes, K., and R. Rigobon. 2002. "No contagion, only interdependence: Measuring stock market co-movements." *Journal of Finance* 57, 2223–2261.

Fry, J. 2018. "Booms, busts and heavy-tails: The story of bitcoin and cryptocurrency markets?" *Economics Letters* 171, 225–229. https://doi.org/10.1016/j.econlet.2018.08.008.

Ghysels, E., and G. Nguyen. 2019. "Price discovery of a speculative asset: Evidence from a bitcoin exchange." *Journal of Risk and Financial Management* 12:4. https://doi.org/10.3390/jrfm12040164.

Gkillas, K., and P. Katsiampa. 2018. "An application of extreme value theory to cryptocurrencies." *Economics Letters* 164:C, 109–111. https://doi.org/10.1016/j.econlet.2018.01.020.

Griffin, J. M., and A. Shams. 2019. "Is Bitcoin Really Un-Tethered?" *SSRN Electronic Journal*.

Hackett, R. 2017. "Blockchain mania." *Fortune* 178:3, 44–59.

Handika, R., G. Soepriyanto, and S. A. H. Havidz. 2019. "Are cryptocurrencies contagious to Asian financial markets?" *Research in International Business and Finance* 50, 416–429. https://doi.org/10.1016/j.ribaf.2019.06.007.

Herrera-Joancomartí, J., and C. Pérez-Solà. 2016. "Privacy in bitcoin transactions: New challenges from blockchain scalability solutions." *Lecture Notes in Computer Science*. https://doi.org/10.1007/978-3-319-45656-0_3.

Houben, R., and A. Snyers. 2018. "*Cryptocurrencies and Blockchain: Legal Context and Implications for Financial Crime, Money Laundering and Tax Evasion*." European Parliament.

Hussain Shahzad, S. J., E. Bouri, D. Roubaud, and L. Kristoufek. 2019. "Safe haven, hedge, and diversification for G7 stock markets: Gold versus Bitcoin." *Economic Modelling July*. https://doi.org/10.1016/j.econmod.2019.07.023.

İçellioğlu, C. S., and S. Öner. 2019. "An investigation on the volatility of cryptocurrencies by means of heterogeneous panel data analysis." *Procedia Computer Science* 158, 913–920. https://doi.org/10.1016/j.procs.2019.09.131.

Ji, Q., E. Bouri, R. Gupta, and D. Roubaud. 2018. "Network causality structures among bitcoin and other financial assets: A directed acyclic graph approach." *Quarterly Review of Economics and Finance* 70, 203–2013. https://doi.org/10.1016/j.qref.2018.05.016.

Joshi, D. 2020. "How Secure is Cryptocurrency and Blockchain Technology? Security Benefits and Issues of DLT." *Business Insider*.

Judmayer, A., N. Stifter, K. Krombholz, and E. Weippl. 2017. "Blocks and chains: Introduction to bitcoin, cryptocurrencies, and their consensus mechanisms." In E. Bertino and R. Sandhu (eds.), *Synthesis Lectures on Information Security, Privacy, and Trust* 9:1. Morgan & Claypool Publishers. https://doi.org/10.2200/s00773ed1v01y201704spt020.

Kajtazi, A., and A. Moro. 2019. "The role of bitcoin in well-diversified portfolios: A comparative global study." *International Review of Financial Analysis* 61, 143–157. https://doi.org/10.1016/j.irfa.2018.10.003.

Katsiampa, P. 2019. "An empirical investigation of volatility dynamics in the cryptocurrency market." *Research in International Business and Finance* 50, 322–335. https://doi.org/10.1016/j.ribaf.2019.06.004.

Kauflin, J. 2019. "The anatomy of a fake cryptocurrency trade: How exchanges create phony transactions." *Forbes*. https://www.forbes.com/sites/jeffkauflin/2019/07/02/the-anatomy-of-a-fake-cryptocurrency-trade-how-exchanges-create-phony-transactions/#2504026e3132.

Kim, C. Y., and K. Lee. 2018. "Risk management to cryptocurrency exchange and investors: Guidelines to prevent potential threats." *2018 International Conference on Platform Technology and Service, PlatCon 2018*. https://doi.org/10.1109/PlatCon.2018.8472760.

Köchling, G., J. Müller, and P. N. Posch. 2019. "Price delay and market frictions in cryptocurrency markets." *Economics Letters* 174, 39–41. https://doi.org/10.1016/j.econlet.2018.10.025.

Konoth, R. K., R. V. Wegberg, V. Moonsamy, and H. Bos. 2019. "Malicious cryptocurrency miners: Status and Outlook." *ArXiv*.

Koops, B.-J., and R. E. Leenes. 2006. "ID theft, ID fraud and/or ID-related crime — Definitions matter." *Datenschutz Und Datensicherheit* 30:9, 553–556. https://ssrn.com/abstract=982076.

Koutmos, D. 2018. "Liquidity uncertainty and bitcoin's market microstructure." *Economics Letters* 172, 97–101. https://doi.org/10.1016/j.econlet.2018.08.041.

Krause, M. J., and T. Tolaymat. 2018. "Quantification of energy and carbon costs for mining cryptocurrencies." *Nature Sustainability* 1, 711–718. https://doi.org/10.1038/s41893-018-0152-7.

Kristoufek, L. 2015. "What are the main drivers of the bitcoin price?" Evidence from wavelet coherence analysis. *PLoS ONE* 10:4. https://doi.org/10.1371/journal.pone.0123923.

Levine, M. 2018. "Is cyber insider-trading illegal?" *Bloomberg*. https://www.bloomberg.com/view/articles/2018-02-02/is-cyber-insider-trading illegal.

Liu, W. 2019. "Portfolio diversification across cryptocurrencies." *Finance Research Letters* 29, 200–205. https://doi.org/10.1016/j.frl.2018.07.010.

Luther, W. J., and A. W. Salter. 2017. "Bitcoin and the bailout." *Quarterly Review of Economics and Finance* 66, 50–56. https://doi.org/10.1016/j.qref.2017.01.009.

Makarov, I., and A. Schoar. 2020. "Trading and arbitrage in cryptocurrency markets." *Journal of Financial Economics* 135:2, 293–319. https://doi.org/10.1016/j.jfineco.2019.07.001.

Martínez-Jaramillo, S., O. P. Pérez, F. A. Embriz, and F. L. G. Dey. 2010. "Systemic risk, financial contagion and financial fragility." *Journal of Economic Dynamics and Control* 34:11, 2358–2374. https://doi.org/10.1016/j.jedc.2010.06.004.

Min, H. 2019. "Blockchain technology for enhancing supply chain resilience." *Business Horizons* 62:1, 35–45. https://doi.org/10.1016/j.bushor.2018.08.012.

Naeem, M., E. Bouri, G. Boako, and D. Roubaud. 2019. "Tail dependence in the return-volume of leading cryptocurrencies." *Finance Research Letters, October*. https://doi.org/10.1016/j.frl.2019.101326.

Nakaso, H. 2017. "Future of central bank payment and settlement systems: Under economic globalization and technological innovation." *Forum Towards Making Effective Use of the BOJ-NET.* Central Bank Speech, Tokyo.

National Internet Finance Association of China. 2020. "*Risk Alert Against the Hype of Overseas Virtual Currency Exchanges*." http://www.nifa.org.cn/nifaen/2955875/2955895/2987315/index.html.

Osterrieder, J., S. Chan, J. Chu, and S. Nadarajah. 2017. "A statistical analysis of cryptocurrencies." *SSRN Electronic Journal*. https://doi.org/10.2139/ssrn.2948315.

Osterrieder, J., and J. Lorenz. 2017. "A statistical risk assessment of bitcoin and its extreme tail behavior." *Annals of Financial Economics* 12:1. https://doi.org/10.1142/s2010495217500038.

Palladino, S. 2017. "*The Parity Wallet Hack Explained*." Security Audits, OpenZeppelin Blog.

Price, J. 2018. "*ASIC Update: Initial Coin Offerings and Cryptocurrency*." https://asic.gov.au/about-asic/news-centre/speeches/asic-update-initial-coin-offerings-and-cryptocurrency/.

Scharnowski, S. 2020. "Understanding bitcoin liquidity." *Finance Research Letters, February*. https://doi.org/https://doi.org/10.1016/j.frl.2020.101477.

Siswantoro, D., R. Handika, and A. F. Mita. 2020. "The requirements of cryptocurrency for money, an Islamic view." *Heliyon* 6:1. https://doi.org/10.1016/j.heliyon.2020.e03235.

Soehartono, U., and K. Pati. 2019. "The regulation of cryptocurrency investation in Indonesia." *3rd International Conference on Globalization of Law and Local Wisdom (ICGLOW 2019)*, 262–266. https://doi.org/10.2991/icglow-19.2019.54.

Stratfor. 2016. "The arduous task of regulating bitcoin." *Stratfor Worldview*. https://worldview.stratfor.com/article/arduous-task-regulating- bitcoin.

Subriadi, A. P., and N. F. Najwa. 2020. "The Consistency Analysis of Failure Mode and Effect Analysis (FMEA) in information technology risk assessment." *Heliyon* 6:1.

Taylor, P. J., T. Dargahi, A. Dehghantanha, R. M. Parizi, and K. K. R. Choo. 2019. "A systematic literature review of blockchain cyber security." *Digital Communications and Networks*. https://doi.org/10.1016/j.dcan.2019.01.005.

Tiwari, A. K., A. O. Adewuyi, C. T. Albulescu, and M. E. Wohar. 2020. "Empirical evidence of extreme dependence and contagion risk between main cryptocurrencies." *North American Journal of Economics and Finance* 51. https://doi.org/10.1016/j.najef.2019.101083.

Transparency Institute Blockchain. 2019a. "*Market Surveillance Report — April*." https://www.bti.live/reports-april2019/.

Transparency Institute Blockchain. 2019b. "*Market Surveillance Report — September*." https://www.bti.live/bti-september-2019-wash-trade-report/.

Twomey, D., and A. Mann. 2020. "Fraud and manipulation within cryptocurrency markets." In C. Alexander and D. Cumming (eds.), *Corruption and Fraud in Financial Markets: Malpractice, Misconduct and Manipulation*, 624. Canada: John Wiley & Sons Ltd.

Urquhart, A., and H. Zhang. 2019. "Is Bitcoin a Hedge or Safe Haven for Currencies?" An intraday analysis. *International Review of Financial Analysis* 63, 49–57. https://doi.org/10.1016/j.irfa.2019.02.009.

Vejačka, M. 2014. "Basic aspects of cryptocurrencies." *Journal of Economy, Business and Financing* 2, 75–83.

Vidal-Tomás, D., A. M. Ibáñez, and J. E. Farinós. 2019. "Herding in the cryptocurrency market: CSSD and CSAD approaches." *Finance Research Letters* 30, 181–186. https://doi.org/10.1016/j.frl.2018.09.008.

Wang, K., C. Bellavitis, and C. M. DaSilva. 2018. "An introduction to blockchain, cryptocurrency and initial coin offerings." *SSRN Electronic Journal*. https://doi.org/10.2139/ssrn.3288059.

Wei, W. C. 2018. "Liquidity and market efficiency in cryptocurrencies." *Economics Letters* 168, 21–24. https://doi.org/10.1016/j.econlet.2018.04.003.

Yeoh, P. 2017. "Regulatory issues in blockchain technology." *Journal of Financial Regulation and Compliance* 25:2. https://doi.org/10.1108/JFRC-08-2016-0068.

Yi, S., Z. Xu, and G. J. Wang. 2018. "Volatility connectedness in the cryptocurrency market: Is bitcoin a dominant cryptocurrency?" *International Review of Financial Analysis* 60, 98–114. https://doi.org/10.1016/j.irfa.2018.08.012.

Zetzsche, D. A., R. P. Buckley, D. W. Arner, and L. FFhr. 2019. "The ICO gold rush: It's a scam, it's a bubble, it's a super challenge for regulators." *Harvard International Law Journal*. https://doi.org/10.2139/ssrn.3072298.

Zięba, D., R. Kokoszczyński, and K. Śledziewska. 2019. "Shock transmission in the cryptocurrency market. Is bitcoin the most influential?" *International Review of Financial Analysis* 64, 102–125. https://doi.org/10.1016/j.irfa.2019.04.009.

https://doi.org/10.1142/9789811239670_0008

Chapter 8

Factors Influencing Individual and Organizational Adoption of Cryptocurrencies

Khouloud Senda Bennani[*,‡] **and Ibrahim Arpaci**[†,§]

[*]*University Tunis Carthage, Tunisia*

[†]*Tokat Gaziosmanpasa University, Turkey*

[‡]*senda.bennani@utctunisie.com*

[§]*ibrahim.arpaci@gop.edu.tr*

Abstract

Cryptocurrencies have gathered a lot of attention since the birth of Bitcoin in 2009. However, less is known about how the characteristics of cryptocurrencies and other factors facilitate and impede their adoption. The objective of this study is to discuss the main conceptual findings on individual and organizational adoption of an innovation and examine the factors influencing the adoption of cryptocurrencies from a holistic perspective. This study proposes two theoretical models. The first model presents the factors impacting the adoption of cryptocurrencies at the individual level. It was derived by combining the eight factors of the Innovation Diffusion Theory (IDT) model with the construct "personal innovativeness." The second model presents the factors impacting the adoption of cryptocurrencies at the organizational level. It was developed based on the Technology–Organization–Environment (TOE) framework. This research allows a better understanding of the current outlook of the cryptocurrency system and predicts its future perspectives. Therefore, this chapter is practically useful for those cryptocurrency users, traders and merchants considering their implementation as an alternative payment method.

Keywords: adoption of cryptocurrencies, individual adoption, organizational adoption, IDT framework and TOE framework

1. Introduction

In an increasingly digital and globalized world, money and its transfer has become increasingly virtual and invisible to the ordinary user (Mikołajewicz-Woźniak and Scheibe, 2015). Nowadays, digital currencies that rely on blockchain technology (Beck *et al.*, 2018) are at the forefront of the media and academic scene. They appear to be rich in potentialities, since they allow transmitting data in a decentralized, secure, transparent way and without intermediary, seeing that they are not regulated by governments or financial institutions. Also, with the expansion of the World Wide Web and the creation of new e-markets, it is becoming increasingly important for people and organizations to adopt cryptocurrencies as a method of payment. However, their diffusion process isn't so fast compared to other innovations (Spenkelink, 2014). Their widespread adoption, as a favored payment mode, by businesses and individuals is still scarce (Polasik *et al.*, 2015; De Nederlandsche Bank, 2014) and their future is very unclear (Spenkelink, 2014), though governments continue to debate their legality (Twomey, 2013). They will need to overcome several challenges in order to experience broader use (Holotiuk *et al.*, 2018). In view of the lack of studies that aim to understand consumer behaviors and intentions in adopting cryptocurrencies (Schuh and Shy, 2016), there is a need to examine the factors that influence their adoption. This research stands out from previous scientific studies by the fact that it examines cryptocurrencies' adoption from a holistic perspective. In particular, this study aims to develop two conceptual models, classifying successively various issues and factors driving the adoption process of cryptocurrencies at the individual and organizational levels. The research question that guided this study is the following: What are the factors influencing cryptocurrencies' adoption as a method of payment by individuals and by organizations?

The Innovation Diffusion Theory (IDT) (Rogers, 1995) is well suited to model the adoption of cryptocurrencies by individuals. Hence, it is used in this study in order to better understand cryptocurrencies' adoption at the individual level. The Technology–Organization–Environment (TOE) framework (Tornatzky and Fleischer, 1990; DePietro *et al.*, 1990) is suited to map the characteristics of cryptocurrencies. Hence, it is used in this study in order to obtain a perspective on both the internal and external factors fostering organizational adoption.

This chapter proceeds as follows: Section 2 provides an overview of the relevant literature on factors influencing the individual adoption of an innovation, by reconciling with cryptocurrencies. Section 3 reviews the studies that have been conducted regarding IT adoption, more particularly, cryptocurrencies' adoption at the organizational level. Section 4 concludes by highlighting the theoretical findings, important implications for research and practice, limitations, and future research avenues.

2. Theoretical Background

Because of the complexities involved in predicting human behavior and in understanding the interaction between humans and technology, apprehending individual and organizational adoption and the use of a new technology or an innovation has emerged as one of the dominant research topics in Information Systems (Benbasat and Barki, 2007; Venkatesh *et al.*, 2017). There have been a variety of theories and models employed in scientific studies to explain the patterns that influence or inhibit technology or innovation adoption at the individual and organizational levels.

2.1 *Cryptocurrencies' Adoption at the Individual Level*

At the individual level, there are five behavioral theories or models that are generally used as a conceptual framework for explaining and predicting the adoption and acceptability of a technological innovation: Theory of Planned Behavior (TPB) (Ajzen, 1991), Technology Acceptance Model (TAM) (Davis, 1989), IDT (Rogers, 1983, 1995, 2003), Theory of Reasoned Action (TRA) (Ajzen and Fishbein, 1980) and Unified Acceptance and Use of Technology (UTAUT) (Venkatesh *et al.*, 2003).

Their wide use is explained by their parsimony and the richness of their empirical validation.

While this study could potentially draw on many of these theories for the purpose of cryptocurrencies' adoption at the individual level, this research will base its assumptions on the IDT adaptation by Moore & Benbasat (1991) that was originally created by Rogers (1983), which considers that the consumer adoption or rejection decision of an innovation is based on beliefs that they form about the innovation (Karahanna *et al.*, 1999). This model considers a range of eight determinants (ease of use, relative advantage, visibility, result demonstrability, compatibility, trialability, image and voluntariness of use) to explain the exact ways in which a population adopts, adapts or rejects a particular innovation. IDT and the other theories mentioned above have many common constructs and complement each other in order to investigate the adoption of innovations.

The feature "Relative Advantages (RA)," which is defined by Moore and Benbasat (1991) as *the degree to which an innovation is perceived to be better than the idea it supersedes*, is similar to "Perceived Usefulness (PU)" of TAM and "Performance Expectancy (PE)" of UTAUT. The feature "Perceived Ease of Use (PEU)," which represents the perceived degree of facility associated with the use of an innovation (Moore and Benbasat, 1991), encompasses the "Perceived Effort Expectancy (PEE)" of UTAUT, the **perceived complexity** of the system derived from the IDT (Rogers, 1995, 2003). The feature "image" that refers to "*the degree to which use of an innovation is perceived to enhance one's image or status in one's social system*" (Moore and Benbasat, 1991) is similar to the "social influence (SI)" of UTAUT, the "subjective norms" of the RAT and the TPB.

The theoretical model proposed for the individual adoption of cryptocurrencies adds a personal trait variable termed "personal innovativeness" to the IDT model adapted by Moore and Benbasat (1991), which focuses only on instrumental beliefs as drivers of an innovation's adoption (Figure 1). This new construct was originally proposed as a moderator of the effects of technology characteristics on its adoption (Agarwal and Prasad, 1998) and it was recently considered by researchers (Jackson *et al.*, 2013; Koivisto *et al.*, 2016) as an antecedent of innovation characteristics and as a construct that has a direct impact on innovation adoption (Lu, J. *et al.*, 2005; Williams, 2018). In this study, "personal innovativeness" is considered as a potentially important factor that influences directly cryptocurrencies' adoption.

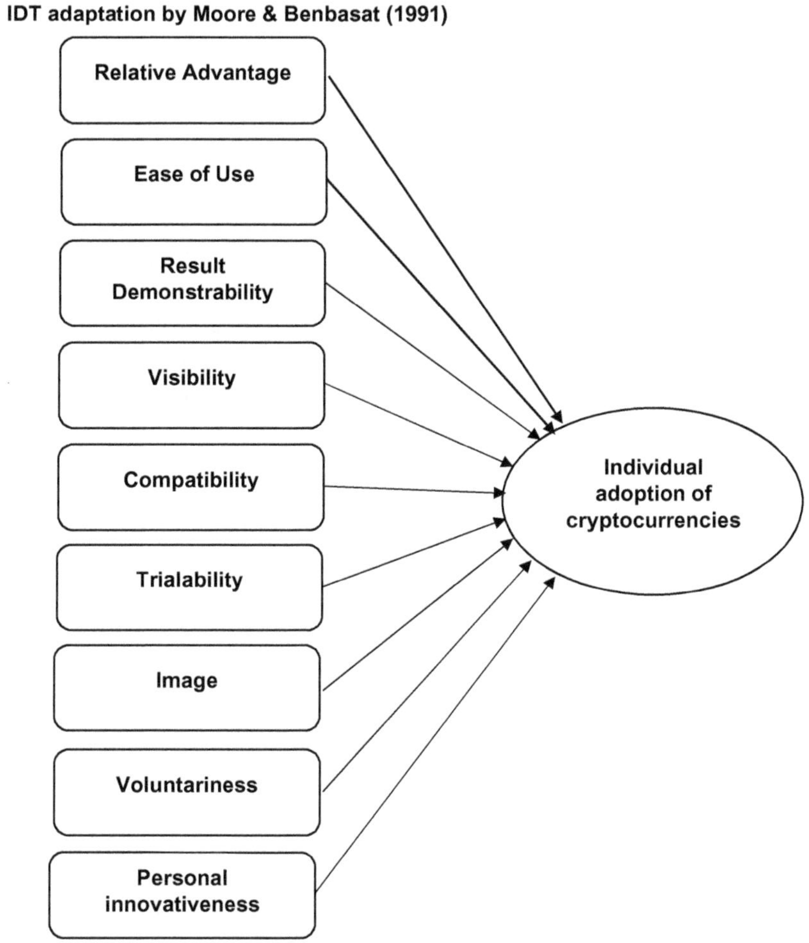

Figure 1: The Theoretical Model for the Individual Adoption of Cryptocurrencies.

2.1.1 *Relative advantage*

Several analyzes determine that cryptocurrency has a lot of advantages such as the transaction speed (Bamert *et al.*, 2013), contrary to traditional banking transactions that take time to complete. These transfers can also be made worldwide without any restrictions. Aside from these advantages, virtual currencies are not subject to government control (Plassaras, 2013), unlike traditional currencies that are managed by states and a central bank. As a result, the commissions charged by virtual currencies are minimal or even non-existent and transaction fees are also much lower than those charged by the various traditional means of payment (e.g., bank cards). This makes it very easy for newcomers to use cryptocurrencies, either as payers or as payees (Spenkelink, 2014). However, just because the cryptocurrencies have no central authority to control them does not mean that there is no security. In contrast, virtual currency is a safe and completely secure payment (Plassaras, 2013; Spenkelink, 2014; Rapport du comité sénatorial, 2015). Indeed, the various transactions carried out are encrypted and validated by software (Open Source) which are distributed on computers throughout the world (Spenkelink, 2014). As a result, each time a transaction is carried out using cryptography, several million computers around the world verify this transaction and keep a record of it. Thus, cryptocurrency is forgery-proof and unbreakable because it is impossible to hack all the computers making up the blockchain. Only the person with the decryption key can use it.

Despite all the benefits associated with cryptocurrencies, individuals may abandon using them if they believe that the gain from adopting them and their feelings about being unique have diminished (Athey *et al.*, 2017).

Despite their many advantages, cryptocurrencies have some drawbacks as well. As an example, the advantage linked to the security of the cryptocurrency can turn into a major disadvantage in the case of loss or theft of the private key (access codes), which would lead to the total loss of the wallet money forever.

Also, the craze and popularity of cryptocurrency are resulting in increased electricity consumption worldwide. Indeed, driven by algorithms, cryptocurrency requires computing power that mobilizes a network of very powerful and therefore energy-consuming computer machines (McCook, 2014).

The bad reputation attributed to the cryptocurrency has caused its relatively low adoption by the general public. Indeed, even if active-cryptos are gradually democratizing, it is not yet possible to buy all the products necessary for everyday life with them. This major drawback could disappear when merchants accept payments in cryptocurrencies.

In addition, the absence of a trusted third party or intermediary in carrying out a transaction using virtual currencies means that there is no possibility of taking out insurance to protect the funds.

Furthermore, the small capitalizations of these digital assets compared to traditional stock market assets make them very volatile products (Bryans, 2014; Kristoufek, 2014; Polasik *et al.*, 2015). This is due to the fact that cryptocurrency operates according to a decentralized system without any structure regulating its price (Birch *et al.*, 2016). The price of financial assets follows the law of the market. It is set according to supply and demand: the more money invested in these crypto-assets, the more stable the price will be and vice versa. This volatility can be a barrier to mass adoption by the general public since they may be afraid of losing all their savings if they see it as an investment for the purpose of storing value.

Another disadvantage is that cryptocurrency transactions are completely irreversible (Ateniese *et al.*, 2017; Cousins *et al.*, 2019). There is no possible cancellation of the transaction after confirmation of sending money. It can only be refunded by the receiving party. That is why it is very important to double check the transaction details to not accidentally send funds to the wrong recipient or send the wrong amount. Also, there is a risk of losing cryptocurrencies' worth if owners lose their passphrase or walled file (Glodman, 2014), because there is no possibility to reset the password.

Aside from this drawback, cryptocurrency is very poorly regulated by legislation (Grinberg, 2011; Cousins *et al.*, 2019). Unlike users of traditional currencies, who are protected by law, users of cryptocurrencies are not. About regulation, cryptomoney has no legal tender. As a result, it is not universally recognized; there is no obligation for sellers and financial institutions, such as banks and payment gateways, to accept payment with crypto-money (Lo and Wang, 2014; Yermack, 2015), and there is no guarantee that crypto-money will be accepted as a means of payment in the future. Exchanges of cryptocurrencies are therefore only possible between players who agree to use them.

2.1.2 *Perceived ease of use*

Research has shown that the ease of use is perceived in different ways, depending on the user profiles. In fact, buying, selling, or sending a virtual currency seems to be easy, convenient and self-explanatory for young people who master technological tools. However, this is still a major weakness concerning old people (Spenkelink, 2014; Baur *et al.*, 2015a), who found the cryptographic system too complex to be understood and to be used. So, this system is not free of effort and users can come across technical difficulties (Baur *et al.*, 2015b). According to Barber *et al.* (2012) and Southurst (2013), the cryptocurrency wallet is often difficult and cumbersome to use, and therefore one needs to be mindful of it before investing. Several individuals are losing their cryptocurrency wallet because of a technical failure or a lack of knowledge and awareness about how to use it (Goldman, 2014). This is what can make the cryptocurrency wallet struggle to gain adoption (Everette *et al.*, 2017). To help them get started with cryptocurrencies, the partisans of this type of currency have put at their disposal tutorials, videos, and training along with marketing activities.

Other researchers have shown that unlike people with a high level of financial knowledge, people with low financial literacy are much less likely to invest in stocks because they are less cautious about their financial decisions (Rooij *et al.*, 2011; Lusardi and Mitchell, 2007; Stolper and Walter, 2017; Arias-Oliva *et al.*, 2019).

2.1.3 *Image*

Regarding cryptocurrencies, individuals may believe that people of their community who use Bitcoin have a more prestigious reputation and have superior profiles than those who are not attached to it (Cousins *et al.*, 2019). Other people think that using cryptocurrencies can affect their reputation in a negative way, since these digital assets have become the currencies of choice for cyber criminals (Everette *et al.*, 2017; Masoni *et al.*, 2016; Extance, 2015; Moore, 2013). These coins are often used for illegal payments, such as buying drugs, money laundering, terrorist financing and tax evasion (Houben and Snyers, 2018). These unlawful acts are facilitated by the fact that cryptocurrencies are decentralized and anonymous. There's no identification required to make transactions (Ober *et al.*, 2013; Levin, 2013). The fear of having a bad reputation associated with the use of cryptocurrencies can explain their low adoption.

The other characteristics of IDT (visibility, compatibility, results demonstrability, trialability, and voluntariness) introduced into major belief constructs that determine people's use of an innovation are best fitting with cryptocurrencies' features. Since these features do not appear in the other models cited above, the researchers think that they do not capture the essence of cryptocurrencies well.

2.1.4 *Visibility*

The feature "visibility" that represents "the degree to which one can see others using the system in the organization" (Moore and Benbasat, 1991) is dealt to be used with cryptocurrencies' adoption, since all types of media channels (internet, televisions, radio stations, magazines, books, etc.) have and continue to have a vast influence on the popularity and credibility of digital currencies. Also, the worldwide installation of cryptocurrency and bitcoin machines (ATM) allowing people to easily purchase bitcoins raises the visibility of cryptocurrencies as they provide more tangible and visible transaction process.

2.1.5 *Compatibility*

The feature "compatibility" that refers to the extent to which "an innovation is perceived as being consistent with the existing values and past experiences of potential adopters" (Moore and Benbasat, 1991) fits well with studying the adoption of cryptocurrencies. On the one hand, the technologies behind cryptocurrencies bring a profound change; therefore, it's difficult for people who are resistant to change and risk-averse to convince them keeping their money on an exchange rather than keeping them in a bank, unlike people who appreciate the fact that the government may not impact the amount of cryptocurrencies in circulation (Grinberg, 2011; Luther, 2013). On the other hand, cryptocurrency fits very well with the globalization and digitalization. In fact, the expansion of the World Wide Web and the creation of new e-markets increase the need for electronic payments and the use of cryptocurrency.

2.1.6 *Result demonstrability*

The feature "result demonstrability," which is defined by Moore and Benbasat (1991) as "the tangibility of the results of using the innovation, including their observability and communicability," is dealt to understand cryptocurrencies' adoption. Their relative advantages such as low cost and fast transactions (karame *et al.*, 2012) are apparent and visible benefits that can be easily communicated to other people. But cryptocurrency wallet users can't see the transaction process and can't understand how it works, what is happening and how mining techniques are generated. This is still a mystery for most of the people; that's why they can't communicate to others the consequences of using it. This makes higher people's perceptions about the probability that something will go wrong with the technical performance of cryptocurrencies.

2.1.7 *Voluntariness*

The feature "voluntariness" that alludes to "the degree to which use of the innovation is perceived as being voluntary or through one's free will" (Moore and Benbasat, 1991) can be employed to examine cryptocurrency adoption. In fact, the decision to purchase things using cryptocurrencies (at least for the moment) is not mandatory and this is made on a voluntary basis. Nowadays, many of the world's retailers and services have started accepting cryptocurrency payments, so people are free to spend digital or traditional currencies. However, this might change in the future, since people can create online stores that only accept cryptocurrency.

2.1.8 *Trialability*

The feature "trialability," which is defined by Moore and Benbasat (1991) as "the degree to which an innovation may be experimented with before adoption," can largely predict and motivate the intention to adopt cryptocurrencies. They are easy to be acquired and tested first-hand by people. For example, trying bitcoin does not require a large amount of virtual currencies. Transactions can be done for a very small amount of cryptocurrencies. Cryptocurrencies can even be experienced without paying money, due to the online free virtual and digital trading simulator. Also, users can have many different wallets and buy, send or mine bitcoins with processes like online banking (Byrne, 2014). Furthermore, the trial phase of cryptocurrencies can be easily done, as a result of the growing number of virtual currency ATMs worldwide that allow an easier option of digital trading in a user-friendly environment. On the other side, the trialability phase of cryptocurrencies can be hardly done by people who are reluctant to adopt new technologies and services. Further, people can be discouraged to try cryptocurrencies because they think that they lack financial and technical knowledge to invest in it. Even purchasing or investing a very small amount of cryptocurrency requires the same actions and knowledge as the purchase of bigger quantities.

The advantages of cryptocurrencies cited above can hold people's attention, at a time when lack of trust is often cited as one of the main obstacles to adapting to change and to growth. But these assets have their flip side. To succeed, the cryptocurrency revolution will have to overcome many barriers, which are technical, organizational and societal.

It should also be noted that "trialability" is very low for most institutions, since compliance barriers to entry for using cryptocurrencies are high. In fact, institutions should collaborate with trusted third parties such as banks and financial companies to hold the assets in legal safekeeping.

2.1.9 *Personal innovativeness*

According to Agarwal and Prasad (1998), personal innovativeness symbolizes the risk-taking propensity of individuals. It has to do with the willingness of individuals to venture into cryptocurrencies. Cryptocurrency is a fairly new innovative mode of payment. Thus, it is highly expected that "personal innovativeness" will play an important role in individuals' behavioral intention to adopt cryptocurrencies. This is because individuals who have a higher personal innovativeness are active information seekers about a new innovation, they are able to cope with high levels of uncertainty and they are most likely to develop attitude toward a new technology and this increases the chance of trying it out.

3. Organizational Adoption of Cryptocurrencies

The systematic review of the literature on the adoption of emerging digital technologies indicated that Technology–Organization–Environment (DePietro *et al.*, 1990; Tornatzky and Fleischer, 1990) is a prominent adoption framework at the organizational level (Arpaci *et al.*, 2015).

3.1 *Technology–Organization–Environment (TOE) Framework*

The TOE framework has been used extensively in order to explain various innovation adoptions including blockchain technology, social commerce, Enterprise Resource Planning (ERP), e-commerce, Customer Relationship Management (CRM) systems, e-business, and Supply Chain Management (SCM) systems, etc. (Arpaci, 2013, 2019). Table 1 reports a systematic review of the studies on the organizational adoption of emerging digital technologies based on the TOE framework.

The TOE framework has "technological," "organizational" and "environmental" contexts. The technological context includes characteristics such as perceived benefits and compatibility of the technology. The organizational context contains the internal issues and resources within the firm. Key factors in the organizational context that can influence the adoption rate include the firm's slack resources, top management support, firm size, organizational readiness, international scope, and financial

Table 1: The Studies that Used the TOE Framework.

References	Innovation	Technological Factors	Organizational Factors	Environmental Factors	Data Collection	Data Analysis
Kulkarni and Patil (2020)	Blockchain	**BCT Infrastructure*, BCT Knowledge, Relative Advantage, Transaction Cost, Perceived Security**	**Organizational Scope, Consumer Readiness**	**Competitive Pressure, Government Policies and Bank Partner Readiness**	407 managers in Indian banks	Partial Least Squares (PLS)-SEM
Wong *et al.* (2020)	Blockchain	**Relative Advantage, Complexity**	Upper Management Support, Cost	Market Dynamics, **Competitive Pressure,** Regulatory Support	194 Malaysian SMEs	PLS-SEM
Abed (2020)	Social commerce	**Perceived Usefulness, Security Concern**	**Top Management Support, Organizational Readiness**	**Consumer Pressure, Competitive Pressure, Trading Partner Pressure**	181 SMEs in Saudi Arabia	SEM
Cruz-Jesus *et al.* (2019)	CRM	**Technology Competence, Data Quality and Integration**	**Top Management Support**		Managers of 277 firms	PLS-SEM
Yeh *et al.* (2015)	e-Business	**IT Maturity, IT Infrastructure**	**IT Human Resource, Top Management Support**	**Partnership Quality, Competitive Pressure**	IT managers from 191 firms	SEM
Lin (2014)	e-SCM	**Perceived Benefits, Perceived Costs**	Firm Size, **Top Management Support, Absorptive Capacity**	Trading Partner Influence, **Competitive Pressure**	IT managers from 283 firms	PLS-SEM
Jia *et al.* (2017)	Enterprise 2.0	**Perceived Usefulness**	Firm Scope, Firm Size, **Subjective Norms**	**Competitive Pressure**	206 responses from 44 firms	PLS-SEM
Bordonaba-Juste *et al.* (2012)	e-Business	**Perceived Benefits**	**IT Expertise**, Firm Size	Pressure Suppliers, Pressure Clients, **Competitive Pressure**	Email Survey of 691 retailers in seven European countries.	t-Test
Ifinedo (2011)	e-Business	**Perceived Benefits**	**Management Commitment & Support**, Organizational IT Competence, Intensity of Competition, Size, Age, Industry Type	**External Pressure**, Financial Resources Availability, IS Vendor Support & Pressure	Questionnaire with 214 SMEs in Atlantic	PLS-SEM
Oliveira and Martins (2010)	e-Business	**Technology Readiness, Technology Integration**	**Expected Benefits and Obstacles of e-Business**, Firm Size, Improved Products/Services/Processes	**Internet Penetration**, Competitive Pressure	Telephone survey with 6964 firms across 27 UE27 countries	SEM

Lin and Lin (2008)	e-Business	**IS Infrastructure, IS Expertise**	Organizational Compatibility, **Expected Benefit of e-Business**	**Competitive Pressure**, Trading Partner Readiness	Email survey of 163 large firms in Taiwan	SEM
Liu (2008)	e-Commerce	**Support from Technology and Human Capital**	**Management Level for Information**, Firm Size (Control: Firm Property)	**User Satisfaction**, **e-Commerce Security**	Online interviews and survey of 156 Chinese firms	Ordinary Least Squares (OLS)
Sparling and Toleman (2007)	e-Commerce	**Relative Advantage Compatibility**	**Technological Opportunism,** Business Category, Size, Technological Readiness **Owner Characteristics, Top Management Support**	Institutional Pressure	Survey of 94 firms in Canada	SEM
Hong and Zhu (2006)	e-Commerce	**Technology Integration**, **Web Functionalities**, EDI Use	**Web Spending**, Perceived Obstacles	**Partner Usage** (Control: **Size**, Industry)	Telephone survey of 838 U.S. and 198 Canadian firms	t-Tests and Logistic Regression
Zhu *et al.* (2006)	e-Business	**Technology Readiness, Technology Integration**	**Firm Size**, Managerial Obstacles, Global Scope	**Competition Intensity**, Regulatory Environment	Telephone Survey with 1857 firms across 10 countries	SEM
Teo *et al.* (2006)	B2B e-Commerce	**Unresolved Technical Issues**, Lack of IT Expertise and Infrastructure, Lack of Interoperability	Organizational Change, Project Management, **Lack of e-Commerce Strategy**, **Lack of Top Management Support**, **Cost-Benefit Assessment**	Fear and Uncertainty, Unresolved Legal Issues	Survey with 249 firms in Canada and North America	Univariate t-tests and Multivariate Discriminant Analysis
Raymond *et al.* (2005)	e-Business	**Manufacturing Technology**	**Manufacturing Context, Managerial Context,** Strategic Orientation	**Networking Intensity**	Questionnaire with 108 SMEs in Canada	PLS
Zhu and Kraemer (2005)	e-Business	**Technology Competence**	**Size**, **Financial Commitment**, International Scope	**Regulatory Support, Competitive Pressure**	Phone interviews of 624 firms across 10 countries	SEM

Note: *Significant factors are shown in bold.

commitment. The environmental context focuses on the external factors, such as the structure of the industry, customers, competitors, business partners, relationships with the government and the regulatory environment.

3.2 *Factors Affecting Organizational Adoption of Cryptocurrencies*

The systematic review of the recent literature on cryptocurrencies and blockchain technology suggested that perceived benefits such as transaction costs and fast transactions, security, privacy, and complexity are important technological factors that may affect organizational adoption of cryptocurrencies (Figure 2). Further, scalability and price volatility would also be important for a wide-scale adoption. Top management support and organizational readiness would be important organizational factors in

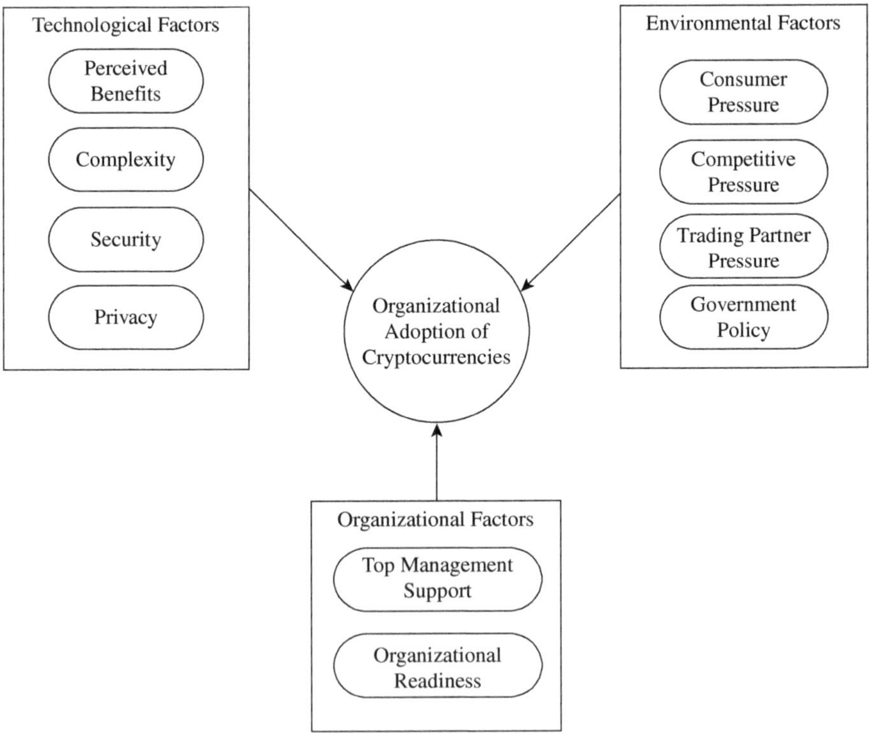

Figure 2: The Theoretical Model for the Organizational Adoption of Cryptocurrencies.

the adoption of cryptocurrencies at the organizational level. Consumer pressure, competitive pressure, trading partner pressure, and government policy would be important environmental factors for the organizational adoption of cryptocurrencies.

3.2.1 *Technological factors*

Blockchain technology provides a distributed infrastructure for the cryptocurrencies (Beck *et al.*, 2018). This technology has a disruptive impact on financial services (Frizzo-Barker *et al.*, 2019; Brühl, 2017). As previously mentioned, blockchain technology provides a decentralized structure, which removes the need for a trusted third party such as banks (Birch *et al.*, 2016). Therefore, one of the most significant benefits of the cryptocurrencies for the companies is lower **transaction costs** and **fast transactions** (Nofer *et al.*, 2017). Further, since all transactions are visible, governments would experience a good audit trail (Decker and Wattenhofer, 2013).

The underlying blockchain technology uses private and public key cryptography, which provides traceability, immutability, and trustworthiness for the cryptocurrencies (Sun *et al.*, 2016). However, the risks that violate **security** and **privacy** such as hacking, identity theft, and cyberattack would be important for the organizational adoption of cryptocurrencies (Xu, 2016). In blockchain technology, miners verify each transaction, if a miner node has an exceptionally strong computational power it can dominate the other nodes in the transaction approval; this may allow fraud, theft, or manipulation (Xu, 2016).

Other challenges or disadvantages include **complexity**, **scalability**, and **price volatility**. Complexity of transaction and price volatility may hinder organizational adoption of the cryptocurrencies. Further, since it was not designed initially for a wide-scale adoption, scalability can be an important issue that needs to be dealt with (Kasireddy, 2017). Another challenge is the amount of energy needed to process a cryptocurrency transaction (Holthaus, 2017). A growing demand for cryptocurrencies would cause a considerable computing-resource waste and confirmation time latency (Zhao *et al.*, 2016), which can hinder their adoption by organizations.

3.2.2 *Organizational factors*

Switching costs are critical challenges that may affect the adoption of cryptocurrencies by organizations. Organizations should accept a switching cost that refers to the budget and labor required to transition from the current system to a blockchain-based system (Frizzo-Barker *et al*., 2019). Therefore, **top management support** and **organizational readiness** would be important organizational factors in the adoption of cryptocurrencies at the organizational level.

3.2.3 *Environmental factors*

Interoperability is another key challenge to the organizational adoption of cryptocurrencies, requiring an effective collaboration among stakeholders (regulators, trading partners, suppliers, etc.) to reach a common industry standard and protocol (de Meijer, 2015, 2016). Thereby, **consumer pressure, trading partner pressure** and **competitive pressure** would be important environmental factors for an organizational level adoption. Further, **government policy** would have a critical impact on the organizational adoption of cryptocurrencies. Governance and regulations easing the adoption process may promote the organizational level adoption.

4. Conclusion

The relevance of disruptive financial innovations such as cryptocurrencies is of the utmost importance to the scientific and professional community. Therefore, a thorough understanding of cryptocurrencies' adoption is needed.

The core objective of this theoretical inquiry is to identify the most important factors driving and hindering the adoption of cryptocurrencies by individuals and companies.

Based on the IDT and on individual psychology, a conceptual model to describe the adoption of cryptocurrencies at the individual level was formulated. The study suggested that relative advantage, ease of use, result demonstrability, visibility, compatibility, trialability, image, voluntariness of use and personal innovativeness are important technological factors that may affect one's attitude toward cryptocurrencies.

Based on the TOE framework, a conceptual model to describe the adoption of cryptocurrencies at the organizational level was formulated. The model suggested that transaction costs, fast transactions, security, privacy, complexity, scalability, and price volatility are important technological factors that may affect individual adoption of cryptocurrencies, whereas top management support and organizational readiness would be important organizational factors in the adoption of cryptocurrencies at the organizational level. Consumer pressure, competitive pressure, trading partner pressure, and government policy would be important environmental factors for the organizational adoption of cryptocurrencies.

This study has resulted in several contributions. First, it contributes to research on cryptocurrencies and broadens the understanding of the individual and organizational factors for the adoption of cryptocurrencies and predicts their future perspectives. Second, this study is expected to determine the possibilities for improvement of the cryptocurrency ecosystem. Third, the findings can be useful for people showing reluctance to adopt cryptocurrency due to the blurred image they have about it. Fourth and final, the results can be used as guidelines for organizations planning to adapt, adopt and become adept at cryptocurrency transactions.

This study does not contain experimental data. Thus, future researchers should conduct an empirical investigation on the adoption of cryptocurrencies. The data can be collected in a variety of ways, such as qualitative in-depth or semi-structured interviews with subject experts and questionnaires in order to validate and test the models proposed in this study. It is important to update these models and to track the evolutionary adoption of cryptocurrencies by conducting longitudinal studies. Also, it would be interesting and relevant in the future to conduct a cross-cultural study by making a comparison between countries with different levels of penetration and usage of cryptocurrencies in order to explore a discrepancy in individual and organizational adoption of cryptocurrencies.

References

Abed, S. S. 2020. "Social commerce adoption using TOE framework: An empirical investigation of Saudi Arabian SMEs." *International Journal of Information Management* 53, 102118.

Agarwal, R., and J. Prasad. 1998. "The antecedents and consequences of user perceptions in information technology adoption." *Decis Support Syst*, 22, 15–29.

Agarwal, R., and J. Prasad. 1998. "A conceptual and operational definition of personal innovativeness in the domain of information technology." *Information Systems Research* 9, 204–224.

Ajzen, I., and M. Fishbein. 1980. *Understanding Attitudes and Predicting Social Behavior*. Englewood Cliffs, NJ: Prentice-Hall.

Ajzen, I. 1991. "The theory of planned behavior." *Organizational Behavior and Human Decision Processes* 50:2, 179–211.

Arias-Oliva *et al.* 2019. "Variables influencing cryptocurrency use: A technology acceptance model in Spain." *Frontiers in Psychology* 10:2019, 475.

Arpaci, I. 2019. "A theoretical framework for IT consumerization: Factors influencing the adoption of BYOD." In E.C. Idemudia (ed.), *Handbook of Research on Technology Integration in the Global World*, 114–129. PA, USA: IGI Global.

Arpaci, I., Y. Yardimci Cetin, and O. Turetken. 2015. "A cross-cultural analysis of smartphone adoption by Canadian and Turkish organizations." *Journal of Global Information Technology Management* 18:3, 214–238.

Arpaci, I. 2013. "*Organizational adoption of mobile communication technologies* (Unpublished Doctorate Thesis)." The Department of Information Systems, School of Informatics of Middle East Technical University.

Ateniese, G., B. Magri, D. Venturi, and E. Andrade. 2017. "Redactable Blockchain — or — Rewriting History in Bitcoin and Friends." *IEEE European Symposium on Security and Privacy (EuroS&P)*, Paris, 2017, 111–126.

Athey, S., C. Catalini, and C. Tucker. 2017. The digital privacy paradox: Small money, small costs, small talk (Working Paper No. 23488). National Bureau of Economic Research, Cambridge, MA.

Bamert, T., C. Decker, L. Elsen, R. Wattenhofer, and S. Welten. 2013. "Have a Snack, Pay with Bitcoins" (pp. 1–5). IEEE; IEEE Commun Soc; Univ Trento.

Barber, S., X. Boyen, E. Shi, and E. Uzun. 2012. "Bitter to better — how to make bitcoin a better currency." In A. D. Keromytis, (ed.), *Financial Cryptography and Data Security: 16th International Conference, FC 2012 Revised Selected Papers [Lecture Notes in Computer Science, 7397]*, 399–414. Germany: Springer.

Baur, A.W., J. Bühler, M. Bick, and C. S. Bonorden. 2015a. "Cryptocurrencies as a Disruption?" Empirical Findings on User Adoption and Future Potential of Bitcoin and Co. In M. Janssen, *et al.* (eds.). *Open and Big Data Management and Innovation.* I3E 2015. Lecture Notes in Computer Science, 9373.

Baur, D., A. Lee, and K. Hong. 2015b. "Bitcoin: Currency or investment?" Available at SSRN 2561183. https://papers.ssrn.com/sol3/papers.cfm?abstract_id=2561183.

Benbasat, I., and H. Barki. 2007. "Quo vadis TAM?." *Journal of the Association for Information Systems,* 8:4, 16. DOI: 10.17705/1jais.00126. Available at: https://aisel.aisnet.org/jais/vol8/iss4/16.

Beck, R., C. Müller-Bloch, and J. L. King. 2018. "Governance in the blockchain economy: A framework and research agenda." *Journal of the Association for Information Systems* 19:10, 1–40.

Birch, D., R. G. Brown, and S. Parulava. 2016. "Towards ambient accountability in financial services: Shared ledgers, translucent transactions and the technological legacy of the great financial crisis." *Journal of Payments Strategy & Systems* 10:2, 118–131.

Bordonaba-Juste, V., L. Lucia-Palacios, and Y. Polo-Redondo. 2012. "Antecedents and consequences of e-business adoption for European retailers." *Internet Research* 22:5, 532–550.

Brühl, V. 2017. "Virtual currencies, distributed ledgers and the future of financial services." *Intereconomics* 52:6, 370–378.

Bryans, D. 2014. "Bitcoin and money laundering: Mining for an effective solution." *Indiana Law Journal* 89:1, 441–472.

Byrne, P. 2014. Overstock CEO, speech at the bitcoin 2014, conference on 15th–17th May at the Passenger Terminal Amsterdam.

Cruz-Jesus, F., A. Pinheiro, and T. Oliveira. 2019. "Understanding CRM adoption stages: Empirical analysis building on the TOE framework." *Computers in Industry* 109, 1–13.

Cousins, K., H. Subramanian, and P. Esmaeilzadeh. 2019. "A value-sensitive design perspective of cryptocurrencies: A research agenda." *Communications of the Association for Information Systems* 45:1.

Davis, F. D. 1989. "Perceived usefulness, perceived ease of use, and user acceptance of information technology," *MIS Quarterly* 13:3, 319–340.

Decker, C., and R. Wattenhofer. 2013. "Information propagation in the Bitcoin network." *In IEEE P2P 2013 Proceedings* 1–10. IEEE.

De Meijer, C. R. W. 2015. "The U.K. and blockchain technology: A balanced approach." *Journal of Payments Strategy & Systems* 9:4, 220–229.

De Meijer, C. R. W. 2016. "Blockchain and the securities industry: Towards a new ecosystem." *Journal of Securities Operations & Custody* 8:4, 322–329.

DePietro, R., E. Wiarda, and M. Fleischer. 1990. "The context for change: Organization, technology, and environment." In L. G. Tornatzky and M. Fleischer (eds.), *The Process of Technological Innovation*, 151–175. Lexington, MA: Lexington Books.

De Nederlandsche Bank. 2014. "DNBulletin: Virtuele valuta's geen bruikbaar alternatief." Retrieved from http://www.dnb.nl/nieuws/nieuwsoverzicht-en-archief/dnbulletin-2014/dnb307263.jsp

Extance, A. 2015. "The future of cryptocurrencies: Bitcoin and beyond." *Nature* 526:7571, 21–23.

Everette, J., Department of the U.S. Treasury, 2017. Risks and Vulnerabilities of Virtual Currency Cryptocurrency as a Payment Method, Public-Private, analytic exchange program.

Frizzo-Barker, J., P. A. Chow-White, P. R. Adams, J. Mentanko, D. Ha, and S. Green. 2019. "Blockchain as a disruptive technology for business: A systematic review." *International Journal of Information Management* 51, 102029. https://doi.org/10.1016/j.ijinfomgt.2019.10.014.

Goldman, S. 2014. "All about Bitcoin." *Goldman Sachs Global Macro Research* 21:25, 1–25. https://cointhinktank.com/upload/All%20About%20Bitcoin-GoldmanSachs-2014.pdf

Grinberg, R. 2011. "Bitcoin: An innovative alternative digital currency." *Hastings Science & Technology Law Journal* 4, 160.

Holthaus, E. 2017. "Bitcoin could cost us our clean-energy future." Retrieved March 10, 2020, from Grist website: https://grist.org/article/bitcoin-could-cost-us-our-cleanenergy-future/.

Hong, W., and K. Zhu. 2006. "Migrating to Internet-based e-commerce: Factors affecting e-commerce adoption and migration at the firm level." *Information & Management* 43:2, 204–221.

Houben, R., and A. Snyers. 2018. "Cryptocurrencies and Blockchain: Legal Context and Implications for Financial Crime, Money Laundering and Tax Evasion, EU Directorate-General for Internal Policies, PE 619.024." Available online: http://www.europarl.europa.eu/cmsdata/150761/TAX3%20Study%20on% 20cryptocurrencies%20and%20blockchain.pdf.

Holotiuk, F., and J. Moormann. 2018. "Organizational adoption of digital innovation: The case of blockchain technology." Research Papers, 202.

Ifinedo, P. 2011. "Internet/e-business technologies acceptance in Canada's SMEs: An exploratory investigation." *Internet Research* 21:3, 255–281.

Jackson, J. D., M. Y. Yi, and J. S. Park. 2013. "An empirical test of three mediation models for the relationship between personal innovativeness and user acceptance of technology." *Information & Management* 50:4, 154–161.

Jia, Q., Y. Guo, and S. J. Barnes. 2017. "Enterprise 2.0 post-adoption: Extending the information system continuance model based on the technology-organization-environment framework." *Computers in Human Behavior* 67, 95–105.

Kasireddy, P. 2017. "Blockchains don't scale. Not today, at least." But there's hope. Retrieved December 8, from Hacker Noon website: https://hackernoon.com/blockchainsdont-scale-not-today-at-least-but-theres-hope-2cb43946551a.

Karahanna, E., D. W. Straub, and N. L. Chervany. 1999. "Information technology adoption across time: A cross-sectional comparison of pre-adoption and post-adoption beliefs." *MIS Quarterly* 183–213.

Karame, G. O., E. Androulaki, and S. Čapkun. 2012. "Double-spending fast payments in Bitcoin." *In Proceedings of the ACM Conference on Computer and Communications Security* 906–917. Raleigh, NC.

Koivisto, K., M. Makkonen, L. Frank, and J. Riekkinen. 2016. "Extending the Technology Acceptance Model with Personal Innovativeness and Technology Readiness: A Comparison of Three Models." In Conference: 29th Bled eConference.

Kristoufek, L. 2014. "What are the main drivers of the Bitcoin price?" Evidence from wavelet coherence analysis. arXiv, 19. Computational Finance; Data Analysis, Statistics and Probability; Statistical Finance.

Kulkarni, M., and K. Patil. 2020. "Block chain technology adoption using TOE framework." *International Journal of Scientific & Technology Research* 9, 1109–1117.

Lin, H. F. 2014. "Understanding the determinants of electronic supply chain management system adoption: Using the technology–organization–environment framework." *Technological Forecasting and Social Change* 86, 80–92.

Lin, H. F., and S. M. Lin. 2008. "Determinants of e-business diffusion: A test of the technology diffusion perspective." *Technovation* 28:3, 135–145.

Liu, M. 2008. "Determinants of e-commerce development: An empirical study by firms in Shaanxi, China." In 4th International Conference on Wireless Communications, Networking and Mobile Computing, Dalian, China, Vol. 1–31, 9177–9180.

Lo, S., and J. C. Wang. 2014. "Bitcoin as money?" *Current Policy Perspectives* 14–4, Federal Reserve Bank of Boston.

Lu, J., J. Yao, and C. S. Yu. 2005. "Personal innovativeness, social influences and adoption of wireless internet services via mobile technology." *The Journal of Strategic Information Systems* 14:3, 245–268.

Lusardi, A., and O. S. Mitchell. 2007. Baby boomers retirement security: The role of planning, financial literacy and housing wealth. *Journal of Monetary Economics* 54, 205–224.

Luther, W. J. 2013. "Cryptocurrencies, Network Effects, and Switching Costs." Available at SSRN 2295134. Retrieved from http://mercatus.org/sites/default/files/Luther_CryptocurrenciesNetworkEffects_v1.pdf.

Masoni, M., M. R. Guelfi, and G. F. Gensini. 2016. "Darknet and bitcoin, the obscure and anonymous side of the internet in healthcare." *Technology Health Care* 24:6, 969–972.

McCook, H. 2014. An Order-of-Magnitude Estimate of the Relative Sustainability of the Bitcoin Network. Working Paper, July 15. https://bitcoin.fr/public/divers/docs/Estimation_de_la_durabilite_et_du_cout_du_reseau_Bitcoin.pdf

Mikołajewicz-Woźniak, A., and A. Scheibe. 2015. "Virtual currency schemes — The future of financial services." *Foresight* 17:4, 365–377.

Moore, T., 2013. "The promise and perils of digital currency." *International Journal of Critical Infrastructure Protection* 6, 147–149.

Moore, G. C., and I. Benbasat. 1991. "Development of an instrument to measure the perceptions of adopting an information technology innovation." *Information Systems Research* 2:3, 192–222.

Nofer, M., P. Gomber, O. Hinz, and D. Schiereck. 2017. "Blockchain." *Business & Information Systems Engineering* 59, 183–187.

Ober, M., S. Katzenbeisser, and K. Hamacher. 2013. "Structure and Anonymity of the Bitcoin Transaction Graph." *Future Internet* 5:2, 237–250.

Oliveira, T., and M. F. Martins. 2011. "Literature review of information technology adoption models at firm level." *The Electronic Journal Information Systems Evaluation* 141, 110–121.

Oliveira, T., and M. F. Martins. 2010. "Firms patterns of e-business adoption: Evidence for the European Union-27." *The Electronic Journal Information Systems Evaluation* 13:1, 47–56.

Omri, M. 2013. Are Cryptocurrencies Super Tax Havens?, 112 Michigan. Law. Review. First Impressions, 38, https://repository.law.umich.edu/mlr_fi/vol112/iss1/2

Plassaras, N. A. 2013. "Regulating digital currencies: Bringing bitcoin within the reach of the IMF." *Chicago Journal of International Law* 14:1, 26 pages.

Polasik, M., A. I. Piotrowska, T. P. Wisniewski, R. Kotkowski, and G. Lightfoot. 2015. "Price fluctuations and the use of bitcoin: An empirical inquiry." *International Journal of Electronic Commerce* 20:1, 9–49.

Raymond, L., F. O. Bergeron, and S. Blili. 2005. "The assimilation of e-business in manufacturing SMEs: Determinants and effects on growth and internationalization." *Electronic Markets* 15:2, 106–118.

Rogers, E. M. 1983. *Diffusion of innovations,* 3rd Ed. New York, NY: Free Press.

Rogers, E. M. 1995. *Diffusion of Innovations*. New York, NY: The Free Press.

Rogers, E. M. 2003. *Diffusion of Innovations,* 5th Ed. New York, NY: The Free Press.

Rapport du comité sénatorial permanent des banques et du commerce. 2015. "Les Cryptomonnaies: Pile ou face?"

Schuh, S., and O. Shy. 2016. U.S. consumers' adoption and use of Bitcoin and other virtual currencies. In De Nederlandsche Bank, Conference entitled "Retail payments: Mapping out the road ahead."

Southurst, J. 2013. "What Do Australia's Biggest Banks Think About Bitcoin?" CoinDesk, iewed 05 March 2020, http://www.coindesk.com/national-australia-bank-turns-back-bitcoincloses-accounts/.

Sparling, L. C. A., and M. Toleman. 2007. "SME adoption of e-commerce in the central Okanagan region of Canada." In 18th Australasian Conference on Information Systems, Toowoomba.

Spenkelink, H. F. 2014. *The Adoption Process of Cryptocurrencies — Identifying factors that influence the adoption of cryptocurrencies from a multiple stakeholder perspective* (Master's Thesis, University of Twente).

Stolper, O. A., and A. Walter. 2017. "Financial literacy, financial advice, and financial behavior." *Journal of Business Economics*, Springer, 87:5, 581–643.

Sun, J., J. Yan, and K. Z. K. Zhang. 2016. "Blockchain-based sharing services: What blockchain technology can contribute to smart cities." *Financial Innovation* 2:1, 26.

Teo, T. S. H., C. Ranganathan, and J. Dhaliwal. 2006. "Key dimensions of inhibitors for the deployment of web-based business-to-business electronic commerce." *IEEE Transactions on Engineering Management* 53:3, 395–411.

Tornatzky, L. G., and M. Fleischer. 1990. *The Processes of Technological Innovation.* Lexington, MA: Lexington Books.

Twomey, P. 2013. "Halting a shift in the paradigm: the need for bitcoin regulation." *Trinity Coll Law Rev.* 16, 67–90.

Van Rooij, M., A. Lusardi, and R. Alessie. 2011. "Financial literacy and stock market participation." *Journal of Financial Economics* 101:2, 449–472.

Venkatesh, V., F. D. Davis, and M. G. Morris. 2017. "Dead or alive? The development, trajectory and future of technology adoption research." *J. AIS* 8:4, 268–286.

Venkatesh, V., M. G. Morris, G. B. Davis, and F. D. Davis. 2003. "User acceptance of information technology: Toward a unified view." *MIS Quarterly* 27:3, 425–478.

Williams, M. D. 2018. "Social commerce and the mobile platform: Payment and security perceptions of potential users." *Computers in Human Behavior* [online]. Available from: https://doi.org/10.1016/j.chb.2018.06.005.

Wong, L. W., L. Y. Leong, J. J. Hew, G. W. H. Tan, and K. B. Ooi. 2020. "Time to seize the digital evolution: Adoption of blockchain in operations and supply chain management among Malaysian SMEs." *International Journal of Information Management* 52, 101997.

Xu, J. J. 2016. "Are blockchains immune to all malicious attacks?" *Financial Innovation* 2:1, 25.

Yermack, D. 2015. "Is bitcoin a real currency? An economic appraisal." In *The Handbook of Digital Currency*, 31–44. Elsevier. doi:10.1016/b978-0-12-802117-0.00002-3.

Yeh, C. H., G. G. Lee, and J. C. Pai. 2015. "Using a technology-organization-environment framework to investigate the factors influencing e-business information technology capabilities." *Information Development* 31:5, 435–450.

Zhao, J. L., S. Fan, and J. Yan. 2016. "Overview of business innovations and research opportunities in blockchain and introduction to the special issue." *Financial Innovation* 2:1, 28.

Zhu, K., and K. L. Kraemer. 2005. "Post-adoption variations in usage and value of e-business by organizations: Cross-country evidence from the retail industry." *Information Systems Research* 16:1, 61–84.

Zhu, K., K. L. Kraemer, and S. Xu. 2006. "The process of innovation assimilation by firms in different countries: A technology diffusion perspective on e-business." *Management Science* 52:10, 1557–1576.

https://doi.org/10.1142/9789811239670_0009

Chapter 9

Crypto-asset Valuation: A Review and Analysis of Current Methods

Chen Liu
School of Business, Trinity Western University, Canada
chen.liu@twu.ca

Abstract

This chapter provides an overview of crypto-asset valuation methods. Specifically, the chapter positions existing crypto-asset valuation methods and techniques within the framework of traditional asset valuation with a particular focus on the income approach, market approach, and cost approach. This income approach considers crypto-assets' features of medium of exchange and storage of value and applies the Quantity Theory of Money, the Crypto J-Curve, the Network Model, and Metcalfe's Law to crypto-asset valuations. The market approach ensembles the price/earnings ratio for the equity market and emphasizes the transaction value and token utilities, with the Network Value-to-Transaction Ratio and the Price-to-Utility Ratio. Finally, the cost approach considers mining costs as the lower bound of crypto-asset valuation. This chapter also discusses empirical tests and related studies with each valuation method. For each valuation framework, this chapter discusses its shortcomings and suggests future research directions.

Keywords: cryptocurrency, bitcoin, valuation, asset pricing, quantity theory of money, network value-to-transaction ratio

1. Introduction

Crypto-assets refer to the digital assets that are generated and regulated by blockchain techniques. There are three main types of crypto-assets: *cryptocurrency coins*, *utility tokens,* and *security tokens*. First, although cryptocurrencies are usually used as a general term and sometimes interchangeable with crypto-assets, this chapter defines cryptocurrencies (or *cryptocurrency coins*) as generally accepted means of payment on blockchain and not specific to any platforms. Examples of cryptocurrency coins include Bitcoin, Bitcoin Cash, and Litecoin. Second, *utility tokens are* platform-specific tokens that give their holders access to products or services of the blockchain platform (Yermack, 2017; Howell *et al.*, 2018). Third, *security tokens* are platform-specific tradable tokens whose primary purpose is to give holders financial returns and therefore mimic traditional financial assets such as debt and equity (Koffman, 2018). While major cryptocurrencies are generated through mining, utility and security tokens represent tokens that are normally issued to their holders in token offering events, i.e., initial coin offerings (ICOs) for utility tokens and security token offerings (STOs) for security tokens (Liu and Wang, 2019b).

This chapter provides an overview of valuation methods for *cryptocurrency coins* and *utility tokens*, the two most common types of crypto-assets. Valuation of security tokens is not within the scope of this chapter as security tokens are still rare and their similarity to equity or debt allows security token valuation techniques to ensemble those of traditional financial assets.

While identifying the determinants of asset prices is one of the most important questions in finance, research on cryptocurrencies is still at its early stage (Makarov and Schoar, 2020). Existing studies focus on cryptocurrency coins as a payment and transaction mechanism and derive their value based on the economics of cryptocurrencies, the blockchain technology, and the mining costs and incentives with a special focus on Bitcoin (e.g., Ciaian *et al.*, 2016; Pagnotta and Buraschi, 2018).

This chapter studies existing crypto-asset valuation approaches and builds the connection to the traditional valuation techniques and principles. Three key motivations call for a rigorous overview and analysis of existing crypto-asset valuation techniques. First, crypto-asset investors need to be able to calculate the crypto-asset value and understand factors that drive valuations. This is particularly challenging as crypto-assets have a wide range of utilities and their valuation requires an understanding of token economics, finance, technical, and legal aspects of the tokens. Each combination of different features may require a different basis of value, which will influence the judgment regarding the most appropriate valuation method to be adopted. This chapter is therefore essential given its comprehensive overview and analysis of various valuation methods and their appropriate and timely use when market exuberance and investor sentiment drive pricing.

Second, token issuers need to be able to value the crypto-assets they allocate to employees, advisors, and investors for financial management and financial reporting purposes. Third, there are also tax implications to both the token issuer and token holders. Furthermore, many issuers and holders of crypto-assets are in the process of altering their legal entity structure in order to resolve historical inefficiencies, relocate, or respond to regulatory changes (Johnson *et al.*, 2019). This may require transfer pricing considerations or the valuation of illiquid tokens being transferred among entities. Therefore, this chapter also provides managerial insights and policy implications.

The chapter is organized as follows. The next section lays a foundation for tokens and token economics and provides a review of existing studies. The sections afterwards discuss the valuation of cryptocurrency coins and utility tokens by first laying out a framework and discussing various techniques of the income approach, the market approach, and the cost approach. In the last section, we conclude the chapter.

2. Fundamentals of Crypto-assets

2.1 *Crypto-assets: An Introduction*

This chapter uses the term "crypto-assets" to refer to digital assets in which blockchain techniques are used to create and regulate the assets. Different crypto-assets have different features, behaviors, and uses. While some behave as a commodity or a form of payment, others behave more akin to a financial asset. This chapter categorizes crypto-assets into three groups: cryptocurrency coins, utility tokens, and security tokens, as listed in Table 1.

Cryptocurrency coins are crypto-assets accepted as a means of payment for the purchase of goods and/or services, or to be used for the money or

Table 1: Three Categories of Crypto-assets.

	Cryptocurrency Coins	Utility Tokens	Security Tokens
Platform	Independent platform	Specific platform	Specific platform
Functions	1. Payment (e.g., Bitcoin, Ether) 2. Smart contract platform (e.g., Ether) 3. Stable coin (e.g., USDT)	1. Payment (e.g., Gemini dollar) 2. Access to product or services (e.g., Filecoin)	A tokenized version of a traditional asset (e.g., BCAP)
Distribution	Mining, token offering	Initial Coin Offerings (ICOs)	Security Token Offerings (STOs)

value transfer. Bitcoin, Bitcoin Cash, Ether, and stable coins (e.g., USDT) are examples of cryptocurrency coins. Cryptocurrency coins are independent of a particular platform and can be used as a form of currency outside their native environment, whereas utility tokens and security tokens, in general, exist on a particular platform that the token issuers create (Blockgeeks, 2018).

Utility tokens are crypto-assets that confirm the rights to access products or services and that generally require the use of a specific blockchain infrastructure (Catalini and Gans, 2019). Utility tokens are usually based on the Ethereum blockchain (Buterin, 2017). A large majority of crypto-assets in the market tend to fall into the categories of utility tokens (Johnson *et al.*, 2019).

Security tokens are crypto-assets that provide financial rights to investors, such as cash flow, real estate, and collectibles such as arts (Koffman, 2018). The most common type is the equity security tokens that possess characteristics similar to those of equities (Marks, 2018). Security tokens are much more heavily regulated by the government than utility tokens (Liu and Wang, 2019a).

As previously discussed, this chapter examines the valuation of cryptocurrency coins and utility tokens. For simplicity, the rest of the chapter uses the term "tokens" or "crypto-assets" interchangeably to refer to cryptocurrency coins and utility tokens.

2.2 *Tokenomics*

The word "tokenomics" (or "token economics") refers to the economic functions of tokens and is therefore important to understand the value derived from tokens (Malinova and Park, 2018; Liu and Wang, 2019a). People buy and hold crypto-assets for three purposes: (1) for access to a company's products or services or future use as a commodity or medium of exchange, (2) for investment returns with the expectation of an increase in the token value, and (3) for both goals simultaneously (Liu and Wang, 2019a, 2019b).

As most tokens, by design, have a limited and fixed amount of supply, the law of demand and supply suggests that token value is mostly driven by an increase in token demand, usually because of an increasing network of token holders (Liu and Wang, 2019a). Specifically, blockchain projects aim to create a network of users and participants often referred to as a "community." Well-designed tokens should provide ways of incentivizing the community and monetizing network effects. Token holders can sell their tokens on a secondary market, receiving cryptocurrencies such as Bitcoin or Ether or fiat money. This is the innovation of ICOs with a liquid resale market for the tokens and thereby enabling the token holders to monetize the network effect (Liu and Wang, 2019b). As long as tokens are kept scarce, any increase in network value will enhance token value because tokens are scarce and are necessary to gain access to the network (Klöhn *et al.*, 2018; Li and Mann, 2018).

2.3 *Literature Review*

While identifying the determinants of asset prices is one of the most important questions in finance (Bhambhwani *et al.*, 2019), academic studies on crypto-asset valuation are still at an early stage. Some early studies hold the perception that cryptocurrency markets are simply plagued with bubbles and speculative trading with the rationale that Bitcoin is intentionally disconnected from direct government oversight, fiscal policy, and monetary policy. Therefore, these studies have attempted to address the "moneyness" of Bitcoin and examine whether it is more analogous to a fiat versus commodity money. Specifically, Yermack (2015) points out the weaknesses in Bitcoin as a currency and claims that Bitcoin (and all cryptocurrencies by association) has no intrinsic value. He also finds that

Bitcoin's dollar price varies significantly among the various exchanges, which can cause problems when trying to analyze price data. These findings are consistent with Hanley (2013) that the value of Bitcoin floats against other currencies with no fundamental value to support it. Similarly, Cheah and Fry (2015) and Corbet *et al.* (2018) claim that Bitcoin has no intrinsic value and that its price has persistently exhibited bubble-like behavior.

On the other side, some authors have identified factors that impact crypto-asset valuation. Currencies have three key functions: a medium of exchange, a store of value, and a unit of account. One strand of studies argues that cryptocurrency coins, such as Bitcoin (BTC) or stable coins, may have a valuable "store of value" feature. For instance, Conley (2017) posits that like any fiat currency, the ecosystem's acceptance, collective belief, and confidence regarding the asset are foundational to crypto-assets' position as a "store of value."

Another group of studies looks at the "medium of exchange" aspect of crypto-assets and the resulting transaction needs and network effect. For instance, Kristoufek (2015) demonstrates that the fundamental factors of usage in trade, money supply, and price level play a role in Bitcoin price over the long term and that Bitcoin price is driven by investors' interests. Ciaian *et al.* (2016) find that market forces and Bitcoin attractiveness for investors and users have a significant impact on Bitcoin price but with variation over time. Peterson (2017) proposes a model that is a function of the network effect using Metcalfe's Law. Bhambhwani *et al.* (2019) argue that consumers value a blockchain as it provides censorship-resistant, border-less, and secure transactions and that a larger network of users implies greater acceptability of tokens as a medium of exchange as well as higher liquidity. Similarly, Grinberg (2011) and Wang and Vergne (2017) conclude the importance of macro factors in determining cryptocurrency value.

Other authors examine the impact of technology and mining costs. For instance, Garcia *et al.* (2014) assert that the cost of production via mining could matter in coming up with a fundamental value for bitcoins insofar as it represents a lower bound. Hayes (2015, 2017, 2019) find that the key value driver for cryptocurrencies is the cost of production, determined by the computational power, coins per minute, and the algorithm used. Bhambhwani *et al.* (2019) posit that computing power and network are positively related to cryptocurrency value.

Table 2: Valuation Framework of Crypto-assets.

Valuation Methods	Traditional Assets	Crypto-assets
Monetary Theory	• Quantity Theory of Money	• The Crypto Quantity Theory of Money
Income Approach	• Discounted Cash Flow	• Quantity Theory of Money • Crypto J-Curve Methodology • Network Model and Metcalfe's Law
Market Approach	• P/E, EV/EBITDA, and other previous/comparable transaction multiples	• Network Value-to-Transaction Ratio (NVT) • Price-to-Utility Ratio
Cost Approach	• Cost of reconstructing	• Cost of mining

3. Crypto-asset Valuation: The General Framework

This chapter provides a comprehensive overview of the existing crypto-asset valuation methods and positions these methods within the traditional asset valuation framework: the income approach, the market approach, and the cost approach, as summarized in Table 2.

The rest of this chapter discusses each valuation method. Studies mentioned here are mostly from the practitioners' side, and the academic studies (e.g., Cong *et al.*, 2019; Makarov and Schoar, 2020; Sockin and Xiong, 2020) are catching up lately.

4. Crypto-asset Valuation: The Income Approach

4.1 *The Crypto Quantity Theory of Money* (*QTM*)

Cryptocurrency coins' payment function in general and utility tokens' function as the only acceptable form of payment within their respective blockchain networks create meaningful parallels with fiat currencies. This leads to the valuation of cryptocurrency coins and utility tokens using the QTM framework (Friedman, 1956).

Specifically, the QTM states that the general price level of goods and services is directly proportional to the amount of money in circulation, or money supply (Friedman, 1956). The QTM is therefore based on the definitional relationship: $MV = PQ$. It states that the money supply (M) times money velocity (V) equals price level (P) times the volume of goods and services transacted in the economy (Q). In practice, the real gross domestic product (GDP) is substituted into the equation as a measure of volume (Q).

Applying the QTM to crypto-assets leads to the following equation:

$$MV = PQ - \rightarrow \text{Token Price} = \frac{1}{P} = \frac{Q}{MV}.$$

Note that P is the price of goods and services in terms of tokens and is therefore the inverse of the token price.

The QTM method states that crypto-asset price is determined by three factors. The first factor is the *economic value of the token transaction* (Q), measured by the number of times that an average token changes hands. In a utility token system, this term Q should equate to the overall value of the services rendered through the system during a specified period.

The second factor is the *token supply* (M), which can be thought of as a combination of two factors:

$$M = M^* \times f.$$

M^* is the total number of tokens coined by issuers, a fixed number written in the smart contract that generates tokens. f is a floating rate, calculated as the proportion of active tokens over the total number of tokens created. f should converge to 100% over the long run. Therefore, the total token supply (M) should be treated as a constant number over the long run for valuation purposes.

This leads to an expanded form of the QTM:

$$\text{Token Price} = \frac{1}{P} = \frac{Q}{MV} = \frac{Q}{M^* \times f \times V}.$$

The third factor of the crypto-asset QTM is the *token velocity* (V): The public nature of the crypto-asset systems makes money velocity an observable quantity. It is the inverse of the average period for which a token is held by one address. Stronger demand for a token would likely lead to increased token liquidity and therefore to easier convertibility into fiat currency.

Table 3 shows the comparison of the QTM approach's application to the traditional versus crypto-assets.

Table 3: The QTM Approach: Comparison of Crypto-assets and Traditional Assets.

QTM Input	Traditional Version	Crypto Version
M	Money supply in the economy (M1)	Size of the crypto-asset, the product of total fixed token supply and the floating rate.
V	Velocity of circulation	Velocity of crypto-asset
P	Price level in the economy	The inverse of token price
Q	Output produced by the economy (GDP)	Quantity of digital resources being provisioned

Because *M* is fixed in the long run, the crypto QTM approach states that token utility and velocity are key value drivers. The implication is that tokens with higher utility (generated through a larger network effect) or low velocity (i.e., those that held owing to speculation) tend to have a higher value.

While the QTM framework is based on the monetary economics, the QTM approach also resembles the classic discounted cash flow (DCF) method and hence falls under the income approach of asset valuation. Under the typical DCF analysis, an asset's value is determined by discounting the future cash flows it is expected to generate to a present value using a risk-adjusted rate of return. However, cryptocurrency coins or utility tokens do not generate cash flows. The QTM method theorizes that the utility a token holder derives from ownership is instead correlated with the size of the economy the token is expected to support and in which the token holder will hopefully participate (i.e., its network value, somewhat similar to a public company's market capitalization) (Bheemaiah and Collomb, 2018).

As discussed above, the QTM approach shares many characteristics with traditional cash flow valuation approaches and monetary theory. However, challenges remain with regard to the estimation of key inputs of the crypto QTM, such as demand and an appropriate reflection of the time value of money. This estimation will inevitably require a careful analysis and a sense of realism about one's confidence in the concluded value range.

4.2 *Crypto J-Curve Methodology*

Burniske (2017) proposes Crypto J-Curve to capture how the market values crypto-assets over time. Based on this framework, crypto-assets have two forms of value: (1) a *current utility value* (CUV) that captures the value driven by their utility and usage today, and (2) a *discounted expected utility value* (DEUV) that represents the value driven by investment speculation for the future (Burniske, 2017). It therefore also falls under the income approach of crypto-asset valuation.

According to Burniske (2017), CUV and DEUV take turns in determining token value as a blockchain project develops and its market perceptions change accordingly. It is therefore a framework for utility tokens only, which are platform- and project-specific. Specifically, when a project and its token are first launched, CUV is low and DEUV dominates as token holders are excited about the technology and expect future price appreciation. When enthusiasm wanes and DEUV drops with inevitable technical roadblocks, the token value drops and is driven more by CUV from the project's early adopters. As the team overcomes technical and business challenges, CUV grows as the token becomes more widely adopted, driving up the token value. DEUV then catches up as speculation and excitement start to grow again. Ultimately, in the steady state of the blockchain project, CUV should drive token price.

Linking back to stock valuation, the notion of DEUV can be considered as a modified version of the DCF valuation method. Instead of measuring expected future cash flow, this model is a first step in estimating CUV and DEUV and their respective dynamic influences on token price (Bheemaiah and Collomb, 2018).

Some adopters of the Crypto J-Curve have begun to use it as a proxy for measuring the different life stages of a crypto-asset. For example, a New York-based VC investment fund uses the Crypto J-Curve to determine which stage a token sale is at: a whitepaper stage is where the team works to define and implement a "minimum viable protocol" and to validate the network's functionality, a release stage is when a token is first made available to the public, and a public stage is when the token begins trading on exchanges (Burniske, 2017). The fund then applies the Crypto J-Curve and estimates token values according to the development stage.

4.3 *Network Model and Metcalfe's Law*

Some authors such as Peterson (2018) and Van Vliet (2018) apply Metcalfe's Law to crypto-asset valuation based on the network effects.

Metcalfe's Law describes the value of a network (*M*) as being proportional to the square of the number of users (Metcalfe, 2013). It indicates that a network becomes more valuable as the number of users increases.

$$M = \frac{n(n-1)}{2}.$$

Whereas the Crypto J-Curve is only for utility tokens, Metcalfe's Law applies best to Bitcoin due to its general application as a method of payment and its peer-to-peer feature. Applying Metcalfe's Law to Bitcoin valuation, Peterson (2018) proposes the following:

$$\text{Value of Bitcoin in dollars } (V) = A \times \left[\frac{n(n-1)}{2} \times \frac{1}{b_t} \right],$$

$$\text{where } b_t \text{ is the number of bitcoins over time: } b_t = b_{t-1} \times ln\left(\frac{B}{b_{t-1}} \right).$$

B is the total number of bitcoins, *B* = 21 million. Using empirical Bitcoin price data Y_t and the number of Bitcoin wallets as a proxy for *n*, *A* is evaluated as the beta coefficient of the linear regression model of

$$ln\, ln(Y_t) = 0 + \beta \left(\frac{ln(B/b_t)}{ln(M_t)} \right) + \varepsilon_t.$$

Peterson (2018) and Van Vliet (2018) empirically tested the model and concluded that Bitcoin's price, in the medium to long term, follows Metcalfe's Law. This method is also based on the income approach by modeling Bitcoin's utility using the network framework.

Peterson (2018) further discusses two limitations of the method. First, this approach does not attempt to explain short-term price movements, which may be driven by a multitude of factors. A second and related caveat is that Metcalfe's Law failed to predict Bitcoin prices in 2013–2014 because prices during that period were not indicative of normal supply and demand under fair competition. Peterson (2018) suggests further research into the application of Metcalfe's Law to cryptocurrency prices.

5. Crypto-asset Valuation: The Market Approach

5.1 *Network Value-to-Transaction Ratio (NVT)*

In traditional stock markets, the price/earnings ratio (P/E ratio) has been a long-standing tool for equity valuation. A high P/E ratio indicates either overvaluation or high growth. Applying the market approach of the P/E ratio to the crypto world, Woo (2017) suggests using money flowing through a token's network as a proxy to "earnings." This leads to the NVT ratio method of token valuation:

$$\text{Network Value to Transaction (NVT) Ratio} = \frac{\text{network value}}{\text{daily transaction volume}}.$$

This valuation ratio compares the network's value (the market cap) to the network's daily on-chain transaction volume. Similar to the P/E ratio, a high NVT ratio indicates that the market cap of the token outpaces the transacted value on its blockchain, suggesting potential token overvaluation. A low NVT ratio caused by an increasing transaction volume indicates a high usage of the token, which, in turn, serves as a signal to buy the undervalued crypto-asset.

The NVT ratio, one of the most popular crypto-asset market-based valuation approaches, may provide a methodology to evaluate the fundamental value of crypto-assets. However, there are some limitations. The first limitation lies in the assumption that the fundamental value of crypto-asset derives only from its function as a *medium of exchange*. The method, therefore, overlooks the *store of value function* of tokens (Liu, 2019). For instance, an increase of the NVT ratio due to a decrease in the transaction volume does not necessarily imply an overvaluation of the token. It could also be the result of an increasing number of long-term holders hoarding more tokens expecting price appreciation in the future, thus causing a decline in transaction volume. Moving forward, using the NVT ratio will require some formal definition of what constitutes a valid transaction in certain networks.

Second, Woo (2017) admits that the NVT ratio is not an effective tool to detect a price bubble *ex ante*. Instead, it is better suited to discern between price collapse and price consolidation retrospectively. Still, it failed to explain the 2017 crypto bull market when the NVT ratio was below its normal range, thus indicating undervaluation (Liu, 2019).

The NVT ratio also failed to identify the 2018 crypto bear market when there was clearly a market collapse while the NVT ratio remained in its normal range (Liu, 2019).

A third limitation of the NVT ratio is the lack of historical data and meaningful comparables. The usefulness of market-based crypto-asset valuation analysis may be limited since drawing meaningful inferences hinges on having access to reliable empirical data, which, given the relative immaturity of the crypto-asset industry, may not yet be available. As with traditional market-based valuation approaches, it is oftentimes challenging to identify reasonable comparable companies, transactions, or assets. This challenge is further compounded in the crypto-asset space where identifying a meaningful comparator among the plethora of crypto-asset offerings (each with varying use cases and slight or considerable technical nuances) can be problematic and may render a relative valuation metric unsuitable for application to the subject crypto-asset.

5.2 *Price-to-Utility Ratio*

To overcome the shortcoming of the NVT ratio, Liu (2019) proposes using the Price-to-Utility (P/U) ratio that incorporates both the medium of exchange and the store of value functions of crypto-assets.

$$\text{Price to Utility Ratio (P/U)} = \frac{\text{price per token}}{\text{utility per token}} = \frac{\text{Market Cap}}{\text{Token Utility}},$$

$$\text{Token Utility} = \frac{\text{token velocity} \times \text{staking ratio}}{\text{dilution rate}},$$

$$\text{staking ratio} = \frac{\text{stake tokens}}{\text{total token supply}}.$$

The *total utility* of a token is determined by three factors: token velocity, staking ratio, and the dilution rate. *Token velocity* measures the percentage of tokens transacted over a specific period relative to the token supply. A large token velocity signifies an increasing usage of and demand for the token, which leads to a high token utility. Not all tokens are being actively traded — quite a substantial number of tokens are inactive for more than a year (the “staked tokens”) and serve as a store of value. Liu (2019) defines the *staking ratio* as the proportion of staked tokens to the total token supply. A high staking ratio suggests that more users are placing long-term faith in the blockchain project. According to Liu (2019), token velocity represents the utility of the token in its role as a medium of exchange that is demanded by daily active users. The staking ratio represents the utility of the token as a store of value, demanded by long-term holders.

Dilution rate measures the annual growth rate of the token supply, and therefore a high dilution rate makes the token less appealing, thus leading to a lower token utility. With the halving event of the BTC supply in 2020, the dilution rate would have fallen below 2%, which is the common inflation rate targeted by major central banks (Liu, 2019). Altogether, the token utility formula shows that a low dilution rate combined with a high token velocity and a high staking ratio leads to a high token utility.

Applying the token utility formula to Bitcoin, Liu (2019) finds that the token utility of Bitcoin has increased significantly over the past five years and that token utility is a leading indicator of the Bitcoin price. An increase in token utility that results from the rise of the token velocity and increases in the staking ratio, along with the decrease of the dilution rate, implies that fewer liquid tokens circulate in the system than are in demand. He shows that a reduction of liquid Bitcoin together with an increasing Bitcoin velocity led to the end of the bearish market of 2018. Liu (2019) also demonstrates that the P/U ratio of Bitcoin lies between 50 and 200 in normal times, above 200 in bubble ages, and below 50 in crypto winters.

Although the P/U ratio was created to solve some of the challenges of the EVT ratio, the concerns over finding comparables still apply to the P/U ratio. Blockchain projects address different issues, provide diverse services, and target various groups of users. For instance, while Bitcoin serves as a decentralized peer-to-peer payment system as well as a storage of value, the value of Ethereum is reflected mostly by the daily active usage of its smart contract platform. Therefore, the P/U ratio is not designed to spot signs of market booms and crashes but it can be instrumental when comparing the valuations of tokens with similar blockchain features.

6. Crypto-asset Valuation: The Cost Approach

From a cost aspect, the most intuitive crypto-asset valuation framework is Hayes' (2015) Cost of Production model. This method postulates that the cost of mining a crypto-asset may provide an indicator of its lower bound of value for crypto-asset valuation.

Specifically, cryptocurrency mining has a fixed cost in the purchase, transportation and installation of the mining machines and a variable cost to cover the direct expense of electricity consumption (Hayes, 2015, 2017). Because miners cannot generally pay for their electricity cost in Bitcoin, they must refer to the currency price of a Bitcoin to measure profitability given a real monetary cost of electricity. Hayes (2015) therefore asserts that miners, operating in a competitive market and incented by the expectation of profits, will continue to produce as long as the total cost of production is less than or equal to the market price of the mined coin.

First, Hayes (2015) estimates the daily production cost, E_{day}:

$$E_{\text{day}} = \text{Electricity Cost}(kwh) \times \text{Mining hours per day} \\ \times \text{Hash Rate} \times \text{Energy Efficiency}.$$

Daily production cost is determined by (1) *the electricity cost* per kilowatt-hour, (2) the *number of hours* the mining machine operates on a given day, usually 24 hours, (3) the *hash rate*: the computational effort expended to solve complex mathematical equations, with a higher hash rate corresponding to an increased likelihood of solving the next block in the blockchain and ultimately earning the block reward, and (4) the *average energy efficiency*, or the amount of energy consumed by the mining machine per unit of mining effort (watts per giga-hashes per second). The more efficient the mining machine, the more likely a miner is to solve a block.

Second, based on the Bitcoin algorithm (Satoshi 2008), the expected number of bitcoins to be produced per day is as follows:

$$\text{BTC/day}^* = \left(\frac{\text{Current block reward} \times \text{Hash Rate} \times \text{Sec}_{\text{hr}}}{\text{Mining Difficulty} \times \text{Prob. of Winning a Block}}\right)$$

$$\times \text{Mining hours per day} = \left(\frac{\text{Current block reward} \times \text{Hash Rate} \times 3600}{\text{Mining Difficulty} \times \frac{1}{2^{32}}}\right) \\ \times 24$$

BTC/day*, the expected level of daily bitcoin production when mining bitcoins directly, is determined by the following: (1) the *current block reward* (expressed in units of BTC/block; see www.Bitcoinblockhalf.com for the current block reward), (2) the *hash rate* per second, based on 3,600 seconds per hour, (3) the current level of *mining difficulty*: cryptographic puzzle mining machines are trying to solve, (4) the *probability of being the first to solve* the block that is $\frac{1}{2^{32}}$ for Bitcoin and is an attribute of the Bitcoin mining algorithm, and (5) the *mining hours* on a given day, usually 24 hours. Because of the framework set-up, the Hayes (2015) model only applies to Bitcoin. Valuation of other mineable crypto-assets needs to take into consideration the mining algorithm and related factors associated with the assets.

The marginal product of mining should theoretically equal its marginal cost in a competitive market, which should also equal its selling price. Therefore, the objective price of production level, p^*, is

$$p^* = \frac{E_{day}}{\text{BTC/day}^*}.$$

Hayes (2015, 2017) therefore suggests that Bitcoin has intrinsic value. Mining for Bitcoin requires the use of electricity to win bitcoins, which can be viewed as similar to running an oil rig in search of oil. Also, Hayes (2017) posits that any opportunities for excess returns are short-lived as competition drives down profit. This is based on two forces. First, miners seek and mine for the most profitable coin which raises the aggregate network hashing power in that coin, causing the *mining difficulty* to increase. Second, as the *mining difficulty* increases, profitability falls per unit of mining effort, and prices will change as mining participants actively produce and subsequently sell relatively overpriced coins.

Empirically, Hayes (2017) applied this formula and found that 92% of Bitcoin's observed market price can be explained by the cost of production model. Using Hayes' (2015) model, Gmitro (2017) presents a market-based analysis on the technological and economic incentives behind cryptocurrency development and calculates the objective price of production level p^* to be \$1875.65. Li and Wang's (2017) empirical analysis also confirms the relevance of mining cost in determining the crypto-asset valuation.

In a more general study, Bhambhwani *et al.* (2019) find computing power to be important for cryptocurrency prices. Specifically, high levels of computing power allow transactions to flow efficiently, secure the blockchain from rogue attackers, and thus increase the trustworthiness of the blockchain. Similarly, Garratt and van Oordt (2019) show that the amount of mining power supplied to currencies that rely on application-specific integrated circuits (ASICs), such as Bitcoin, responds less to adverse exchange rate shocks than other currencies.

The cost of production model has some limitations. First, as previously discussed, Hayes' model is best tested and applied to the Bitcoin. One needs to update the parameters to fit for the other Proof-of-Work (PoW) system that requires the cost of electricity. Still, this model may have limited applicability under a PoS protocol, which does not use electricity-based mining but relies on a forger's relative network stake to establish consensus (Singh and John, 2019). Second, this model assumes that miners are only incented by the expectation of profits and will stop producing once the marginal cost exceeds prices. It, therefore, ignores other incentives such as miners' philosophical belief in an unregulated, transparent financial system and that they may be willing to operate at a loss to develop and maintain this network (Ige, 2018). Third, the model assumes that miners operate in a perfectly competitive market. However, due to the high cost of mining equipment, miners appear to be capitalizing on economies of scale, which has led to a certain degree of centralization and has the potential to impact both the market price of the coin and the individual miner's cost to produce it (Singh and John, 2019).

7. Conclusion

This chapter provides an overview of the valuation of crypto-assets, with a special focus on cryptocurrency coins and utility tokens under the framework of the monetary theory and the income approach, market approach, and cost approach. The appropriate approach for each crypto-asset will depend on the specific facts and circumstances of each case, the time available for the analysis, the purpose and the required level of reliance to be placed on the valuation.

The valuation approaches examined herein are still in the early stages of development and, given the various noted limitations, this chapter calls for significant refinement as the crypto-asset market matures. We believe that a rigorous analysis will help provide insight into value creation itself and that a quantitative analysis based on realistic assumptions can give investors a useful sense-check in their decision-making. The crypto-asset valuation will inevitably require careful analysis and a sense of realism about one's confidence in the concluded value range.

References

Bhambhwani, S., S. Delikouras, and G. M. Korniotis. 2019. "Do Fundamentals Drive Cryptocurrency Prices?" Working Paper, Available at SSRN 3342842.

Bheemaiah, K., and A. Collomb. 2018. "Cryptoasset Valuation." Working Paper.

Blockgeeks. 2018. "What Are Security Tokens?" Retrieved from https://blockgeeks.com/guides/security-tokens/.

Burniske, C., and J. Tatar. 2017. *Cryptoassets: The Innovative Investor's Guide to Bitcoin and Beyond.* New York: McGraw-Hill Education.

Burniske, C. 2017. "The Crypto J-Curve." Retrieved from https://medium.com/@cburniske/the-crypto-j-curve-be5fdddafa26.

Buterin, V. 2017. "Ethereum Research Update." Saatavissa (viitattu 13.2). https://blog.ethereum.org/2016/12/04/ethereum-research-update.

Catalini, C., and J. S. Gans. 2019. "Initial Coin Offerings and the Value of Crypto Tokens." Working Paper, National Bureau of Economic Research.

Cheah, E.-T., and J. Fry. 2015. "Speculative bubbles in bitcoin markets? An empirical investigation into the fundamental value of bitcoin." *Economics Letters* 130, 32–36.

Ciaian, P., M. Rajcaniova, and d'Artis Kancs. 2016. "The economics of bitcoin price formation." *Applied Economics* 48:19, 1799–1815.

Cong, L. W., Y. Li, and N. Wang. 2019. "Tokenomics: Dynamic Adoption and Valuation." Working Paper, Becker Friedman Institute for Research in Economics.

Conley, J. P. 2017. "Blockchain Cryptocurrency Backed with Full Faith and Credit." Working Paper, Vanderbilt University Department of Economics.

Corbet, S., B. Lucey, and L. Yarovaya. 2018. "Datestamping the bitcoin and ethereum bubbles." *Finance Research Letters* 26, 81–88.

Friedman, M. 1956, "The quantity theory of money: A restatement." *Studies in the Quantity Theory of Money* 5, 3–31.

Garcia, D., C. J. Tessone, P. Mavrodiev, and N. Perony. 2014. "The digital traces of bubbles: Feedback cycles between socio-economic signals in the bitcoin economy." *Journal of the Royal Society Interface* 11:88, 20140623.

Garratt, R., and M. R. C. van Oordt. 2019. "Why Fixed Costs Matter for Proof-of-Work Based Cryptocurrencies." Working Paper.

Gmitro, M. 2017. "Computational Aspects of Cryptocurrency Valuation." Working Paper.

Grinberg, R. 2011. "Bitcoin: An innovative alternative digital currency." *Hastings Science & Technology Law Journal* 4, 160.

Hanley, B. P. 2013. "The False Premises and Promises of Bitcoin." arXiv preprint arXiv:1312.2048.
Hayes, A. S. 2015. "A Cost of Production Model for Bitcoin." Working Paper, SSRN 2580904.
Hayes, A. S. 2017. "Cryptocurrency value formation: An empirical study leading to a cost of production model for valuing bitcoin." *Telematics and Informatics* 34:7, 1308–1321.
Hayes, A. S. 2019. "Bitcoin price and its marginal cost of production: Support for a fundamental value." *Applied Economics Letters* 26:7, 554–560.
Howell, S. T., M. Niessner, and D. Yermack. 2018. "Initial Coin Offerings: Financing Growth with Cryptocurrency Token Sales." Working Paper, National Bureau of Economic Research.
Ige, L. 2018. "Cryptoasset Valuation Techniques." Working Paper.
Johnson, R., J. Bufton, and J. Daniel. 2019. The Valuation of Crypto-assets: Minds Made for Shaping Financial Services." EY. Retrieved from https://assets.ey.com/content/dam/ey-sites/ey-com/en_gl/topics/emeia-financial-services/ey-the-valuation-of-crypto-assets.pdf.
Klöhn, L., N. Parhofer, and D. Resas. 2018. "Initial Coin Offerings (ICOs): Economics and Regulation." Working Paper, Available at SSRN 3290882.
Koffman, T. 2018. "Your Official Guide to the Security Token Ecosystem." Retrieved from https://medium.com/@tatianakoffman/your-official-guide-to-the-security-token-ecosystem-61a805673db7.
Kristoufek, L. 2015. "What are the main drivers of the bitcoin price? Evidence from wavelet coherence analysis." *PloS one* 10:4.
Li, J., and W. Mann. 2018. "Initial Coin Offerings and Platform Building." Working Paper.
Li, X., and C. A. Wang. 2017. "The technology and economic determinants of cryptocurrency exchange rates: The case of bitcoin." *Decision Support Systems* 95, 49–60.
Liu, C., and H. Wang. 2019a. "Crypto Tokens and Token Offerings: An Introduction." In S. Goutte, K. Guesmi, and S. Saadi (eds.), *Cryptofinance and Mechanisms of Exchange*, 125–144. Cham: Springer.
Liu, C., and H. Wang. 2019b. "Initial Coin Offerings: What Do We Know and What Are the Success Factors?" In S. Goutte, K. Guesmi, and S. Saadi (eds.), *Cryptofinance and Mechanisms of Exchange*, pp. 145–164. Cham: Springer.
Liu, Y. 2017. "Cryptocurrency Valuation." Retrieved from https://www.forbes.com/sites/wwoo/2017/09/29/is-bitcoin-in-a-bubble-check-the-nvt-ratio/#18bdb3bf6a23.
Makarov, I., and A. Schoar. 2020. "Trading and arbitrage in cryptocurrency markets." *Journal of Financial Economics* 135:2, 293–319.
Malinova, K., and A. Park. 2018. "Tokenomics: When Tokens Beat Equity." Working Paper, Available at SSRN 3286825.

Marks, H. 2108. "The Future of US Securities Will Be Tokenized." Retrieved from https://hackernoon.com/the-future-of-us-securities-will-be-tokenized-c469d41d81a1.

Metcalfe, B. 2013. "Metcalfe's law after 40 years of ethernet." *Computer* 46:12, 26–31.

Pagnotta, E., and A. Buraschi. 2018. "An Equilibrium Valuation of Bitcoin and Decentralized Network Assets." Working Paper, Available at SSRN 3142022.

Peterson, T. 2018. "Metcalfe's Law as a model for bitcoin's value." *Alternative Investment Analyst Review Q2*, 9–18.

Singh, T. K., and T. St. John. 2019. "Decrypting crypto: An introduction to cryptoasset and a study of select valuation approaches." *Journal of Business Valuation* 1–87.

Sockin, M., and W. Xiong. 2020. "*A Model of Cryptocurrencies.*" Working Paper, No. w26816. National Bureau of Economic Research.

Van Vliet, B. 2018. "An alternative model of Metcalfe's Law for valuing bitcoin." *Economics Letters* 165, 70–72.

Wang, S., and J.-P. Vergne. 2017. "Buzz factor or innovation potential: What explains cryptocurrencies' returns?" *PloS one* 12:1, e0169556.

Woo, W. 2017. "Introducing NVT Ratio (Bitcoin's PE Ratio), Use it to Detect Bubbles." Retrieved from https://woobull.com/introducing-nvt-ratio-bitcoins-pe-ratio-use-it-to-detect-bubbles/.

Yermack, D. 2015. "Is bitcoin a real currency? An economic appraisal." In *Handbook of Digital Currency*, 31–43. Cambridge: Academic Press.

Yermack, D. 2017. "Corporate governance and blockchains." *Review of Finance* 21:1, 7–31.

https://doi.org/10.1142/9789811239670_0010

Chapter 10

The Nexus between Cryptocurrencies, Currencies and Commodities: A Primer

Siavash Taheri[*,‡], **Janelle Mann**[*,§], **and Austin McWhirter**[†,||]

[*]*Department of Economics University of Manitoba, Winnipeg, Manitoba, Canada*

[†]*Vancouver School of Economics University of British Columbia, Vancouver, British Columbia, Canada*

[‡]*taheris@myumanitoba.ca*

[§]*janelle.mann@umanitoba.ca*

[||]*austin.mcwhirter@alumni.ubc.ca*

Abstract

This primer provides a pairwise comparison of cryptocurrency characteristics with those of fiat currency and hard commodities to shed light on the nexus between cryptocurrencies, fiat currency, and hard commodities. Then, it synthesizes methods and results from empirical research that investigate the nexus. The findings reveal that the existing literature has not reached a consensus on the nature of cryptocurrencies, in particular whether they should be categorized as a currency or a commodity which indicates the research area is not yet saturated.

Keywords: Bitcoin, commodity, cryptocurrency, currency, returns, volatility

1. Introduction

Cryptocurrencies have grown dramatically in terms of trading volume, market capitalization, and the number of independent cryptocurrencies since Bitcoin was introduced in 2008. The growth of cryptocurrencies has brought about a conversation on the nature of cryptocurrencies, in particular whether they should be categorized as a currency or a commodity. This chapter is a primer on the nexus between cryptocurrencies, currencies, and commodities. The nexus crosses disciplines and motivates this chapter. The purpose of this primer is to act as a springboard to encourage and inspire future research that contributes to the conversation on the nature of cryptocurrencies.

The chapter is structured as follows. Section 2 compares the characteristics of cryptocurrencies to those of currencies and commodities with a focus on the nexus between all three. The next two sections synthesize empirical research that incorporates at least one data series for each of the following categories: cryptocurrency, currency, and commodity. Section 3 focuses on returns and Section 4 focuses on volatility. Section 5 concludes the chapter.

2. The Nexus

This section sheds light on the cryptocurrency, currency, and commodity nexus. The first subsection compares the characteristics of fiat currencies with cryptocurrencies. The second subsection compares the characteristics of hard commodities with cryptocurrencies. The nexus crosses disciplines and motivates this chapter and the empirical research synthesized in Sections 3 and 4.

2.1 *Cryptocurrencies Versus Currencies*

There are both similarities and differences between cryptocurrencies and government-backed fiat currencies which fulfill a monetary role. The latter possess three main characteristics: they function as a medium of exchange, a unit of account, and a store of value. Yermack (2015) used these three characteristics to evaluate the extent to which cryptocurrencies are similar to fiat currencies. The following paragraphs follow suit.

The first characteristic of a currency is that it functions as a medium of exchange. In other words, people should be able to use a currency for daily transactions. Cryptocurrencies are widely used in online transactions but the number of transactions is far fewer than fiat currencies with a comparable market capitalization. For example, Bitcoin and the Danish Krone had a similar market capitalization in 2019 (FiatMarketCap, 2020). However, the average daily transactions of Bitcoin were approximately 340,000 bitcoins (nearly $3 billion), while the Danish Krone had average daily transactions of $42 billion (Countries-ofthe-World, 2020). Although there are similarities between cryptocurrencies and currencies as a medium of exchange, it is unclear if cryptocurrencies can fully satisfy this function because they lack widespread acceptance (Carrick, 2016). However, Hazlett and Luther (2020) argue that Bitcoin satisfies the medium of exchange function albeit over a smaller domain than USD, but perhaps larger than Guatemalan quetzal. Ammous (2018) posits cryptocurrencies will not become a medium of exchange until they are either a unit of account, store of value, or both.

The second characteristic of fiat currency is that it functions as a unit of account. This means fiat currency must be divisible, mutually interchangeable, and countable (Carrick, 2016). Most importantly, a unit of account is something that can be used to value goods and services (Doepke and Schneider, 2017). Cryptocurrencies are divisible and countable. They can be divided into any desirable fraction and merged back into a whole piece. Cryptocurrencies are also interchangeable. They are created equally and there is no difference between any two units of a cryptocurrency. Whether or not cryptocurrencies can serve as a unit of account is more contentious. While cryptocurrencies seem to meet the unit of account characteristic, some disagree (Wu and Pandey, 2014; Ammous, 2018). High volatility in the price of cryptocurrencies makes it challenging to consistently value goods and services using a cryptocurrency. For example, in 2019 the average sales price for a new single-family house in the U.S. was $373,100 in January, $388,000 in July, and $384,500 in December (U.S. Census Bureau, 2019a, 2019b, 2019c). When valued in bitcoins the average single-family house was approximately 100 bitcoins in January, 36 bitcoins in July, and 51 bitcoins in December.

The third characteristic of a currency is that it functions as a store of value. Cryptocurrencies generally do not satisfy this characteristic due to their highly volatile and unpredictable demand, which results in unpredictable purchasing power. However, Ammous [2018] notes that the store of value characteristic of fiat currencies is closely tied to the predictability of their supply; lower growth makes a better store of value. This is because a predictable money supply leads to a more consistent inflation rate and therefore less volatility. Bitcoin experienced high growth in its early years, but is only expected to grow by 1% in 2020. This compares to an average fiat currency growth of 5% for advanced economies between 1990 and 2015 and hints at Bitcoin's potential to function as a store of value in the future (Ammous, 2018).

To conclude this section, it is important to note several similarities between cryptocurrencies and fiat currencies because they tend to motivate the empirical literature comparing these two assets. Firstly, neither possess an intrinsic value (Baur *et al.*, 2018). The government's authority to enforce the use of a fiat currency, along with citizen willingness to use it, gives fiat currency value. Cryptocurrencies derive their value from their expected future demand, which is likely to be determined by perceptions surrounding its future use as a medium of exchange (Hazlett and Luther, 2020). Thus, both assets do not have underlying value absent of social context. Secondly, cryptocurrencies and fiat currencies are scarce. The mining process of Bitcoin amongst other major cryptocurrencies combined with their supply cap gives them a synthetically scarce characteristic that is similar to fiat currencies, whose scarcity is determined by its central bank (Corbet *et al.*, 2018). Finally, cryptocurrencies are hard to forge. With fiat currencies, the government ensures there are no forgeries by keeping a ledger and by equipping the physical bills with unique characteristics. Cryptocurrencies maintain a similar ledger (the blockchain) by keeping track of each transaction in nodes (Corbet *et al.*, 2018). This way, every unit of cryptocurrency mined is accounted for. For the remainder of this chapter, "fiat currency" will be shortened to "currency."

2.2 *Cryptocurrencies Versus Hard Commodities*

There are both similarities and differences between cryptocurrencies and hard commodities such as gold, copper, and crude oil, which are mined or extracted. One obvious link is that both cryptocurrencies and commodities are classified as a commodity by the U.S. Commodity Futures Trading Commission and have futures contracts that are traded on the CME Group. Cryptocurrencies have been referred to as the new gold or digital gold (Popper, 2016). It follows that gold is the most common commodity with which cryptocurrencies are compared. Empirical research incorporating gold and cryptocurrencies tend to compare their safe haven properties, specifically whether they are "uncorrelated with stocks and bonds in a market crash" (Baur and Lucey, 2010). Cryptocurrencies have also been compared to Western Texas Intermediate (WTI) crude oil, Brent crude oil, natural gas, silver, and copper.

Hard commodities possess four main characteristics: they are costly to mine or extract, they are storable, no single government or institution controls their global supply, demand, or price and they have an intrinsic value, i.e., they can be consumed or used as inputs in the production of other consumable goods. The extent to which cryptocurrencies are similar to hard commodities depends mainly on whether they possess these characteristics. The following three paragraphs elaborate on this point.

The first characteristic of a hard commodity is that they are costly to mine or extract. The mining process for cryptocurrencies involves solving a complicated math problem that requires time, money, computational power, and energy consumption (Gandotra *et al.*, 2019). The number of remaining coins to be extracted is known with certainty, while the stock of unmined hard commodities is not. Despite stark differences in mining techniques, mining cryptocurrencies is similar to hard commodities in that their mining technologies are constantly evolving. One innovation in the case of Bitcoin is mining pools, where Bitcoin miners combine their computational resources to increase their odds of successfully mining Bitcoin, then split the profits (Gandotra *et al.*, 2019). Another similarity is that mining prospects can fail. Even successful efforts to find a block solution by cryptocurrency miners can take months. Therefore, much like hard commodities, cryptocurrency mining prospects are subject to a degree of uncertainty (Narayanan *et al.*, 2016).

The second and third characteristics of a hard commodity are that they are storable and their global supply, demand and prices are not controlled by a single government or institution. Cryptocurrencies share these characteristics. The fourth characteristic of a hard commodity is that it has an intrinsic value. Cryptocurrencies do not share this characteristic. It is important to note that this dichotomy with respect to intrinsic value is a similarity between cryptocurrencies and currencies and brings about the nexus between cryptocurrencies, currencies, and commodities. For the remainder of this chapter, "hard commodity" will be shortened to "commodity."

3. Empirical Research Investigating the Nexus

This section presents empirical research that investigates the cryptocurrency, currency, and commodity nexus with returns being the focus of the first subsection and volatility being the focus of the second subsection.

Existing empirical research differs substantially in the choice of empirical method and data, e.g., time period, currency timeseries, and commodity timeseries. All of the empirical research incorporate Bitcoin, but very few incorporate any of the other 2,500 cryptocurrencies (CoinMarketCap, 2020). Most cryptocurrencies do not hold much relevance. Total market capitalization is widely used to identify major actively traded cryptocurrencies, e.g., Catania *et al.* (2019); Charfeddine and Maouchi (2019); Fry (2018); Fry and Cheah (2016); Gil-Alana, Abakah, and Rojo (2020); Gkillas and Katsiampa (2018); Guesmi *et al.* (2019); Koutmos (2018); and Peters *et al.* (2016). Table 1 displays the set

Table 1: Cryptocurrencies whose Market Capitalization Exceeds $1 Billion.

	2014		2017		2020	
	Market Cap	% of Total Market Cap	Market Cap	% of Total Market Cap	Market Cap	% of Total Market Cap
Bitcoin	$7.53	88.4	$18.86	86.1	$180.96	62.6
Ethereum	—	—	$1.29	5.8	$30.06	10.4
XRP	$0.12	1.4	$0.21	0.9	$12.36	4.2
Bitcoin Cash	—	—	—	—	$7.34	2.5
Bitcoin SV	—	—	—	—	$5.38	1.8
Litecoin	$0.4	4.7	$0.19	0.8	$5.10	1.7
Tether	—	—	$0.02	0.1	$4.63	1.5
EOS	—	—	—	—	$4.18	1.4
Binance Coin	—	—	—	—	$3.55	1.2
Tezos	—	—	—	—	$2.46	0.8
Cardano	—	—	—	—	$1.59	0.5
Stellar	—	—	$0.01	0	$1.48	0.5
Chainlink	—	—	—	—	$1.48	0.5
Monero	—	—	$0.16	0.7	$1.48	0.5
TRON	—	—	—	—	$1.42	0.5
Ethereum Classic	—	—	$0.11	0.5	$1.13	0.4
Huobi Token	—	—	—	—	$1.11	0.4
Neo	—	—	$0.01	0	$1.01	0.3
Dash	$0.1	1.1	$0.2	0.9	$1.01	0.3

Source: CoinMarketCap (2020). All numbers are in billions of USD.

of cryptocurrencies whose market capitalization exceeds $1 billion for the years 2014, 2017, and 2020. The number of major actively traded cryptocurrencies is increasing over time. Bitcoin continues to have the highest total market capitalization and, if it were a currency, would fall in the third quartile of the market capitalization for all currencies.

3.1 *Returns*

A starting point for investigating the behavior of cryptocurrency, currency and commodity returns is to calculate pairwise correlation coefficients. Wu and Pandey (2014) created a pairwise correlation matrix for the daily returns to holding Bitcoin and six currencies between 2010 and 2013. The correlation coefficient for only one of the pairs containing Bitcoin was statistically significant, although it was only 0.07. The pairs involving two currencies were positive and statistically significant. This pattern suggests that the returns to Bitcoin and currencies do not necessarily move in tandem. Wu and Pandey (2014) continue by creating a pairwise correlation matrix for the daily returns to Bitcoin and major asset classes, including gold and a commodity index. Pairwise correlation coefficients involving either or both of Bitcoin and gold were the only major assets whose coefficients were close to zero. As a result, Wu and Pandey (2014) continue by investigating Bitcoin as a diversification tool for an investment portfolio. Henriques and Sadorsky (2018) also created a pairwise correlation matrix for daily returns to Bitcoin, five ETFs, and gold between 2011 and 2017; Baur, Dimpfl and Kuck (2018) created a pairwise correlation matrix for daily and weekly returns to Bitcoin, gold futures price, gold cash price, USD relative to the pound, USD relative to the euro, and equity market index returns; and Baur *et al.* (2018) created a pairwise correlation matrix for daily returns to Bitcoin, six currencies, and four commodities between 2010 and 2017 with the findings from all three studies being similar to Wu and Pandey (2014) in that the pairwise correlation coefficients closest to zero were those that involved Bitcoin. This provides preliminary evidence that Bitcoin may be useful as a diversification tool for investment portfolios.

Another way to investigate correlation is to calculate dynamic correlations from a generalized autoregressive conditional heteroskedastic (GARCH) model. Shahzad *et al.* (2020) estimate the asymmetric generalized dynamic conditional correlation (DCC) variant of the GARCH model to compare the hedging effectiveness of Bitcoin and gold for G7 stock indexes between July 2010 and December 2018. The calculated daily dynamic correlations for gold are approximately double that of Bitcoin and range between 0.40 and 0.45 with the exception of the gold–Japan pair whose correlation is similar to that of the Bitcoin–Japan pair. Shahzad *et al.* (2020) continue by using the asymmetric generalized DCC-GARCH model to calculate a hedging effectiveness index.

The mean equation from a GARCH model can offer additional insights into the behavior of returns. Dyhrberg (2016) takes this approach and models the returns to holding Bitcoin with a GARCH model and an exponential GARCH model. The mean equations for both models incorporate currencies (USD relative to the pound and USD relative to the Euro), commodities (gold futures and gold cash price), the Financial Times Stock Exchange index, and the federal funds rate. Results are not included because the econometric models are misspecified as described in Baur *et al.* (2018). In their replication and extension of Dyhberg (2016), they estimate independent asymmetric-GARCH models following Glosten *et al.* (1993) termed GJR-GARCH for each of the variables included in the mean equation of Dyhberg (2016). The only variables in the correctly specified mean equation are an autoregressive component and the USD trade-weighted index. The USD trade-weighted index is negative and statistically significant for all models except those with returns to Bitcoin as the dependent variable, indicating that the USD is negatively related to all assets except Bitcoin. The authors posit that Bitcoin's volatility may dominate the impact of the movements in the USD on the returns to Bitcoin.

Bouri *et al.* (2018) also use the mean equation from a GARCH model to investigate the behavior of returns with a focus on return spillover during bull and bear market conditions. The research incorporates daily returns to holding Bitcoin, currency (USD index), and commodities (gold, S&P GSCI commodity, and S&P GSCI energy) amongst various stocks and bonds to estimate a STVAR-BTGARCH-M model with a logistic transition function for bull and bear market conditions. Results for the Bitcoin–currency and Bitcoin–commodity pairings differ. There is no spillover effect from Bitcoin to currency in either market condition but there is a positive spillover effect from Bitcoin to commodities during bear markets and a negative spillover effect during bull markets. The results agree that there is positive spillover from currency to Bitcoin and commodities to Bitcoin in bear market conditions, but in bull market conditions the spillover from currency to Bitcoin is negative.

The mean equation is not the only way for GARCH models to offer insights into the behavior of commodity and cryptocurrency returns. Multivariate GARCH models can also be used to select optimal weights for investment portfolios. Henriques and Sadorsky (2018) apply the optimal weights from the multivariate DCC-GARCH, asymmetric DCC-GARCH, and generalized orthogonal GARCH to two investment portfolios. The first investment portfolio includes five ETFs and gold as a safe haven. The second replaces gold with Bitcoin. The investment portfolios containing Bitcoin rank highest with respect to the following risk-adjusted measures: Sharpe ratio, Omega ratio, Sortino ratio, and information ratio. The results are robust to the inclusion of trading costs and allowing for short sales.

Wu and Pandey (2014) compare investment portfolios that allow Bitcoin to be included with those that do not using weekly returns between 2010 and 2013. Major world currencies (Bloomberg Dollar Spot index), commodities (S&P CME spot commodities index), stocks (S&P500 index), bonds (Bloomberg USD Investment Grade Composite Bond index), and real estate (FTSE NAREIT total return index) make up the remainder of the investment portfolio. Optimal weights were selected by simulating 1,000 investment portfolios subject to several constraints for five different objective functions: minimize total variance, minimize semi-variance, maximize Sharpe ratio, maximize Sortino ratio, and maximize Omega ratio. The weight for commodities in the investment portfolio that allowed Bitcoin was always equal to or greater than those that did not allow Bitcoin to be included and the investment portfolios allowing Bitcoin rank highest in terms of return across all risk-adjusted measures. The optimal investment portfolios continue to include Bitcoin even after the Black-Letterman approach was used to incorporate varying levels of pessimistic views towards Bitcoin.

Corbet *et al.* (2018) investigate pairwise spillover between returns to cryptocurrencies (Bitcoin, Ripple, and Litecoin), currency (USD broad exchange rate), and commodities (gold and MSC GSCI total returns index), amongst other assets using daily data from 2013 through 2017. First, they employ a generalized variance decomposition method following Diebold and Yilmaz (2012). The pairwise spillover from USD and commodities to cryptocurrencies is the largest for USD to Bitcoin at 4.18% followed by gold to Litecoin at 4%, and the commodities index to Bitcoin at 2.38%. These values reveal that returns to cryptocurrencies are isolated from returns to currency and commodities. The pairwise spillovers from cryptocurrencies to the USD and commodities are higher, with the largest pairwise spillovers being 15.25% from Bitcoin to USD, 10.63% from Bitcoin to the MSC GSCI total returns index, and 9.64% from Litecoin to USD. Next, they employ frequency domain analysis following Barunik and Krehlik (2015) and find that cryptocurrencies, USD, and commodities are not connected at short frequencies but display similar patterns to the pairwise spillovers from the generalized variance decomposition. Combined, the findings indicate that cryptocurrencies are not connected to the USD or commodities.

Shahzad *et al.* (2020) compare the ability of Bitcoin and gold to be a safe haven for G7 stock indexes using three principal regression equations following Baur and McDermott (2010). They find gold to be a superior safe haven during periods of large stock market downturns and overall for almost all G7 countries. Specifically, gold is classified as a strong safe haven for Germany and the U.S. and a weak safe haven for France, Italy, Japan, the U.K., and an aggregate stock market index for G7 countries. Bitcoin is only a weak safe haven for Canada and France. The authors acknowledge that these findings differ from most previous research. This paper does not include commodity data but is included here as a recently published paper that sheds light on the large body of literature that compares the safe haven properties of cryptocurrencies with those of gold.

Panagiotidis *et al.* (2018) provide one final take on comparing the cryptocurrency returns to the behavior of currency and commodity returns. They employ the Least Absolute Shrinkage and Selection Operator (LASSO) framework to examine 21 possible determinants of daily Bitcoin returns between 2010 and 2017. Two of the possible determinants are commodities and four are currencies. Gold is found to be the second most important determinant for the full sample and Brent crude oil is found to be the 14th most important determinant. The averaged ranking for the currencies is 15.25 with eleventh being the highest ranking. All commodities and currencies have a positive effect on the returns to holding Bitcoin. Results from splicing the full sample into three subperiods reveal gold as one of the least important determinants in the third period while Brent crude oil becomes the eighth most important determinant. The averaged ranking of the exchange rates increased to 11.75 with eighth being the highest ranking. The change in ranking of gold when moving from the full sample to the spliced sample hints that the nexus may be evolving.

The variance equation from a GARCH model is commonly used to investigate cryptocurrency, currency, and commodity volatility. Dyhrberg (2016) takes this approach and models the returns to holding Bitcoin using both a GARCH model and an exponential GARCH model. The mean and variance equations for both models incorporate currencies (USD relative to the pound and USD relative to the euro), commodities (gold futures and gold cash price), the Financial Times Stock Exchange index, and the federal funds rate. In the replication and extension by Baur *et al.* (2018), independent GJR-GARCH models are estimated for each of the variables included in the mean equation of Dyhberg (2016) with a variance equation that includes only the ARCH and GARCH terms and an indicator function to allow for asymmetric volatility. The coefficient estimates for the ARCH and GARCH terms reveal that volatility is the most persistent for Bitcoin. The coefficient estimate for the indicator function in the GJR-GARCH model is positive for Bitcoin but negative for the other assets (with the exception of the USD relative to the pound, which is not statistically significant). This means that positive shocks increase the volatility of Bitcoin by more than a negative shock. The GARCH models also indicate that the behavior of Bitcoin is different than that of currencies and commodities.

Bouri *et al.* (2018) also use the variance equation from a GARCH model to investigate volatility with a focus on volatility spillover to returns during bull and bear market conditions. The research incorporates Bitcoin, currency (USD index), and commodities (gold, S&P GSCI commodity, and S&P GSCI energy) amongst various stocks and bonds to estimate a STVAR-BTGARCH-M model with a logistic transition function for bull and bear market conditions. The results find that the volatility effects of currency and commodities on Bitcoin returns have a larger role than Bitcoin volatility during both bull and bear market conditions. The results for the Bitcoin–currency and Bitcoin–commodity pairings indicate a positive effect from Bitcoin volatilities to gold returns during bear market conditions. This effect reverses during bull market conditions. There is also a positive effect from Bitcoin volatilities to currency returns during bear market conditions. The results for the currency–Bitcoin and commodity–Bitcoin pairings are more consistent. There is a positive effect from currency and commodity volatility to Bitcoin returns during both bull and bear market conditions. These findings reveal that Bitcoin is connected with currency and commodities to an even lesser extent via volatility than returns.

The variance equation is not the only way for GARCH models to offer insights into the behavior of cryptocurrency, currency, and commodity volatility. Guesmi *et al.* (2019) use a VARMA(1,1)-DCC-GJR-GARCH model to select optimal weights for investment portfolios containing Bitcoin, currency (euro and yuan exchange rate), commodities (gold bullion and WTI crude oil), stocks (MSCI emerging markets index and MSCI global market index), and the VIX (implied volatility index to proxy U.S. market volatility). The DCC-GJR-GARCH model employs daily returns between 2012 and 2018 to create a benchmark. Then, a constant expected return is imposed to determine the mean–variance optimal weights for the portfolio containing Bitcoin. The optimal weights were highest for WTI crude oil, gold, and the VIX and resulted in a lower risk investment portfolio than that which precludes Bitcoin. The GARCH model provides two other insights: there are significant volatility spillovers and a shock to currencies or commodities increases the volatility of Bitcoin returns.

Bouri *et al.* (2017) provide one final take on the use of GARCH models to investigate cryptocurrency, currency, and commodity volatilities. They estimate a bivariate DCC-GARCH model for both daily and weekly data between 2011 and 2015 and extract the pairwise conditional correlation between Bitcoin and a currency (USD index) and commodities (SPGS commodity index, gold spot price, and the Brent Crude oil spot price), amongst other assets. A regression for each pairwise conditional correlation is estimated as a function of extreme movements which are proxied by dummy variables representing returns in the tenth, fifth and first percentile of the distribution. For weekly data, Bitcoin is found to be an effective diversifier for the currency and commodities. For daily data, Bitcoin is found to be an effective diversifier only for the currency and a strong hedge for the SPGS commodity index.

Corbet *et al.* (2018) investigate pairwise volatility spillovers between cryptocurrency (Bitcoin, Ripple, and Litecoin), currency (USD Broad Exchange Rate), and commodities (gold and MSC GSCI total returns index), amongst other assets using daily data from 2013 through 2017. First, they employ a generalized variance decomposition method following Diebold and Yilmaz (2012). The pairwise volatility spillovers from currency and commodities to cryptocurrencies is the largest for MSC GSCI total returns to Ripple at 2.05%, followed by gold to Bitcoin at 1.55% and MSC GSCI total returns index to Litecoin at 1.11%. These values reveal that cryptocurrency volatilities are more isolated than returns with respect to spillovers from currency and commodities. The pairwise volatility spillovers from cryptocurrencies to currency and commodities is the largest for Litecoin to gold at 4%, followed by Bitcoin to the MSC GSCI total returns index at 1.22%, and Ripple to MSC GSCI total returns index at 1.08%. Next, they employ frequency domain analysis following Barunik and Krehlik (2015) and find pairwise volatility spillovers to cryptocurrencies and from cryptocurrencies to be less than that from the generalized variance decomposition method. Combined, the findings indicate that cryptocurrencies are not connected via volatility spillovers to the USD broad exchange rate.

4. Conclusion

When this chapter was at the proposal stage, the plan was to synthesize the literature on the nexus of cryptocurrencies, currencies, and commodities and conclude by clearly presenting the consensus as to whether cryptocurrencies should be categorized as a currency or a commodity. Existing empirical research covers many different time periods, with a wide range of empirical methods and currency timeseries but has not reached a consensus. This may be due to an evolving nexus, or perhaps another asset class all together is more comparable, such as synthetic commodity money as proposed by Selgin (2015). Thus, the chapter evolved into a primer in hopes that it will encourage and inspire future research that contributes to the conversation on the nature of cryptocurrencies.

References

Ammous, S. 2018. "Can cryptocurrencies fulfil the functions of money?" *Quarterly Review of Economics and Finance* 70: 2016, 38–51. https://doi.org/10.1016/j.qref.2018.05.010.

Barunik, J., and T. Krehlik. 2015. "Measuring the frequency dynamics of financial and macroeconomic connectedness." *SSRN Electronic Journal*. https://doi.org/10.2139/ssrn.2627599.

Baur, D. G., T. Dimpfl, and K. Kuck. 2018. "Bitcoin, gold and the US dollar — A replication and extension." *Finance Research Letters* 25, 103–110. https://doi.org/10.1016/j.frl.2017.10.012.

Baur, D. G., K. H. Hong, and A. D. Lee. 2018. "Bitcoin: Medium of exchange or speculative assets?" *Journal of International Financial Markets, Institutions and Money* 54, 177–189. https://doi.org/10.1016/j.intfin.2017.12.004.

Baur, D. G., and B. M. Lucey. 2010. "Is gold a hedge or a safe haven?" An analysis of stocks, bonds and gold. *Financial Review* 45:2, 217–229. https://doi.org/10.1111/j.1540-6288.2010.00244.x.

Baur, D. G., and T. K. McDermott. 2010. "Is gold a safe haven? International evidence." *Journal of Banking and Finance* 34:8, 1886–1898. https://doi.org/10.1016/j.jbankfin.2009.12.008.

Bouri, E., M. Das, R. Gupta, and D. Roubaud, 2018. Spillovers between bitcoin and other assets during bear and bull markets. *Applied Economics* 50:55, 5935–5949. https://doi.org/10.1080/00036846.2018.1488075.

Carrick, J. 2016. "Bitcoin as a complement to emerging market currencies." *Emerging Markets Finance and Trade* 52:10, 2321–2334. https://doi.org/10.1080/1540496X.2016.1193002.

Catania, L., S. Grassi, and F. Ravazzolo. 2019. "Forecasting cryptocurrencies under model and parameter instability." *International Journal of Forecasting* 35:2, 485–501. https://doi.org/10.1016/j.ijforecast.2018.09.005.

Charfeddine, L., and Y. Maouchi. 2019. "Are shocks on the returns and volatility of cryptocurrencies really persistent?" *Finance Research Letters* 28:2018, 423–430. https://doi.org/10.1016/j.frl.2018.06.017.

CoinMarketCap. 2020. *Historical Snapshots*. Accessed June 2020 at https://coinmarketcap.com/historical/.

Corbet, S., A. Meegan, C. Larkin, B. Lucey, and L. Yarovaya. 2018. "Exploring the dynamic relationships between cryptocurrencies and other financial assets." *Economics Letters* 165, 28–34. https://doi.org/10.1016/j.econlet.2018.01.004.

Countries-ofthe-World. 2020. "*Top 25 most traded currencies*." Accessed June 2020 at https://www.countries-ofthe-world.com/most-traded-currencies.html.

Diebold, F. X., and K. Yilmaz. 2012. "Better to give than to receive: Predictive directional measurement of volatility spillovers." *International Journal of Forecasting* 28:1, 57–66. https://doi.org/10.1016/j.ijforecast.2011.02.006.

Doepke, M., and M. Schneider. 2017. "Money as a unit of account." *Econometrica* 85:5, 1537–1574. https://doi.org/10.3982/ECTA11963.

Dyhrberg, A. H. 2016. "Bitcoin, gold and the dollar — A GARCH volatility analysis." *Finance Research Letters* 16, 85–92. https://doi.org/10.1016/j.frl.2015.10.008.

FiatMarketCap. 2020. "*Top fiat currencies by market capitalization*." Accessed June 2020 at https://fiatmarketcap.com/.

Fry, J. 2018. "Booms, busts and heavy-tails: The story of Bitcoin and cryptocurrency markets?" *Economics Letters* 171, 225–229. https://doi.org/10.1016/j.econlet.2018.08.008.

Fry, J., and E. Cheah. 2016. "Negative bubbles and shocks in cryptocurrency markets." *International Review of Financial Analysis* 47, 343–352. https://doi.org/10.1016/j.irfa.2016.02.008.

Gandotra, V., F.-E. Racicot, and A. Rahimzadeh. 2019. *Cryptocurrency mining*. In S. Goutte, K. Guesmi, and S. Saadi (eds.), "Cryptofinance and mechanisms of exchange." *Contributions to Management Science*, 51–67. Cham: Springer.

Gil-Alana, L. A., E. J. A. Abakah, and M. F. R. Rojo. 2020. "Cryptocurrencies and stock market indices. Are they related?" *Research in International Business and Finance* 51(March 2019), 1–11. https://doi.org/10.1016/j.ribaf.2019.101063.

Gkillas, K., and P. Katsiampa. 2018. "An application of extreme value theory to cryptocurrencies." *Economics Letters* 164, 109–111. https://doi.org/10.1016/j.econlet.2018.01.020.

Glosten, L. R., R. Jagannathan, and D. E. Runkle. 1993. "On the relation between the expected value and the volatility of the nominal excess return on stocks." *The Journal of Finance*. https://doi.org/10.2307/2329067.

Guesmi, K., S. Saadi, I. Abid, and Z. Ftiti. 2019. "Portfolio diversification with virtual currency: Evidence from bitcoin." *International Review of Financial Analysis* 63:2017, 431–437. https://doi.org/10.1016/j.irfa.2018.03.004.

Hazlett, P. K., and W. J. Luther. 2020. "Is bitcoin money? And what does that mean." *The Quarterly Review of Economics and Finance* 77, 144–149. https://doi.org/10.1016/j.qref.2019.10.003.

Henriques, I., and P. Sadorsky. 2018. "Can bitcoin replace gold in an investment portfolio?" *Journal of Risk and Financial Management* 11:48, 1–19. https://doi.org/10.3390/jrfm11030048.

Koutmos, D. 2018. "Return and volatility spillovers among cryptocurrencies." *Economics Letters* 173, 122–127. https://doi.org/10.1016/j.econlet.2018.10.004.

Narayanan, A., J. Bonneau, E. Felten, A. Miller, and S. Goldfeder. 2016. *Bitcoin and Cryptocurrency Technologies: A Comprehensive Introduction*, Princeton University Press, ISBN 0691171696. https://press.princeton.edu/books/hardcover/9780691171692/bitcoin-and-cryptocurrency-technologies.

Panagiotidis, T., T. Stengos, and O. Vravosinos. 2018. "On the determinants of bitcoin returns: A LASSO approach." *Finance Research Letters* 27, 235–240. https://doi.org/10.1016/j.frl.2018.03.016.

Peters, G. W., A. Chapelle, and E. Panayi. 2016. "Opening discussion on banking sector risk exposures and vulnerabilities from virtual currencies: An operational risk perspective." *Journal of Banking Regulation* 17:4, 239–272. https://doi.org/10.1057/jbr.2015.10.

Popper, N. 2016. *Digital gold: Bitcoin and the inside story of the misfits and millionaires trying to reinvent money*. Harper.

Selgin, G. 2015. "Synthetic commodity money." *Journal of Financial Stability* 17, 92–99. https://doi.org/10.1016/j.jfs.2014.07.002.

Shahzad, S. J. H., E. Bouri, D. Roubaud, and L. Kristoufek. 2020. "Safe haven, hedge and diversification for G7 stock markets: Gold versus bitcoin."

Economic Modelling 87, 212–224. https://doi.org/10.1016/j.econmod.2019.07.023.

U.S. Census Bureau and the U.S. Department of Housing and Urban Development. 2019a. "*Monthly New Residential Sales, March 2019*." https://www.census.gov/construction/nrs/pdf/newressales_201901.pdf.

U.S. Census Bureau and the U.S. Department of Housing and Urban Development. 2019b. "*Monthly New Residential Sales, August 2019*." https://www.census.gov/construction/nrs/pdf/newressales_201908.pdf.

U.S. Census Bureau and the U.S. Department of Housing and Urban Development. 2019c. "*Monthly New Residential Sales, December 2019*." https://www.census.gov/construction/nrs/pdf/newressales_201912.pdf.

Wu, C. Y., and V. K. Pandey. 2014. "The value of bitcoin in enhancing the efficiency of an investor's portfolio." *Journal of Financial Planning* September, 44–52.

Yermack, D. 2015. *Is Bitcoin a Real Currency? An Economic Appraisal*, D. Chuen (ed.), Academic Press. https://doi.org/10.1016/B978-0-12-802117-0.00002-3. Additional details can be found here: https://www.sciencedirect.com/science/article/pii/B9780128021170000023.

https://doi.org/10.1142/9789811239670_bmatter

Index

www.ingramcontent.com/pod-product-compliance
Ingram Content Group UK Ltd.
Pitfield, Milton Keynes, MK11 3LW, UK
UKHW020357150926
8624IPUK00004B/205

9 789811 239663